ROUTLEDGE LIBRARY EDITIONS:
PRISON AND PRISONERS

Volume 14

SOCIAL SKILLS IN PRISON
AND
THE COMMUNITY

SOCIAL SKILLS IN PRISON
AND
THE COMMUNITY

Problem Solving for Offenders

PHILIP PRIESTLEY, JAMES McGUIRE,
DAVID FLEGG, VALERIE HEMSLEY,
DAVID WELHAM
AND
ROSEMARY BARNITT

Routledge
Taylor & Francis Group

LONDON AND NEW YORK

First published in 1984 by Routledge & Kegan Paul plc

This edition first published in 2024
by Routledge
4 Park Square, Milton Park, Abingdon, Oxon OX14 4RN

and by Routledge
605 Third Avenue, New York, NY 10158

Routledge is an imprint of the Taylor & Francis Group, an informa business

British Library Cataloguing in Publication Data
A catalogue record for this book is available from the British Library

ISBN: 978-1-032-55549-2 (Set)
ISBN: 978-1-032-57112-6 (Volume 14) (hbk)
ISBN: 978-1-032-57116-4 (Volume 14) (pbk)
ISBN: 978-1-003-43786-4 (Volume 14) (ebk)

DOI: 10.4324/9781003437864

Publisher's Note
The publisher has gone to great lengths to ensure the quality of this reprint but points out that some imperfections in the original copies may be apparent.

Disclaimer
The publisher has made every effort to trace copyright holders and would welcome correspondence from those they have been unable to trace.

Social Skills in Prison and the Community
Problem solving for offenders

Philip Priestley, James McGuire, David Flegg,
Valerie Hemsley, David Welham and Rosemary Barnitt

Routledge & Kegan Paul
London, Boston, Melbourne and Henley

First published in 1984 by
Routledge & Kegan Paul plc
39 Store Street, London WC1E 7DD,
9 Park Street, Boston, Mass. 02108, USA,
464 St Kilda Road, Melbourne,
Victoria 3004, Australia and
Broadway House, Newtown Road,
Henley-on-Thames, Oxon RG9 1EN
Printed in Great Britain by
Thetford Press, Thetford, Norfolk

Library of Congress Cataloging in Publication Data

Social skills in prison and the community
Bibliography: p.
Includes index.
1. Prisoners - Education - Great Britain - Case studies.
2. Social skills - Study and teaching - Great Britain -
Case studies. 3. Rehabilitation of criminals - Great
Britain - Case studies. I. Priestley, Philip.
HV8883.3.G7S262 1984 365'.66 83-21160

ISBN 0-7100-9272-5

Contents

ACKNOWLEDGMENTS   vii

1   THE PROBLEM AND A PROJECT   1

2   DESIGN AND DEVELOPMENT   12

3   TRAINING THE STAFF   22

4   THE OFFENDERS AND THEIR PROBLEMS   35

5   METHODS AND MATERIALS   60

6   THE CONDUCT OF THE COURSES   92

7   THE RESULTS OF THE COURSES   111

8   AFTERWARDS   135

9   PROBLEMS AND PROSPECTS   166

    APPENDIX 1   176

    APPENDIX 2   178

    NOTES   180

    BIBLIOGRAPHY   187

    INDEX   192

Acknowledgments

We are grateful to more people than can properly be thanked here.
Firstly, the Home Office Research Unit which funded the whole project
for more than three years, and secondly Dr Eunice Belbin of the
Industrial Training Research Unit, Cambridge, who secured and administered the grant, and made the enterprise possible. The Prison
Department gave us access to their prisons and seconded four full-
time officer posts to the release courses, and the Day Training Centre
of the South Yorkshire Probation and After-care Service invited us to
work with their staff and members. The Governors of Ranby and Ashwell
prisons made us welcome in their establishments. We would like to
thank Peter Soord, director of the Sheffield Day Training Centre, who
made us welcome there and greatly facilitated our work, together with
the staff of the Centre who were involved in running groups at various
times over the duration of the project: Jack Binks, Jon Clennell, Jim
Cowley, Linda MacLeod, Jack Quinn and Antonia Savage.

The burden of the work was carried out in all these places by
prison officers and probation officers; we would like to thank also
John Clenell, Barry Commons, Bob Cordiner, Bill Cossar, Clive Gostelow,
Brian Needham, Roger Needham, Ken Poulton, Pete Simms, Derek Skinner,
Ray Taylor, Larry Townsend, Bill Wallace and Ken Wilford; without
their efforts, nothing would have been achieved.

Thanks also to Dr Mary Edwards for help with the staff training
and at Ashwell Prison; to Robin Smith who supplied some of the test
data quoted in chapter four and to Lesley Furness whose help in com-
piling both background and follow-up information was invaluable; to
Richard Tilt, Brian Emes, Ralph Skrine, Dr Michael Doran, Erzsi
Hurley, Philip Bartlett, Rodney Cox, Ken Jones, Sonia Coats, Peter
Dawson, Tom Douglas, and last, but far from least, all the men in
Ranby and Ashwell, Cardiff, Nottingham and Leicester prisons, and
Glen Parva Borstal, and at the Sheffield Day Training Centre, from
whom we learned so much.

Chapter 1

The problem and a project

From the end of the Second World War until the mid-1970s, English penal policy was broadly characterised by an emphasis on keeping people out of custodial institutions. The making of this policy was a complex business to which many agencies and organisations and individuals contributed, and its results were to be seen in a series of legislative measures, and in the changing practices adopted in penal establishments and community services for offenders. (1) In prison, the emphasis took the form of activities known collectively as 'treatment and training'. 'Treatment' was represented briefly in the 'Norwich experiment', when basic grade prison officers attempted to reproduce under English conditions the therapeutic groupwork conducted in Californian prisons under the guidance of Norman Fenton. (2,3) More permanently, Grendon Underwood Prison embodied the idea of a therapeutic community for prisoners classified as in need of psychiatric treatment, or as psychopaths. (4) The 'training' element was represented in trade and vocational courses which have a long history in the prison service, and which have waxed and waned, and been born again, most recently in the guise of the 'industrial' prison. (5) And a third strand of the 'treatment and training' approach was provided by a variety of schemes to prepare prisoners, and especially longer-sentence ones, for the transition from inside to outside. Pre-release hostels and working-out schemes linked vocational training and preparation directly to work in the community. (6)

They also complemented the parallel development of pre-release preparation, which increasingly involved probation officers in the provision of services inside as well as outside prison. (7)

In the community, voluntary after-care was added to the statutory supervision already given by the probation service to Borstal boys, young prisoners, preventive detainees, and life sentence offenders released on licence. (8) Voluntary after-care hostels and other schemes to help ex-prisoners also proliferated. (9)

There is little evidence, however, to suggest that any of these and other innovations, either singly, or in combination, had any measurable or repeatable effects on the reconviction rates of the offenders who experienced them. (10) In fact a declining use of imprisonment as a proportion of all sentences passed in both the

magistrates' and higher courts was accompanied by a steady growth
in the numbers of men and women held in prison, which led, in the
late 1960s and early 1970s, to one of the now familiar 'overcrowd-
ing' crises. (11)

Suspended sentences, available from 1967, had made no permanent
impression on the prison population, appearing like other such
measures to act more as an alternative to fines or probation than
to prison. (12) It was against this background that the Criminal
Justice Act of 1972 introduced a number of new measures, designed,
amongst other things, to divert offenders from custodial sentences.
They included deferred sentences, criminal bankruptcy, community
service, and day training centres. Deferred sentences had the
effect of lengthening the tariff available to the courts; criminal
bankruptcy and community service were both based on the deliber-
ations of the Advisory Council on the Penal System, under the chair-
manship of Lady Wootton, and they sought to strengthen that part of
the criminal law which stresses restitution and reparation; directly in the case of bankruptcy, and indirectly through the community
service order. (13) Day training centres owed more to the 'treatment and training' model. This book is an account of an action-
research project which took place in the period following the implementation of the 1972 legislation. Its main aim was to develop and
try out some new ways of helping offenders to tackle some of their
problems both in and out of prison. These were to be incorporated
in full-time courses, lasting for several weeks, for men about to
be released from two Midland prisons, Ranby and Ashwell, and for
offenders attending one of the experimental day training centres
established under the 1972 act; the one at Sheffield run by the
South Yorkshire Probation Service. Course materials were developed,
prison and probation officers were trained to use them, and they
were tried out with thirty-six groups of offenders - nineteen groups
in the two prisons, comprising 224 men, and seventeen groups at
Sheffield day training centre, containing 123 members, a combined
total of 347.

This book outlines the origins of the project, the design and
development of course materials and the training of staff; looks at
the characteristics of the offenders who took part in the experiment, and at some of their self-reported problems; details the content and conduct of the courses in practice; and reports some evaluative data by which the effectiveness of the work may be gauged.

In this chapter some of the problems of men leaving prison are
considered, as well as the difficulties of doing innovative work in
penal establishments; and the origins and nature of the day training centre at Sheffield are described.

LEAVING PRISON

'Gate fever' is the name of a non-medical syndrome said to infect
men in prison as the day of their discharge draws near. Its symp-
toms are euphoria and anxiety mixed with irrational thinking; and
the unfailing cure of the condition is the cold douche of reality
which awaits the victim outside the prison gate. (14)

The problems which confront the newly released prisoner are dif-

ferent for each individual but the most common and immediate of them
are the practical difficulties of finding somewhere to live, getting
and keeping a job, and negotiating the social security system in
order to keep afloat financially. (15)   Behind these tangible problems lie the less visible but no less real ones of re-establishing
relationships with family and friends and neighbours. (16)   To the
tackling of these dilemmas many ex-prisoners bring a deeply rooted
sense of belonging to a legally disadvantaged and socially stigma-
tised minority. (17)   And depending on how long a man has spent in
prison he will emerge more or less ill-equipped to cope with his
problems and to compete in the obstacle race which appears to separate him from the elusive goal of personal rehabilitation. (18)

It may be significant that the annual reports of the Prison Department record in detail the number and complexion of receptions
into prison establishments during any year, but fail to mention any-
where how many men are discharged on completion of their sentences.
And that preparing men for release has tended to be seen as a mar-
ginal activity of little concern to main grade prison staff.   One
of the aims of this research was to involve uniformed officers in
providing an improved level of service to men about to be released
from prison.   In order to understand the development of the project,
it may be useful to look at some of the forces that help to shape
the predicament of the recent ex-prisoner.

The purpose of imprisonment

Perhaps the most important thing to acknowledge is that despite some
tentative official rhetoric to the contrary, prisons remain first
and foremost places of punishment. (19)   Men and women are sent
there, partly to protect society by removing them from its midst,
but mainly so that they can be made to suffer the pains of imprisonment for as long as the courts have decreed at the time of their
sentences.   Two ideas are commonly invoked to justify the imposition
of suffering on offenders;   desert and deterrence.   Desert is a
polite word for revenge.   It is rarely put so crudely nowadays as in
the lex talionis - an eye for an eye - but the effect is the same.
Sentences are supposedly calculated so as to equate the damage
caused by an offence with the suffering which must be undergone by
the offender so that he can 'pay off his debt to society'.   It is
an idea which has deep roots in everyday thinking about law and
order, is historically linked with the blood feud and Saxon notions
of compensation (20) and may on occasion even make sense to offenders who feel contrite about what they have done. (21)

But whereas desert looks back to past events, deterrence is concerned with future behaviour;   both with that of the particular offender and with that of other potential offenders.   Specifically,
the theory of deterrence holds that a painful or punitive experience
will persuade an individual to avoid in future the behaviour which
has brought it upon him. (22)   And, the argument continues, others
who are made aware of these unpleasant consequences will themselves
be deterred from engaging in that sort of behaviour.   So deterrence
also incorporates a primitive theory of reform, and forms one of the
cornerstones of current penal practice.   Prisons are organised to

give expression to these ideas; not by inflicting physical pain and
suffering of the kind associated with earlier models of justice, but
essentially by imposing a number of social and psychological deprivations on the convicted person. (23)

The subjective experience of imprisonment

The most fundamental of these deprivations is loss of freedom;
freedom of movement, freedom of association, freedom of choice. It
is not simply that custody has to be endured; what determines the
quality of life in prison is the extent to which choices about virtually everything are curtailed. (24) Most of the major elements
of the prison routine are not open to negotiation; things to do
with time, getting up in the morning, going to bed, mealtimes, association periods, governor's applications, the earliest date of
release; and things related to place, the prison where the sentence
is served, location within it, furnishings, work options and so on.
In addition severe restrictions are placed on the quantity and
quality of communication which the prisoner can maintain with the
outside world. Add to these deprivations the absence of money in
realistic amounts, of the opposite sex and alcohol, and of most
normal leisure pursuits, then extend the picture it conveys through
time, through months and years; and something of the meaning of imprisonment emerges quite graphically. (25) Even so the subjective
experience of a prison sentence cannot be properly appreciated by
inspecting a straightforward catalogue of items of this sort. From
the inside, prison life is most often seen, and felt, in terms of
frustration; of being at the mercy of a blind bureaucracy, and of
personal helplessness. (26) Personal adaptations to this situation
can assume radically alternative forms. A few prisoners rebel,
either in individual campaigns of insubordination, (27) or collectively in riots. (28) Most adopt a posture of passive conformity
towards a system which is clearly beyond their control. In extreme
cases this passivity can become what has been recognised as 'institutional neurosis'. And even in cases which fall short of this
diagnosis there may be perceptible attrition of the personality and
character. (29)
     The longer that men spend in prison the more likely it becomes
that they will suffer some degree of damage, and the more difficult
it becomes for them to manage successfully the transition from captivity to freedom. It has been the recognition of this damage which
has provided some of the motive power for the slow reform of the
prison system over the past century and a half. (30) This process
can best be described as a humanitarian drift away from the milita-
ristic rigidities and cruelties of the silent system, but in more
recent years it has been broadened out and speeded up by the addition of ideas and practices designed to reform or 'cure' the individual offender. (31)
     These have been introduced into the prison system by imported
specialists, priests, doctors, psychiatrists, education officers,
psychologists, welfare officers; professionals and semi-profession-
als possessing competences and loyalties rooted in the world outside
prison. And they have brought with them an ideology of treatment

which conflicts sharply with the traditional view of imprisonment
based on utilitarian notions of deterrence and repentance. (32)

The role of the prison officer

Since custody has been, and remains, the most important function of
the prison service, its internal organisation, which closely follows
a military model, has changed little in any of its essential features. Within this hierarchic, bureaucratic and rule-bound framework the actual duties of the basic grade prison officer have also
remained relatively static, although the style in which they were
carried out until quite recently was more relaxed than was the case
prior to the Second World War. (33) But by comparison with the work
of the 'treatment' intruders their tasks have come to assume an increasingly custodial appearance.
        Since 1963, it has been the official policy of the Prison Offi-
cers Association to press for the greater involvement of its members
in rehabilitative tasks. In its policy statement, 'The role of the
modern prison officer', the work of typical uniformed officers is
described as being that of 'mere fetchers and carriers of men for
the people who come inside from the various bodies which interest
themselves in prison work'. (34) And of his ordinary daily routine
it says 'there is little in this procedure that is different from
the work of the turnkey in the last century, and the Prison Officer
class as a whole is tending to become thoroughly institutionalised
as a result.'
        It is not clear to what extent these views reflected those of
the grass-roots membership of the association, nor how far they
simply represented some sort of lever for securing higher status
and pay. But they did constitute an explicit challenge to the assumed expertise of the treatment professionals. The claim that
prison officers could perform their duties just as well remains to
be tested in practice since only limited opportunities have been
created for officers to undertake rehabilitative work with serving
prisoners. (35) Nor have they been prepared for such a role by the
basic training they have received on entering the prison service.
Although there is an expectation that officers will be 'a good influence' on their charges, no time is allocated during the ordinary
daily routine for this to take any form more specific than a kind of
'moral osmosis'. And officers are not trained in the specific
skills they might need to engage in individual counselling or group-
work with prisoners.

'Screws' and 'cons'

One of the reasons for this may be a reticence on the staff side to
relinquish the predictability of discipline and standing orders for
the uncertainties of personal involvement with men in prison. Another and probably more important obstacle to innovation in this
direction is provided by serving prisoners themselves.
        The 'inmate subculture' in English prisons is less virulent and
less articulated than that which is reported to exist in American

gaols but there is a code of values which commands quite wide assent amongst the prisoner group. (36) Externally this code declares war on the forces of law and order, and in particular it defines the prison officer as 'the enemy' with whom contact is permitted only for purposes of exploitation. (37) These sentiments are summarised in the phrase 'All screws are bastards', and despite the distinction which most prisoners can make in practice between 'good screws' and 'bad screws', it is clear that there are powerful constraints against any activity which resembles fraternisation with the enemy. (38)

Innovation in prison

Any attempt at innovation within the prison system must therefore contend with a set of conditions which are almost always less than encouraging, and quite often directly destructive. The difficulties include:

1 The confused and contradictory nature of the purposes which the prison system is supposed to serve.
2 The primacy of custodial and punitive aims over those of re-habilitation and reform.
3 A lack of consensus amongst prison staff about the nature of their proper role.
4 The deep organisational divisions which exist between officers and prisoners.

'Release courses'

The release course project originated in discussions with the Home Office Research Unit and the Prison Department between 1973 and 1975, about possible ways of preparing prisoners for release, with a particular emphasis on finding and keeping work in the community. Initially it was thought that this would be an educational enter-prise, best undertaken by part-time teachers recruited specially for the purpose. At some point during the development of the pro-ject proposal, it was suggested that prison officers could be trained to perform these tasks, thus allowing some test of the as-pirations expressed in the POA paper, 'The role of the modern prison officer'.

In order to evaluate the effectiveness of the training model which eventually emerged, it was proposed that courses be run in a variety of establishments: a local prison dealing with very short-sentence men; a medium sentence training prison; and a long-term prison. Outside prison courses were to be organised in a probation home or hostel, and if possible, a day training centre.

It was agreed that two, full-time, basic grade officer posts would be allocated to the project in each of the prisons, and that four officers from each establishment would be trained to work in pairs, running alternate courses of twelve weeks' duration, for groups of twelve men nearing their earliest dates of release (EDRs). In the event the 1975-6 squeeze on public expenditure curtailed the number of prison sites to two, which turned out to be Ranby and Ashwell.

Ranby prison, near Retford, Nottinghamshire was opened in July 1971 as a closed, low-security (category 'C') establishment, based on a former RAF camp, but in the process of being rebuilt by prison labour. In 1975 its population was still expanding and around the four hundred mark. Trade training courses were available in painting and decorating, construction work, and basic electronics. Expensively equipped workshops were intended for the production of electrical-mechanical products, and for wood machining and assembly work, although there were difficulties in securing regular supplies of work, especially for the woodwork.

Ashwell is an open prison near Oakham in Leicestershire operating since 1955 in a former army camp. There is no perimeter security, and the four hundred or so men there, drawn from Midland Region local prisons, are serving sentences of less than five years, and are security category 'D'. The men are housed in army-style billets, and in one hundred purpose-built rooms. In 1975, a number of sixteen-week vocational training courses were available to prisoners, including electrical work, bricklaying, construction, painting and decorating, plastering, and carpentry. Many of the graduates of these courses were subsequently employed on outside working parties building the new Borstal at Glen Parva near Leicester. Other men worked on the prison farm or on domestic duties within the prison.

As for the proposal to run courses outside prison, funding was not forthcoming for the hostel option, and it appeared at first as though none of the existing day training centres would be willing to incorporate any of the intended course contents into their regimes. At Sheffield, however, a change of director was taking place in 1975 and the basic programme of the centre was under review.

After discussions, the centre agreed to collaborate in the research by attempting to integrate the course content developed for use in the prisons into its own programme and to monitor and evaluate its feasibility and effectiveness for offenders not undergoing sentences of imprisonment.

DAY TRAINING CENTRES

Origins

The idea of non-residential alternatives to prison is not new; fines, probation orders, and attendance centres are long-standing examples in this country. The extension of attendance centre sentences from juvenile to adult offenders has frequently been urged by the Magistrates' Association, and Dr R.G. Andry proposed a non-residential form of treatment for persistent petty offenders in his book 'The Short Term Prisoner'. (39)

The specific impetus for the day training centres established in the 1972 Criminal Justice Act came from a survey of '614 men leaving local prisons' carried out by Kate Vercoe, in collaboration with prison welfare officers at Swansea, Cardiff, Bristol and Gloucester; all of them busy local prisons with a rapid turnover of short-sentence offenders. (40) The survey, commissioned by the south-western regional council of the National Association for the Care and Resettlement of Offenders, revealed a process of drift into social isolation, drink dependence, and chronic petty recidivism. A working party of the regional council, at its meeting on 15 April 1970, recommended that proposals for a non-residential alternative to prison be drawn up. This was described as 'a community training centre, which men could be required to attend within the conditions of a probation order', and which could operate as 'a viable alterna-tive to imprisonment for a considerable proportion of those now com-mitted for short sentences only. The centre would provide a wide range of courses and experiences in the general areas of health, re-medial education, vocational training and preparation, and personal development.' (41)

A fuller proposal was published as a NACRO Regional Paper, 'The problem of the short term prisoner', and later presented to a Howard League conference in November 1970, chaired by Lord Gardiner, the former Lord Chancellor, and attended by senior Home Office offi-cials. (42)

Section 20 of the Criminal Justice Act provided for convicted of-fenders to be required to attend a day training centre for a period not exceeding sixty days, as part of a probation order which would continue after the statutory attendance had been completed. Four day training centres were set up on an experimental basis in four probation areas; Inner London, Mid-Glamorgan, Liverpool, and South Yorkshire. Sheffield was the first of the four to open, taking its earliest group of offenders in March 1973. Each of the centres sub-sequently developed along different lines; and for some consider-able time after their inception they appear to have had little in common with each other beyond an overall aim 'to advise, assist and befriend'.

Sheffield day training centre

At Sheffield, the aims of training during the sixty-day period cen-tred around some basic notions: of developing self-awareness; of examining personal problems; and of preparing for work. In ad-dition the centre sought to develop a strong sense of community, through which, in part, some of its other goals could be achieved. Staff and probationers were to work together to solve problems, whether individual or communal.

Briefly, the programme could be described in terms of three cen-tral elements: first, a set of rules governing its basic organisa-tion; second, a range of resources and activities that supplied the content of each day; and third, a specific way of working which in-fluenced most of what happened to staff and probationers alike.

First, with reference to rules and basic procedures; those at-tending the centre were expected to stay for sixty working days, or five days a week for twelve weeks; from 8.30 in the morning until 5.00 (now 4.30) in the afternoon. Each day was divided into four sessions, the exact timetabling of which has varied over the years.

The centre was designed for fifteen probationers at a time; all
adult males who might otherwise be sent to prison. Initially these
were to be drawn from the Sheffield area, but the catchment boundaries have slowly expanded, to include Rotherham, then the rest of
South Yorkshire, and more recently even the occasional man from
Leeds or Nottingham. Men in attendance at the centre could leave
five days early if they showed evidence of having a job. In addition the centre had some ground rules concerning behaviour - for
instance, no physical violence was tolerated - which have of course
been retained and could hardly be discarded.

Referral

The basic mechanism by which men arrived in the centre was referral
by a field probation officer prior to a court appearance. Those
referred were invited to spend a day in the centre deciding whether
or not they wanted to come. During this day, the centre exercised
its own selection procedure, consisting of interviews carried out
by the director and another probation officer; tests of intelligence and personality administered by a visiting psychologist; and
a case conference, involving the director, the staff probation officer who has seen the offender, the psychologist, and the referring
probation officer from outside. The decision to accept or reject
the man was taken by the director; if accepted, the man could in
turn only be sent for day training if he himself consented; and of
course, only if the court saw fit to send him.
     Some types of offenders, including all those under twenty-one,
those with a history of psychiatric illness, or those suffering from
severe alcoholic or drug addictions, were not accepted. (43)
     If sentenced to probation with a day training condition attached,
the offender could start his sixty days on the first Monday following his court appearance. This led to a 'staggered' intake system;
the small numbers starting together on a given day remained together
for an initial period, after which they were allocated to other activity groups. This feature of the centre was altered at the beginning of the period of experimental work being described here, and a
'block intake' system installed in its place.

Activities

A second major element in the day training centre's programme at
that time was, of course, the assorted group activities that went
to make up each day. Though the exact nature of these inevitably
changed between 1973 and 1975, in essence they were of two principal
kinds: group discussions, and practical activities of various
sorts. Each day began with a community meeting involving all members of the centre; staff probation officers, ancillaries, secreta-
ries, and men on probation. This was followed after a break and
staff review session, by smaller group discussions with individual
probation officers. In the afternoon, a wide range of other activities was available, depending partly on the day of the week as some
staff were employed on a sessional basis; these included woodwork,

enamelling, pottery, restoring furniture, maintenance work in a
local industrial museum, and games and exercises in the centre's
gym. Outside community work, such as gardening or home repairs for
old people, was available to most men at some time during their
stay. During one period a family group was run on one afternoon a
week, and relatives and probation officers of the men attending the
centre were invited. Finally, a man in the centre would see his own
outside field officer two or three times during his twelve weeks -
certainly during initial and final assessments, and probably on at
least one other occasion in between.

Rationale

These are, however, only the superficial aspects of the centre's
life, and to make sense of them we must turn to a third element, the
way of working, which provided the rationale for the rest of the
centre's activity. Like other centres, Sheffield adopted a 'treatment' orientation towards its work, and looked towards psychiatry
for inspiration which it found in the concept of the 'therapeutic
community'. The 'therapeutic community' idea has had some currency
in psychiatry in this country for over twenty years; and has followed a related notion - that of casework, with which it shares a
number of assumptions - in being put to work in the offender field.
At its core is the principle that all members of a community (whatever it may be) - whether staff or patients - should join forces in
an egalitarian fashion to solve members' problems. The therapeutic
community is associated particularly with the name of Maxwell Jones,
and Clark (44) has given us a sketch of such a community in Belmont
Hospital where Jones did much of his work:

> The centre of Belmont life was the morning meeting, attended by
> all members of the community, where all matters of general inter-
> est were analysed. There was a system of feedback of the events
> of the previous twenty-four hours. This was followed, always,
> by a staff review session, where the main meeting was analysed
> and personal contributions and reactions assessed. Throughout
> the day there was a pattern of meetings and discussions which
> varied over the years, but included workshop groups, domestic
> groups, small psychotherapy groups, staff sensitivity groups,
> assessment sessions etc. In all these there was some immediate
> business, but the main task was the social analysis of the 'here
> and now' - what was happening amongst the members of the groups
> at that time - always with the eventual aim of increasing the
> individual's awareness and understanding of what he was doing to
> himself and to other people.

This description could well be taken, with the staff review session
and the staff sensitivity group included, to be a description of
Sheffield day training centre during the period 1973-5. Sheffield
operated, therefore, as a therapeutic community, based, as one staff
member expressed it, on 'the generation of incident for discussion'.
Its treatment ethos rested on identical assumptions to those held by
similar communities working in psychiatry.

In many respects it is questionable whether some of these assumptions are valid for work with offenders. First, the intense focus
on interpersonal relations, and linked to this, the community's preoccupation with itself, bordering on self-absorption, can arouse
hostility amongst those not accustomed to them; this was a common
experience at the centre. Second, the notion of personal or emotional damage intrinsic to the idea of therapy is not wholly appropriate to an understanding of most offenders' problems. And third,
to a group with such an acute sense of 'them' and 'us', the presence
of staff who proclaim egalitarian ideals while simultaneously holding separate review sessions, might seem something of a contradic-
tion.

This thumbnail sketch of the regime at Sheffield day training
centre cannot fully convey what was going on there in 1975, but the
important point to be made is that existing staff had come to feel
some dissatisfaction with it as a way of working with the offenders
they were receiving, in none too large numbers, from the local
courts. As the directorship of the centre changed hands there was
an inclination to add new activities drawn from different theoretical perspectives to the daily work of the centre, and in particular
to try out some of the materials then under development for use in
release courses at Ranby and Ashwell.

Project timetable

The timetable for the project was for staff training, of prison and
probation officers, to take place at the end of 1975 and for experimental courses to take place at Ranby, Ashwell and Sheffield during
1976 and 1977. These were to be monitored and evaluated by members
of the research team. But prior to all that it was necessary to
make some decisions about the content of the proposed courses and
to gather some possible materials for inclusion in the 'package'.

Chapter 2

Design and development

THE AIMS OF THE PROJECT

The original commission from the Home Office Research Unit set two principal objectives for this research:

1　'To develop, test and evaluate a training package which will equip selected offenders with skills relevant to keeping them out of trouble. These will include work, survival and social skills.'
2　'To develop training materials and training courses for instructors so that the package can be administered by personnel normally available in the prison setting.'

It asked, in other words, for answers to two broad questions: first, what can be done to prepare men more effectively for release from prison, and to help them and other offenders to survive and stay out of trouble in the community? Second, and more specifically, what part can prison officers play in this process?

The precedents for answering either question in the affirmative were not promising. There have been many attempts, employing a wide range of theoretical perspectives and practical methods to 'rehabilitate' or 'reform' the offender. (1) So far they have failed to come up with any incontrovertible evidence of systematic change in people's attitudes or subsequent behaviour. (2) One of the reasons for this failure may be the insistence of such studies on using rates of reconviction as the sole, or even the major, criterion of success. Two problems arise from this approach. In the first place, concentration on so global a measure may leave undetected smaller, but no less significant movements in the direction of desirable goals, e.g. towards longer intervals between the commission of offences; to more minor forms of offences; to greater job stability or satisfaction; to increments of any kind in human happiness. Second, and more critically, despite the best efforts of social scientists, it has not as yet proved possible to construct a foolproof methodology for measuring the effects of any kind of intervention on human behaviour. Virtually all research that purports to do this can be shown to be flawed in one detail or another of its design, so that critics can dismiss as unfounded or untypical

of its design, so that critics can dismiss as unfounded or untypical
any findings which appear to indicate success. (3) By the same
token, the supporters of particular therapies or approaches can continue to insist that more reliable or sophisticated research designs
would be certain to demonstrate the beneficial results which they
claim to achieve in their work with given individuals or groups.

One response to these difficulties would be to abandon altogether
the search for better ways of working with offenders or other groups
of people who have problems. Another would be to pitch the aims of
research and development at a more modest level than, for example,
that of reducing gross rates of recidivism; and to set aside the
quest for 'scientific proof' in favour of more descriptive accounts
which draw on as many kinds of evidence as possible.

There are in any case other persuasive arguments for abandoning
reconviction rates as an exclusive measure of success. It appears
to be the case that homelessness, unemployment, alcohol abuse,
mental illness and other indices of social and personal disorgan-
isation are statistically related to higher probabilities of reconviction. (4) But many people who get into trouble again do not display these characteristics, whilst many of those who do escape reconviction. So helping offenders to find work and accommodation,
or to cope better with personal problems may have no bearing whatsoever on whether particular individuals re-offend or not. But
that is no argument for not doing any of these things. It is self-
evidently desirable to assist the homeless find somewhere to live,
the jobless to get work, the anxious to worry less, the addicted to
become less dependent on alcohol or drugs, and so on. Most of the
services currently provided for serving prisoners can only be justi-
fied on these grounds; the maintenance of a minimum dietary, medical services, educational facilities, vocational training, the
ministrations of the clergy, the visits of the prison visitors, or
the assistance offered by prison welfare officers. Such facilities
promote ends thought desirable in themselves. If the strict test
of recidivism were to be rigorously applied to them, or indeed to
the whole of the prison service, both they and it would be abandoned
without further ado. Similarly with the outcomes of innovative
programmes; decisions to adopt them on a larger scale are only
rarely influenced by evidence of their proven effectiveness.

So the main aim of the work at Ranby and Ashwell was not simply
to demonstrate that recidivism can be reduced, but to show that
prison officers can undertake a rehabilitative role in their work
with serving prisoners towards the ends of their sentences. Signs
of success for this less ambitious programme were to be sought in
what happened in the prison and afterwards; in the quality of the
day-to-day contacts as well as between officers and men engaged in
the project, and in the reactions of both of them to what they were
doing.

In essence this book describes a feasibility study rather than a
controlled experiment. But the feasibility of what? An equation
had to be found which somehow matched the known problems of released
prisoners with the as yet unknown capacities of prison officers,
none of them with previous training or experience of working in a
rehabilitative way with prisoners. And a way also had to be found
of not reproducing the problems and pitfalls which have dogged past

efforts to prepare prisoners for release. Of these, the most important by far concerned the acceptability to serving prisoners of
the service they were to be offered. Prison welfare officers who
are administratively responsible for helping men with their release
problems occupy a peculiar place in the prison structure, working
within it, yet not of it, and the object of suspicion and obstruc-
tion from discipline staff and serving prisoners alike. Prisoners
tend to resort to 'the welfare' in order to pass messages to the
outside world, to get information about what is going on at home,
and to secure help with tangible problems such as abandoned suit-
cases or negotiations with the tax authorities. It is unlikely that
many of the men, or indeed many of the welfare officers would argue
that the transactions between them were seriously aimed at helping
individuals to change their attitudes or behaviour.

There had been in most establishments sporadic efforts by prison
welfare departments to mount pre-release courses, typically in the
form of voluntary evening sessions looking at things like social
security, the role of the probation and after-care service, tax
matters and so on. The attractiveness of these proceedings to most
men in prison can be measured directly by their attendance figures,
which in most cases can best be described as disappointing.

The 'education' model

The search for something better as the basis of this project focused
first on three existing models for working with people. The most
obvious of them was a conventional model of 'education'; the organisation of classroom situations in which a teacher imparts knowledge
to students. The knowledge may be of a factual or a conceptual
nature and the methods employed to impart it can range from stand-up
teaching, rote learning, note-taking, reading, and watching films,
to programmed learning, multi-media presentations, and project work
of various kinds. Existing pre-release courses often conformed
closely to the traditional pattern of a lecture by a visiting
expert, followed by an opportunity for questions and discussion.
It is a perfectly respectable way of helping some people to learn
about some topics, but as a model for pre-release preparation it
can only be a partial one since it stresses the giving of information at the expense of other and equally important items. It also
posed a problem of expertise for prison officers none of whom was
likely to possess either the expert knowledge required, or experience of teaching methods. It was desirable however that course
tutors develop the ability to prepare and present factual material
to their members in an interesting and appealing way. And that they
should be able to devise opportunities for acquiring and assimi-
lating information from a wide range of other sources. It would be
presumptuous to designate these as formal teaching skills, but the
distinction was likely to be an academic one to prison officers, and
even probation officers, to whom the idea of standing in front of a
group of people and telling and showing them things placed them in-
escapably in the role of 'teacher'.

The 'social work' model

Social work provided a second possible model; one which concen-
trates more on feelings and attitudes than on information. In its
pure form it is an adaptation of psychotherapy, using one-to-one
counselling and group work to promote insight and self-awareness and
to help individuals make decisions and cope with difficulties by
talking through them. Like teaching it presupposes long professional training; but unlike education it also demands that its practi-
tioners subscribe to specific bodies of 'theory' about human psychology and the development of the personality in both its normal
and abnormal forms. (5) It posed therefore the same question of
expertise as did the educational model, and added to it the difficulty that the aims and methods of social work are less widely
understood and far less widely accepted both amongst prison staffs
and by prisoners themselves. (6) It could even be argued that the
model disqualified itself for use in pre-release situations in terms
of the vigorous resistance of many offenders to the idea that they
are 'sick' or in need of treatment.
      Two elements of social work practice were nevertheless essential
for helping offenders cope better with their problems; namely one-
to-one counselling, and group discussion. The use of both of these
'verbal' methods can be thought of as lying somewhere along a con-
tinuum that extends from informal chat at one end to arduous and
technically difficult 'therapies' at the other. Highly trained and
professionally employed counsellors or group therapists might wish
to draw an absolute distinction between the work that they themselves do with their 'clients' or patients and the apparently aim-
less and unstructured conversation that goes on between lower-order
staff in institutions and helping agencies and the people they are
trying to assist. But there is an increasing quantity of evidence
that this is not the case. In so far as the positive effects of
verbal methods of helping can be measured at all it appears that
naive, briefly trained, or even untrained, helpers can achieve results which are not only as good as those achieved by professionals,
but in some cases even better. (7) There is also an accumulating
body of experience which suggests that individuals with problems
can become prime agents in their own and others' therapy by taking
part in self-help groups and activities and by engaging in co-
counselling procedures. (8)
      There were good reasons therefore for including these elements
in the programme and they were added to a growing list of activities
and skills which the project staff were expected to master before
and during the courses they were to run with prisoners and day
training centre members.

The 'training' model

A third model for working with people is that of training - most
familiarly used in the transmission of manual and occupational
skills. Trade training is fairly widely available in prisons, and
it was not intended in this research to duplicate that provision.
But the basic notions which underlie the 'training' tradition proved

to be of more direct relevance in their more recent guise of 'social
skills training'. This became in fact one of the principal sources
for the contents of the 'package' that was being assembled, and because of its importance to the project and the relative novelty of
the methods - more pronounced in 1975 than today - a fuller account
of social skills training is given at this point.

Social skills methods

Social skills training methods were initially developed and used in
the field of mental health, and their overall aim was to help
psychiatric patients by enabling them to improve their ability to
deal with other people and to form relationships with them. It had
been noted, for example by the psychoanalyst Harry Stack Sullivan
(9,10) in his work with psychiatric patients, that many of their
illnesses could be characterised by, and perhaps even traced to,
disturbed patterns of relationships between patients and other
people. If an individual failed to communicate with others in a
satisfactory manner, his or her social behaviour could become dis-
torted as a result. Sullivan elaborated this view of illness in
his 'interpersonal theory of psychiatry', which placed the repair
of personal relations, and the enhancement of the individual's conception of him or herself with regard to others, at the centre of
the therapeutic process.
    But the impetus to look at social skills as such, at complex,
learned sequences of social behaviour and response, came not from
psychoanalysis but from social learning theory, and social skills
training was devised in the beginning as a technique of behaviour
modification. Current concepts of social skills training however
differ from traditional notions of psychotherapy, where the accent
may be on the promotion of insight, or the shaping of behaviour by
punishments and rewards, in that the starting-point is the individual's own expressions of discomfort vis-à-vis particular social situations, and in that what follows is not 'treatment', but 'training'
of a specific kind.
    Such training begins with assessment, just as do other forms of
social work or psychotherapy, but in this case it is designed primarily to help the individual pinpoint those areas of social life
in which a lack of confidence or an inability to act appropriately
is somehow damaging to him or herself, to others, or to relations
between the two. Assessment might be accomplished by asking the
individual to complete a questionnaire on his or her interpersonal
problems or social behaviour, by interviewing the individual, and
by informal observation of his or her typical social response in
common everyday situations or by more systematic scrutiny of role-
played versions of them. From this there emerges a picture of the
individual's capacities in dealing with others; and in particular,
those areas in which he or she would like to become more skilled
can be located with some accuracy. The net result is that the individual is helped to arrive at some decisions about those aspects of
social skills which he or she would like to alter in some respect.
    What follows next is the training element of the process, in-
tended to enable individuals to extend their range of social skills,

improve particular skills, or find new ways to approach specific encounters that they have previously misconstrued, mishandled, or dealt with to their own disadvantage. In some cases this may mean helping someone obtain enough courage and confidence to cope with others on even the simplest and least threatening level. In others it may mean teaching someone the real meaning of a gesture or other social signal which he or she has consistently misinterpreted. In still others, it may mean analysing a complex and very stressful encounter in the hope of finding alternative ways to handle it.

Whichever of these may be the case, a number of training methods will be used to develop social skills. The first is instruction, or advice-giving, about the nature of social interaction, about the expectations of people in particular well-defined situations (job interviews, dates, or court hearings, for example), or about the messages conveyed by social signals of various kinds. A second method, which takes the process of instruction a stage further, is known as modelling; this entails the actual demonstration, in a specially prepared role play (live or on videotape), of how some situation might be dealt with, the demonstration being given by someone (or by several people) confident enough to deal with the situation in question. The focus of attention then shifts to the learner. For having explored different ways in which such-and-such an encounter might be handled, he or she must then try out the necessary skills, and must practise them as thoroughly as possible, first in informal role plays, and later in real situations or in role plays made as lifelike as possible. In some cases, individuals may be asked to monitor their everyday transactions with others and report to the therapist or worker on the progress they are making. Finally, to make the person's own attempts to acquire skills as effective as possible, feedback must be given on how well he or she is doing; in other words, comments must be supplied by other people on their reactions to the person's gradually changing social behaviour. This complete training sequence must be followed as often as possible, for as many skills as is necessary, until individuals are both more confident about their ability to deal with others, and are also actually more socially competent in the eyes of others as well as themselves.

How effective is this kind of training in helping people to make real improvements in their social skill? Research work, conducted mainly with psychiatric patients, has so far proved fairly encouraging. Groups of psychiatric patients from various diagnostic categories, including the 'socially phobic', those suffering from depression or anxiety states, and schizophrenics have derived benefit from specially prepared courses of social skills training mounted and evaluated by numerous workers (e.g. 11,12,13 and 14). The training has also proved to be effective with various handicapped groups - children, (15) adolescents, (16) and adults. (17) Modelling and related exercises have also been shown to be valuable for social skills training with a variety of non-psychiatric populations. They have been used, for instance, to teach dating skills to students, (18) in assertiveness training for women, (19) to help individuals overcome shyness and social anxiety (20) and to help children and adolescents acquire conversation, friendship-making, and other social skills. (21,22,23) Finally, the training has been successfully applied not only to the promotion of socially valuable behaviour, but also to the skilled control of socially undesirable behaviour, such as aggressiveness (24) and excessive drinking. (25) Thus there seems to be a broad spectrum of socially skilled behaviour which can be developed and improved through training. It includes basic skills like self-expression and communication, holding conversations, and talking to the opposite sex, as well as more complex kinds of skill like assertiveness or self-control in the face of different kinds of pressure from others. The training also often has the by-product (in some cases an end in itself) of helping individuals judge themselves and others more accurately. Clearly, all these kinds of skill would be of considerable value to offender groups, to help them cope with various situations, which, by their own testimony they find problematic.

The few research projects which have investigated the use of social skills training with offenders have in fact produced generally positive results. Most of the work that has been done has employed modelling as a key technique, though this is often supplemented by the use of instructions, giving feedback, and 'reinforcement' of successful or appropriate responses. The format for the modelling usually consists of a series of role plays. First, a social situation which individuals or groups handle badly is identified. A role play is then run in which inappropriate, awkward, or unsuccessful strategies for dealing with the situation are examined. Next, models, who may be the people running the group or group members themselves, demonstrate more effective ways of dealing with it. Those who find the situation problematic are then encouraged to imitate the models, and are given feedback by others on how well they are doing. This kind of format has been used to train offenders both in very basic skills such as the use of eye contact, and in more complex skills that might be deployed in everyday (but slightly difficult) encounters.

To date, most of the evidence that this kind of training can be effective has come from work with adolescent offenders. For example, Spence and Marzillier (26) ran a series of training sessions with a group of five young male offenders in a regional assessment centre. Concentrating on very elementary skills such as the use of eye contact, the making of appropriate head movements, and so on, it was found that training could produce short-term positive effects on the behaviour of the five boys, though some skills were affected more than others and different boys showed different kinds of improvement over time. Looking at more complex skills, Thelen, Fry, Dollinger and Paul (27) used pre-recorded videotaped models to illustrate appropriate ways of dealing with sticky situations, e.g. being accused of something, or asking for help with a problem. Having viewed these tapes, the boys who took part in the experiment were then asked to role-play the model's part in a re-enactment of the situation. The boys, residents of a children's home, were subsequently judged as being better socially adjusted by teachers and social work staff who rated their behaviour 'blind', though these effects were somewhat short-lived, a result which prompted the authors to suggest that the staff might also be included in the training.

A longer-term study, with a much larger sample and firmer results, was carried out by Sarason and Ganzer. (28,29) Once again, a modelling - role play - feedback sequence was used; this time to look at a whole series of social situations over a training course of sixteen, one-hour sessions. The work was carried out in a reception and diagnostic centre for delinquent boys. Sixty-four boys were given social skills training incorporating modelling exercises, and were compared in their subsequent performance with sixty-four boys assigned to a discussion group and sixty-four assigned to a 'control' group. Follow-up of the three sub-samples showed that the 'modelling' and 'discussion' groups made significant gains as compared to the control group, in their attitudes, social behaviour, degree of self-control, and most significantly of all, in their rate of recidivism after a three-year period had elapsed. 'Modelling' group members in particular had a clearer recollection than 'discussion' group members of the content of their training sessions; and were more likely to attribute changes in their behaviour to what they had learned in the group.

But it is not only with adolescent offenders that social skills training has had worthwhile effects. Crawford (30) undertook a series of training sessions with three sex offenders in Broadmoor Hospital. The sessions, sixteen in all over a three-month period, focused initially on the basic components of social interaction such as non-verbal communication, voice intonation, etc. and progressed to more 'advanced' skills that might be called into play in fairly intricate situations, including, for this group, interacting with members of the opposite sex. The results, collated from questionnaire responses, and from ratings made by external observers of the patients' performances in role plays and on videotaped talks, showed that the three individuals who took part had become substantially more socially skilled than members of an untrained 'control' group. They spoke more clearly and fluently, behaved with more friendliness and confidence, and reacted more appropriately towards others.

Various other pieces of research have shown, for example, that it is possible to lessen conflict between juvenile offenders and their parents by training both parties in negotiating skills, (31) and that it is also possible to decrease 'egocentrism' amongst chronic juvenile offenders, and to increase their capacity to appreciate situations from another person's point of view, by inviting them to enact a series of role plays in which they successively take different parts. (32) In the second of these studies, an eighteen-month follow-up of the boys who participated in these role plays indicated that they were significantly less offence-prone than members of comparison 'placebo' and 'control' groups.

The use of social skills training is now becoming more widespread in work with offenders, but since much of this occurs at practitioner level, and is not research-orientated in purpose, it rarely appears in reports. Skills training methods have however recently been tested for feasibility in a number of social work settings, ranging from intermediate treatment, (33) to social work in prison. (34) Explorations like these suggest that the use of social skills training is not a strategy restricted to the psychologist's armoury alone: sessions can be organised on a fairly informal basis and run by staff of many different social work agencies.

To employ social skills methods with offenders, however, often means that the training has to be directed at fairly concrete social situations, rather than at components of social skill isolated from their familiar everyday settings. The concern of most individuals is with how they will solve a day-to-day problem involving another person or group of people. Skills viewed in the abstract, divorced from their contexts in everyday reality, may seem irrelevant and trivial. Social skills training must be applicable very directly to ordinary encounters if it is going to make much sense to adult offender groups.

For this reason, much of the material incorporated in release and day training centre courses consisted of what is known as 'life skills training'. Although founded on the same ideas as social skills training, and employing the same methods, life skills training is concerned principally with helping individuals to deal with the complexities of present-day existence; it could be summarised in a phrase as 'learning how to cope with the system'. This is not to say that it focuses exclusively on the dealings between citizens and officialdom; while negotiating with bureaucracy would certainly be seen as a 'life skill', so would a great many other competencies such as budgeting, job-seeking, making family decisions, or obtaining satisfaction from leisure time. Life skills training is then the counterpart of social skills training at the 'raw' end of the scale: attempting to help individuals take decisions and implement them in the midst of the rough-and-tumble of their daily lives.

One particular source proved especially fruitful for both general ideas and ready-made materials in the running of courses. This was the 'Life Skills Coaching Manual' produced by the Training, Research and Development Station of the Department of Manpower and Immigration, Saskatchewan, Canada. (35) This department had launched a large-scale compensatory education programme, known as Saskatchewan Newstart, in the late 1960s, the aim of which was to provide special training programmes for disadvantaged adults and adolescents in the state of Saskatchewan. Over a period of several years, the project developed a large quantity of materials for helping individuals, many of them unemployed, with low incomes, low levels of literacy, and other problems which often accompany these, to take a fresh look at their lives and to acquire a range of problem-solving skills which would help them manage their difficulties more effectively. A set of manuals was produced and a number of life skills courses were run on the basis of them; the 'Life Skills Coaching Manual' was one of these. Although the starting-point of many of these courses and their associated materials was the idea of training in interactive skills, they subsequently went on to deploy these skills in the solving of real-life problems connected with money, rights, accommodation, family, work and leisure. While much of this material had to be translated and adapted for use in release-type courses, the basic ideas it supplied contributed a great deal to the construction of many individual exercises.

A curriculum

Amongst these ideas, the most fundamental was the, perfectly obvious, but at the time peculiarly elusive, notion that it is possi-

ble to design a course that will deal with people's concrete, everyday problems, that will take them through a series of sessions which
can impart to them the skills they need for achieving greater control over themselves and their lives. This was the notion of a life
skills or problem-solving 'curriculum' and it subsequently became
the cornerstone of course design in both prisons and the day training centre.

It is tempting to report that this eventually emerged as a neat
amalgam of the three models outlined above, and in a form which lent
itself to strict empirical testing in controlled field trials; but
that would be misleading. As with most social research it is only
possible *after* the events in question to formulate elegant proposi-
tions about what went on. But during the planning of the project
some basic assumptions were made and a basic structure was evolved
within which the activity which followed was to take place.

The key to the project design was the adoption of a 'learning'
approach to the problems of the newly released prisoner. Learning
is used here, not in any narrow behaviourist sense, but in the
broadest possible definition of the word, to include any activity
whatsoever which could help men cope better with some of their problems in the community.

Educational, social work and training activities can all be incorporated within the compass of a 'learning' framework, and it has
the added advantage that it avoids the idea of therapy or treatment,
something from which both offenders and many prison officers are
likely to shy away. 'Therapy' implies that there is something wrong
with the individual, that he is a 'head case'; learning on the
other hand is a morally neutral activity which need imply no stigma
whatsoever for the learner.

The most obvious format for any kind of learning activity is
that of a 'course', a block of time or a series of discontinuous
sessions devoted in this case to preparing men for release.

In the envisaged release courses, the curriculum was conceived
from the outset as something more than a set of taught materials
about the problems men face when they are released from prison.
It was conceived as a multi-method learning experience from which
men might acquire the information, the attitudes and the skills
they required in order to survive more successfully in the outside
world. The curriculum was to consist of those activities, methods
and materials which would equip course members with 'take-away'
assets in the hope that they would then fend for themselves rather
than become unnecessarily dependent on after-care or other social
agencies. And the purpose of the research was to test and evaluate
in practice as wide a range of these materials as possible.

The overall shape of the curriculum, its aims and internal organisation, the specific nature of its contents, and the style in which
they were to be presented were the product of a number of interacting factors. These included the personal characteristics of the
offenders who were to take part in the courses, and the nature of
their self-perceived problems. Almost equally critical were the as
yet unknown capabilities of the prison officers to administer any
or all of the curriculum content, and of the probation staff at the
day training centre to adapt it to their own quite different ways
of working. Training the staff was the first step in finding
answers to some of these questions.

Chapter 3

Training the staff

Conventional wisdom insists that fully operational social workers
cannot be produced in less than two academic years, teachers in not
less than three, and group psychotherapists can take up to ten
years to come to professional maturity. The prisons involved in
this project had decided that release course officers could be produced in seven weeks. It is not unusual, of course, for raw entrants to be pitched into the fray of residential social work with
even less preparation than that. But their position is entirely
different from that of the men who were about to become release
course officers. New residential workers join established organisations with more or less successful records of surviving on a day-
to-day basis. And they bear, as junior members of staff, only a restricted degree of responsibility for ensuring that it continues to
do so. By contrast, the nine officers who came on the first of the
training courses held at Vaughan College, Leicester, (1) and the
National Marriage Guidance College at Rugby, in November and December, 1975, were being asked to:

1 Master a formidable battery of skills and techniques for working
   with people who have problems.
2 Become knowledgeable in a number of the problem areas faced by
   recent ex-prisoners, e.g. work, welfare rights, accommodation.
3 Blend these ingredients together in a sophisticated format for
   which no precise previous models existed.
4 Extend and develop existing materials to meet the needs of course
   members.
5 Establish from scratch, in a basically hostile environment, a
   workable educational course of some complexity.
6 Overcome the deep and entrenched hostility that marks the staff-
   prisoner relationship in most establishments.

The personal characteristics which the officers brought to this task
varied widely. The Ranby officers were, with one exception, relative newcomers to the service, none of them having more than two and
a half years' experience. The members of the Ashwell contingent, on

the other hand, were of longer standing, with four or five years'
service on average, an advantage in some respects but decidedly dis-
advantageous in another (namely, their eligibility for promotion to
senior officer which normally means transfer to a different establishment). The same broad difference was also true of the batch of
officer trainees from the two prisons who attended the second training course a year later.

The two groups of officers were different in one further and
crucial way: the four from Ashwell were the self-selected survivors
of a group of eleven officers who had attended an earlier presentation of the aims of the project. The Ranby officers, on the other
hand, had been 'invited' to apply for training by their Governor and
had then been briefed in detail about what the work would entail.

For the most part, both groups consisted of men in their late
twenties and early thirties, whose previous employment had been in
craft and technical work, regular service in the armed forces, unskilled factory work, driving, clerical, administrative and service
jobs. They had joined the prison service for a variety of motives,
but chiefly for the money and the security. 'Deep down,' said one
of them, 'it was the security aspect of it. I thought I'd be better
off in a service with a bit of security.' But their expectations of
what they would be doing as prison officers were far from identical.
One thought the job would consist of 'locking people behind bars'
and was surprised to find there was 'more social welfare than I had
imagined'. Another had joined with high hopes of working with
people and was disappointed that 'It didn't happen. I was quite
disillusioned. No one seemed interested in getting anything done.'

Their experience in the prison service itself had been varied
too; general discipline duties, detached service in Northern Ire-
land, clothing exchange store, labour control, chief's clerk, running an induction unit; a good cross-section from the daily round
of the modern prison officer, and one from which direct rehabilitative work with prisoners is conspicuously missing. Not all of
the officers however, had been content to let matters rest there.
'There was a lot of scope for satisfaction and interest,' claimed
one of the longer-serving officers, who had tried to encourage
prisoners 'to look at life in a realistic way'. He had had some
success in this but also found there was a price to pay, because
'It made me a loner. I've faced a lot of criticism from people of
higher rank than myself. They didn't see the officer's role as I
see it. It's almost as though a lot of staff are afraid they may
lose control; that you can't mix discipline with the human approach.' His own answer to such criticism was unequivocal: 'It
can be done, and it ought to be done, every day by every officer.'

Despite the efforts which had been made to communicate the
nature of the project and of the training which was to precede it,
the officers arrived at Leicester for the first training course
with mixed and basically unclear ideas about what they had let
themselves in for. They ranged from almost total ignorance: 'I
hadn't a clue what to expect,' and 'I didn't know much about it,'
to misconceptions about the style of the course: 'I thought we'd
be in classroom situations. I didn't realise that we'd be learning
by doing things ourselves,' and also about the nature of the content: 'I took with me a wrong anticipation of what I was going to

be taught. I thought I would come away with everything laid out A
to Z; that I could open a book when we got back and everything
would be ready to go. I found that I'd have to formulate it from
scratch.'

The statements by these last two officers identify two key
features of the training course, which were that it was based on,
first, the acquisition of basic skills, and second, equipping the
course members to write and run their own programmes rather than
relying on prescriptive packages of materials, which did not in any
case exist at that time.

The overall aim of the course was, then, to equip officers with
the skills, knowledge and confidence they need to run effective release courses.

A full list of these skills and areas of knowledge would be for-
biddingly long, but the principal items on it are:

Skills	Areas of knowledge
Interviewing	Work and vocational guidance
Counselling	Social skills training
Administering tests	Accommodation
Leading group discussion	Rights
Teaching	Violence
Conducting role play and simulations	Leisure
Using video	Money
Writing materials	Family matters
Planning and running courses	
Evaluating course activities	

It was clear that this agenda could not be covered adequately in the
time available and that some priorities needed to be established.
These were accordingly defined as the basic skills and the subject
areas of work and social skills, interpreted broadly enough to cover
some, at least, of the areas of knowledge which could not be dealt
with as fully as was thought desirable.

At the beginning of the staff training a session was devoted to
making as clear as possible the aims and assumptions of the project.
(2) The assumptions were concerned with expectations of the people
who were to take part in the project, with the conditions under
which they were to work, and with the style of the proceedings. It
was assumed, first, that most people are capable of acquiring new
skills and of extending the legitimate control they exert over their
immediate environments, and second, that most offenders dislike
being in trouble, and in prison, and would prefer to avoid it if
possible. The conditions under which they were to work included an
insistence on voluntarism, that men would be free to choose whether
they participated in the prison courses or not, and that both there
and in the day training centre, they would be free not to partici-
pate in any of the course activities which they did not find attractive or relevant. And in order to make these choices easier
there was to be a determined effort to make clear to prisoners and
probationers the aims both of the courses as a whole and of their
specific parts. The style of the enterprise was to be one in which
course members assumed a great deal of responsibility for their own

learning, for assessing their own problems, formulating their own goals, and helping each other to achieve them. The effectiveness of these procedures was to be continuously monitored through a variety of evaluative devices.

Both the staff training courses followed the same basic pattern of two blocks, the first of them concentrating on assessment methods and practice, followed by a one-week exercise with serving prisoners, and the second looking at substantive areas of course content such as work, accommodation, etc., also followed by a one-week prison exercise. The differences between the first and second officer training courses are of two kinds: superficially, the first course was one week longer than the second, and contained a higher proportion of contributions by outside tutors on subjects such as counselling, group leading and vocational guidance. But a more profound change had undergone the content of the second officer's course which was based on the solid practical experience of their colleagues from the first course, in working with groups of prisoners during the preceding year. It was, therefore, more direct, more economically delivered, and hopefully easier to absorb than its predecessor. The bulk of the teaching on the two officer training courses was done by members of the research team. Their previous experience was in occupational therapy, academic psychology, consumer ergonomics, engineering, personnel work, social work and retail training. On the first course there were specialist inputs in vocational guidance by a team from the careers officer training course at Bristol Polytechnic (3) on group work by a senior lecturer in social work at Keele University; (4) and on personal counselling by tutors of the National Marriage Guidance Council college at Rugby. (5) Weeks four and five of the first course were residential, as was the fourth week of the second course.

The logic of the courses was to start with the fundamentals of interviewing and assessment, and to try these out, first of all in the relative safety of the classroom, then on one afternoon with inmates at local penal establishments (Glen Parva Borstal and HM Prison, Nottingham, respectively); and finally within the compass of a one week 'mini-course' planned and carried out by the prison officers themselves. Within each skill and knowledge area an attempt was made to work to a format and in a style which might act as an analogue of the release courses which officers were themselves to run later, and to provide teaching and practice models which could be followed as directly as possible in their own work. The format was as follows:

1   A statement of aims. The purpose of the activity and what the student should have achieved when it is completed.
2   A stimulus. A film or illustration of some kind to dramatise the subject in hand and to capture the interest of the student, e.g. a film of a bad interview to introduce interviewing technique.
3   An exposition of the skill or topic, accompanied where appropriate by handouts or other illustrative material.
4   A demonstration of the skill or technique or exercise.
5   Opportunities for practice, firstly with colleagues on the course and then with 'live' cases.
6   Feedback on the performance of the skill or technique via video-tape recordings or ratings by observers.

	Monday	Tuesday	Wednesday	Thursday	Friday
Week 1	Introduction to course	Assessment methods	Assessment	Assessment	Assessment
	Aims and values of project	Interviewing skills	Speaking skills	Counselling	
	Assessment methods	Projects	Tutorials	Prison visit	Weekly evaluations
Week 2	–	Assessment	Assessment	Assessment	Feedback on visit
	Teaching skills	Use of video	Interviewing skills	Counselling	Assessment
	Objective planning	Group leading		Planning	Planning
	Project planning	Project planning	Project planning	Prison practice	Weekly evaluations
Week 3	Project in Nottingham prison				
Week 4	Introduction to materials on 'work'	'Work' materials	'Work'	Social skills methods	Social skills methods
			Social skills methods		Project planning
		Simulations	Simulations		Weekly evaluations
Week 5	Objective setting Exercise 1	Objective setting	Assessment	Assessment	Assessment
			Programmed learning	Project planning	Tutorials
		Project planning	Project planning	Presentation of programmes	Discussion and review
Week 6	Project in Nottingham prison				

Figure 3.1 Second staff training course: timetable

7 Further practice.
8 Discussion and evaluation of the learning which has taken place.

This was an ideal, not achieved in every case, but the end product of even its partial application was a packed training day of varied activity, group discussions, films, tape and video recordings, rehearsal and practice, speakers, visits, projects and presentations.

Time did not permit, and the course content was not appropriate for, a leisurely liberal education type of approach. Its pace was therefore brisk; the officers would have said 'breakneck'. But no concessions were made to the inexperience of the officers, nor was any attempt made to reduce the difficulty of the subject matter. The assumption had been made that prison officers would be capable of absorbing the information and acquiring the skills necessary for running courses. Time for training was strictly limited and the ground to be covered was extensive. If the assumption had turned out to be mistaken then the project as conceived had little future.

COURSE CONTENTS

Interviewing

Interviewing was an obvious choice as the starting-point for the officer training course. It is the nearest helping activity to everyday life, and something of which most people have some experience, from both sides. And yet despite its importance as a tool for working with people it has attracted surprisingly little attention from those who train and educate new entrants to 'people' work.

The officers would require interviewing skills for selecting course members, for helping in the assessment process, and as a basis for any individual counselling and vocational guidance they might undertake. What they needed therefore was a simple outline, a framework and a set of principles, and some practice in actually doing it.

The proposed framework for interviewing skills was:

1 Have a purpose. Be able to state the purpose of an interview to the person on the receiving end, e.g. the purpose of this interview is to find out whether you would be a suitable release course member.
2 Be prepared. Take along a list of the areas you wish to cover during the interview, and some of the specific questions you wish to ask.
3 Be friendly and polite. Adopt a relaxed but courteous attitude and treat the interviewee with respect.
4 Listen. Take an interest in what the person is saying. Encourage the flow of his contributions with nods and grunts and smiles, and open-ended questions.
5 Summing up. Summarise the content of the interview at the end and recite it to the interviewee.
6 Writing up. If necessary and if there is time, make a written summary of the interview.

A videotape of a bad and a good interview was shown, (6) the guidelines above were discussed, and a handout of Alec Rodger's 'Seven
point plan' was distributed. (7) The officers were then set to
interviewing each other, using video and audio tape recorders followed by feedback and group discussion of their technique. Practice
interviews were then conducted with inmates at local prison establishments, on subjects such as work histories, leisure and release
problems, also followed by feedback sessions.

Group leading

Training for group leading followed a similar pattern to the one
employed for interviewing. A definition of aims or purpose, some
simple rules of procedure and as much practice as possible within
the limited time available.

   Group discussion was of paramount importance to the future success of the courses since all the other activities could be seen in
one sense simply as the stimuli to discussion between the members
of the course about their problems. The group was seen in fact as
a primary learning resource, and the experience, knowledge and expertise of its members as something which they should be encouraged
to share as much as possible with each other. The assumption was
that in any group of twelve prisoners, there would be individuals
with weaknesses or deficits alongside individuals with strengths
and assets in the same area. For example, a man with poor job
search skills can learn a great deal from someone with good job
search skills, not by having the latter deliver a lecture on the
subject but by so organising things that he contributes what he has
to offer in a group discussion, a peer interview or a role play, or
even an informal conversation.

   Some effort was made on both courses to acquaint officers with
the theoretical background to group work, but this was not over-
emphasised since the intention was not to produce group therapists,
but discussion leaders capable of stimulating and maintaining a
useful and rational discussion about particular release problems.
Practice was given therefore in starting off a discussion, using a
short verbal presentation, or a cartoon or other pictorial starter,
or a handout. As with interviewing, extensive use was made of video
and audio tape recording and officers were encouraged to rate their
own and each others' performances, and to identify those aspects of
them which they wished to improve by further practice.

   Attention was also given to some of the things that customarily
go wrong in groups; silences for instance, withdrawn or dominant
members and aggressive confrontations either between group members
or between group members and the group leader.

Assessment

Although interviewing and group discussion can easily be treated as
extensions of the ordinary experience of talking to other people
either singly or in larger numbers, the giving of pencil and paper
tests is something quite different. Most people have had to fill in

a variety of forms and tests during their lives, ranging from application forms for driving licences to lengthy intelligence or personality tests. The intention in this project was not to equip officers to administer the latter sort, but it was proposed to use a
number of simpler pencil and paper techniques for assessment purposes during release courses, and it was essential that they feel
at ease in this relatively novel situation. Some of the methods
were to be of an unstructured kind, e.g. sentence completion or
pattern notes; and some were more structured, e.g. a social skills
problem checklist taken from the Canadian Life Skills Manual, (8) or
attitude inventories like those in Eysenck's 'Know your own personality'. (9) After an initial introduction to tests and test-taking,
the topic was tackled by setting aside the first part of each day in
the staff training course to the completion and discussion of a
single pencil and paper procedure. This provided familiarity with a
good cross-section of methods; but of all the contents of the officer training courses this was the part that caused the most difficulty initially. This was significant because it probably reflects
a deep-rooted suspicion of pencil and paper methods, and the uses to
which they are customarily put; and it was something which would
also have to be overcome amongst the prison and day training centre
course members if the methods were to be at all useful.

Pencil and paper procedures covered during the courses included:

Sentence completion
Brainstorming
Pattern notes
Mooney problem checklist
Social skills problem checklist
Skill survey
Connolly Occupational Interests Questionnaire
Self-perception rating scales
Diary forms
Occupational history sheets
Alcohol problem checklist
Speaking skills rating sheet
Interacting with police
Telephone skills checklist
Picture tests
Saleable skills

Copyrighted tests which have to be administered by qualified testers
were also tried out, e.g. 16PF, (10); EPI, (11); Rotter Scale,
(12); AH2 Intelligence Tests. (13)

Teaching

Teaching in the sense intended for use in release courses did not
mean the technical mastery of a corpus of knowledge, of concepts and
facts, and their transmission through lectures, and writing on the
board and setting essays, subsequently examining the students for
the knowledge they have gained. The 'formal' teaching consisted of
the ability to stand up in front of a group in order to introduce

and then manage competently the administration of a variety of activities from pencil and paper tests, films and role plays, to group discussions, speakers or visits; and projects.

The skills of preparing and presenting material were introduced and practised in the same way as interviewing, group leading and testing. But the art of teaching is above all one that must be mastered in front of a live audience, and opportunities for the officers to do this were provided at the ends of each of the two course blocks.

Vocational guidance

Since 'work' was the number one problem on most prisoners' priority lists it was essential for the officers to become familiar with some of the materials they could use in this area. These included CODOT, a Department of Employment classification of jobs; (14) Signposts, a card index system which does the same job but which lends itself to project work with groups of prisoners; (15) assessment materials additional to those already covered in earlier sessions; lectures on vocational guidance resources; and practice in helping individuals to make occupational choices. Given the limited amount of time that could be devoted to this important topic the emphasis was placed on encouraging the officers to make use of external experts and resources rather than attempting to become 'experts' in their own right. And they were urged to ensure that their own course members in their turn assumed as much responsibility as they could for collecting their own information related to work and training.

Social skills

The social skills perspective was central to the design of the project, and it was one that was likely to be least familiar to the officers. A considerable portion of the available training time was therefore devoted to it. The aims of this section of the course were to:

1 Introduce some basic concepts in the social and life skill areas.
2 Practise some assessment methods in social skills.
3 Try out some social skills training packages.
4 Attempt the design and development of new packages for use in release courses.

Part of the conceptual background to social skills concerns the idea of systematic problem-solving and this was used as the framework around which the specifics of social skills training - behavioural assessment, role play, modelling, critical incidents analysis, successive approximation and simulation - could be explored. Great attention was paid to the provision of feedback on behaviour using videotape recording. And finally officers were asked to work in teams to compile their own social skills programmes on topics of their own choosing, and incorporating new methods and materials of their own devising. Subjects chosen for this project included

money, complaining, and alcohol, and the presentation of the results provided yet another opportunity for the practice of the basic
skills of teaching, testing and group discussion leading.

Projects and placements

The pivot of the officer training, however, lay in the practical
projects and extended placements which were designed to provide opportunities for learning 'on the job' how to be release course instructors. These ranged from small-scale tasks such as finding out
some factual information about work or leisure or social problems
and presenting the findings to the rest of the group, to larger-
scale enterprises such as the two four-day programmes in local prisons which the officers were asked to plan and carry out.

In between these two extremes the officers were asked to arrange
an evening event on some topic of concern to released prisoners,
during which they were expected to use as many skills as possible.
One group invited the warden and a resident from the local pre-
release employment hostel to describe the scheme and to take part
in a group discussion. Another team made a film of a personnel officer talking about his policy towards the employment of ex-prisoners; also followed by discussion; others presented an extended
role play of a typical ex-prisoner's progress during his first few
days of freedom. And another group filmed a tour of the local skill
centre at Leicester with a commentary by one of the centre staff
about the various courses and how to get on them.

It was during the longer placements, however, that all the elements of the training course had to be knitted together in front of
a critical and potentially hostile audience after only two weeks of
preparation.

The first real test of the ideas behind the project, and of the
value of the officers' training course came on Monday 17 November
1975 when the Ranby officers arrived at HM Prison, Nottingham, and
the Ashwell officers at HM Prison, Leicester, to run four-day assessment exercises of their own design, with groups of twelve inmates. They felt, as one officer put it, 'very apprehensive'. 'Of
all the course it was the part I was least looking forward to - a
group of strange prisoners and having to present it.' The appre-
hension did not stem only from fears about his own performance, but
about the possible response of the prisoners. 'Knowing prisoners
as I do, I know from bitter experience that they can be pretty per-
verse. With strangers and especially with someone who doesn't exude
an air of confidence, then they will destroy him, no doubt about
that.' For a prison officer this kind of fear is not just one of
embarrassment, or of being made to look slightly foolish, it is a
threat to the whole of his credibility as an officer. Many of them
were afraid that being cast in a teaching role for which they were,
and felt, ill-equipped would expose them to ridicule by prisoners
who were possibly more intelligent or learned than themselves.

'In actual fact,' according to the same officer, 'it was great.
They accepted everything. They responded in such a positive way.
I knew then that this was the thing.' Other officers shared his
view of this first week's work with serving prisoners. And so did

many of the prisoners who had taken part in the exercise at the two prisons, on the evaluation forms they filled in at the conclusion of the four days. What they appeared to have appreciated most was 'being able to talk freely' and 'the easy-going atmosphere between con and staff'. They were also complimentary about the performance of the officers, and about 'the friendly and constructive way the officers have presented their material'. One man even declared, 'Before this class, I feel I must have been blind.'

The same responses were evoked during the second officers' training course in 1976, and the comment of the probation officer from Sheffield who was a fellow student was, 'An amazing demonstration of what wasted potential there must be in the prison service if six officers can achieve this level of competence within three weeks on this course.'

It was noticeable, moreover, during the first of these 'mini-courses', that the men who had been assembled at Leicester and Nottingham prisons were of radically differing complexions. The Leicester group comprised what an officer who escorted them to the classroom referred to as 'a right load of rubbish', by which he meant an odd assortment of men from unimportant work-parties, or who had been refusing labour. They ranged from the very intelligent to the borderline educationally subnormal, and included men with a representative range of personality types and personal and social handicaps. At Nottingham, all the men were volunteers who had responded to an advertisement, and they were, as a group, much more intelligent and presentable than their Leicester colleagues. They included a proportion of professional criminals, and some men who held key posts in the prison, in official jobs and in the informal structure of the inmate subculture. Neither was an easy audience to please, and some of the Nottingham men in particular admitted later that they had come along for a laugh and to witness the discomfiture of the officers, but that as the week had progressed they had found themselves becoming interested in the contents of the course and that they had gained something from it which they had not expected.

By this midway stage then, the results of the officers' training were encouraging but scarcely conclusive. Four days in a strange prison with a group of men in 'holiday' mood did not predict how a ten- or twelve-week course in the workaday environment of the home establishment might go down. The remainder of the training was devoted to the substantive contents of the courses; to work and vocational guidance materials, to social skills techniques and to teaching, course planning and materials writing. As in the earlier parts of the course the emphasis was on learning by doing rather than by listening to lectures, or being spoonfed with pre-digested information. The second one-week placement in the same prisons, with substantially the same prisoner groups, received similar, but rather more muted responses.

Each week's activities on the staff training courses were evaluated by their members on standard questionnaires, which included some open-ended questions on what they had liked or disliked, measures of usefulness for specific items on the timetable, and confidence ratings about running release courses. The confidence ratings of six officers on the second training course ran as follows:

TABLE 3.1 Officers' training course 2

How confident do you feel about running a release course?

	Very					Not very	
Week 1			1	5			
Week 3			4		2		
Week 4	1	5					
Week 6	4	2					

At the end of weeks two and five this question referred to confidence about running the prison 'mini-courses' during the weeks following, rather than a full release course, and has been omitted from
this table. There is a clear movement towards greater confidence as
the course progresses, and the ratings are reinforced by comments
made by the officers in answer to the open-ended questions on the
evaluation forms about things they had liked, e.g. 'acquiring new
knowledge', 'having to think again', 'the change that I feel has
come to me solely due to being on this course', 'personal growth
gained from the course', 'the way we were motivated'. These obser-
vations about personal growth were not confined to the officers
themselves; the deputy governor at one of the prisons described
them as 'transformed' when they returned from the training course.

But within the general spirit of confidence and personal development that marked the end-of-course comments of the officers, there
were considerable variations concerning their evaluations of its
component parts.

TABLE 3.2 Course contents rank-ordered by degree of confidence
Second staff training course

---

 1 Interviewing
 2 Use of video
 3 Counselling
 4 Group discussion leading
 5 Assessment
 6 Social skills/role play
 7 Setting objectives
 8 Vocational guidance
 9 Programme construction
10 Teaching

And the officers on both courses had specific criticisms to make of
the training they had just received. The most common ones were of
the amount of material that had been condensed into six or seven
weeks, the pace at which they had to cover it, and the need for more

time to take in and feel confident about so many new things. On the
first course too there was criticism of the 'unstructured' group experiences provided by tutors at the National Marriage Guidance
Centre in Rugby as being too 'therapeutic'.

But the interesting thing about the comments of the officers is
how far they were in parallel with those made by the prisoners they
had worked with during the course. They liked, for instance, 'the
atmosphere created by students and tutors', 'learning about myself',
'learning about others', 'the fact that I was never bored', 'practice at subjects rather than theory only', 'the people', 'the enthusiasm'. This suggests that the aim of making the staff training
so far as possible analogous with the release courses had succeeded
to some extent, and that the same model appeared to have some merits
for both groups.

Suggestions for improving the course centred mainly on the shortage of time to absorb all the material; most of its graduates
wanted to see a longer course, and some of them thought that more
would get done if the whole of the course were to be run residen-
tially. Other members of the first course thought that seven weeks
of continuous training was too tiring and suggested that it be
broken in the middle. This idea was adopted for the second training
course and appeared to have the desired effect. But at the end of
the first staff training course the question remained to be answered
whether a way had been found not just of working with men at the
ends of their sentences, and in the day training centre, but also
of equipping basic grade prison officers to do this kind of work
effectively.

Chapter 4

The offenders and their problems

Although some decisions had already been made about the basic shape
of the curriculum which was to be developed for use in the prisons
and the day training centre, its final form was to be determined in
use with large numbers of offenders. Their personal characteristics, the ways in which they perceived their own problems, and their
responses to the methods and materials, would all help to shape the
package of tried and tested methods that was to emerge at the end of
the project.

This chapter presents some basic information about the men who
took part in the courses during the project; 224 in the prisons,
and 123 at the day training centre. The Ranby and Ashwell course
members are compared with unsuccessful applicants for places, and
with random samples of prisoners who did not apply at all; and men
who attended the day training centre in 1977 are compared with those
who were referred to the centre at the same time, but were subsequently given different sentences, usually custodial ones. The results of a survey are also reported which asked 250 men in three
prisons to specify the problems they thought they would face after
their release.

RECRUITING PRISONERS FOR COURSES

During the two years of the project, from January 1976 to December
1977, nineteen courses of varying lengths were run by officers at
the two prisons: eleven at Ranby and eight at Ashwell. Recruitment
for these courses was never a very highly organised business. Advertisements were placed on noticeboards in the dining halls or billets or wing offices; at Ashwell two open meetings were held for
prospective candidates; and there was a certain amount of informal
recruitment carried on by existing and former course members amongst
their friends and billet-mates. Eligibility was determined by dates
of release; all those men due to be released between the end of the
course being advertised and the end of the one following it could
apply. It is difficult to give gross figures for applicants, since
numbers of men at both prisons made inquiries and indicated that
they intended to apply for a course place, but subsequently with-

drew or were found to be ineligible because of their release dates, or the work they did, or for other reasons.

Serious contenders for course places varied between 20 per cent and 50 per cent of the eligible populations at the two prisons. With more determined efforts, the courses could probably have attracted higher proportions of the populations at the two prisons but it might have proved counter-productive to stimulate much more demand than could be met in practice. However, if about one-third of the men in any prison are willing to spend several weeks working on their release problems, meeting that demand alone would require a considerable re-allocation of resources within the prison service. It had been hoped originally that release courses would be run at quite different kinds of prison establishments to see whether differences in populations implied the need for changes in curriculum or course organisation, and to test whether the same general format could be used successfully with both long- and short-term prisoners under different conditions of security. In the event, Ranby and Ashwell turned out to be similar in some respects in both regime and recruitment.

We were interested in describing the course members at each prison, and in finding out to what extent they were typical of the wider populations from which they were drawn. Biographical and criminal record data were collected, therefore, for three groups of men: course members, unsuccessful applicants for course places, and a random sample of men at each prison who had not applied. (1) These data were collected from the official records of the men concerned. Some of the information, such as previous convictions, is of considerable reliability, but some items are of more doubtful quality: descriptions of jobs held prior to conviction for example, which are often simply noted down in the records on the say-so of the newly received prisoner to the reception officer.

The numbers of men falling into these three categories at Ranby and Ashwell were as shown in Table 4.1.

TABLE 4.1

	Course members	Unsuccessful applicants	Sample of non-applicants
Ranby	132	41	110
Ashwell	92	44	113

COURSE MEMBERS AT RANBY AND ASHWELL

There were some clear differences between the populations of course members at the two prisons, differences deriving from the security classifications of the two establishments, and the differential recruitment of prisoners to meet their separate security and training criteria. The course members at Ranby, for example, with a mean age of 28 years 11 months, were somewhat older than those at Ashwell - mean age 27 years 5 months, although around half the men at both places were less than 26 years old.

TABLE 4.2

Age - years	Under 21	21-25	26-30	31-35	Over 35
% Ranby (n=132)	3.8	40.9	29.5	12.9	12.9
% Ashwell (n=92)	2.2	52.2	23.9	9.8	12.0

There were also significant differences in the kinds of offences for which they were currently serving terms of imprisonment, as shown in Table 4.3.

TABLE 4.3   Present offence

Offence	% Ranby (n = 132)	% Ashwell (n = 92)
Violence against person	13.6	6.5
Burglary	43.2	20.7
Theft/handling	23.5	38.0
Fraud/deception	3.8	17.4
Take vehicle	11.4	5.4
Traffic offence	0	4.3
Drugs	0.8	4.3
Sex	0	1.1
Other	3.8	1.1

$X^2 = 59.89$. $df = 4$. $p < .001$.

Men at Ranby were more likely to have committed offences of violence, or burglary and taking vehicles, than their counterparts at Ashwell, who for their part were more likely to have been convicted of fraud, traffic and drug offences.

The current sentences of the men also reflected these differences; a majority at Ranby serving between 7 and 18 months, and small but significant fractions at Ashwell serving less than 6 and more than 24 months; the latter group being responsible for the longer average sentences of 16.3 months compared to 13.6 months at Ranby.

TABLE 4.4   Present sentence

Sentence (months)	less than 6	7-12	13-18	19-24	more than 24
% Ranby (n = 132)	6.9	57.7	23.1	8.5	3.8
% Ashwell (n = 92)	13.2	37.4	25.3	9.9	14.3

X^2 = 22.12.   df = 4.   p < .001.

One determinant of sentence length is the seriousness of current offence, as measured by the damage done to the victim or the amount or value of the goods involved in property offences.   Another influential factor is the length and nature of the offender's previous criminal history.

TABLE 4.5   Number of previous convictions

No. convictions	0	1	2-5	6-10	11-15	16-20	21+
% Ranby (n = 124)	0.8	3.2	21.8	40.3	21.0	5.6	8.1
% Ashwell (n = 80)	10.0	6.3	36.2	30.0	8.7	7.5	1.2

X^2 = 34.18.   df = 5.   p < .001.

The average number of previous convictions at Ranby was 10.9, and at Ashwell 7.6;   almost twice as many of the Ranby men had eleven or more previous convictions.   Course members' previous criminal histories also varied between the two prisons.   Many more of the Ranby men had committed violence at some time in the past (35 per cent compared to 12 per cent) and more of them had records of burglary, and taking vehicles.   Ashwell men on the other hand had a slight lead in matters of fraud, and had infringed the traffic laws much more frequently.

TABLE 4.6   Previous offences

Offence	% Ranby (n = 125)	% Ashwell (n = 89)
Violence against person	35.2	12.4
Burglary	76.0	53.9
Theft/handling	74.4	65.2
Fraud/deception	23.2	27.0
Take vehicle	49.6	24.7
Traffic offence	25.6	48.4
Drugs	18.4	12.4
Sex	1.6	1.1
Others	12.0	18.0

Their experience of the penal system varied too; the more recidivistic Ranby population having been through the mill more
thoroughly than the Ashwell one, having been sent to prison and
to Borstal much more frequently, but, somewhat surprisingly, mar-
ginally less frequently to approved schools.

TABLE 4.7   Previous sentences

Sentence	% Ranby (n = 123)	% Ashwell (n = 88)
Discharge	35.8	33.0
Fine	87.8	76.1
Probation	72.4	55.7
Approved school	18.7	19.3
Detention	21.1	18.2
Borstal	33.3	15.9
Prison	71.5	47.8
Suspended sentence	49.6	33.0
Community service order	5.7	4.5
Deferred sentence	4.9	5.7

Social background and intelligence

Approximately one-third of the men at both prisons were currently
married, but more of the Ranby men were single, and more of the
Ashwell ones separated or divorced.

TABLE 4.8   Marital status

	Married	Sep/divorced	Single
% Ranby (n = 130)	33.1	18.5	48.5
% Ashwell (n = 90)	37.8	28.9	33.3

$X^2 = 11.27$. df = 2. p < .01.

Prison records systematically collect information about the previous job histories of convicted offenders, either in response to
direct questions from reception officers, or from the police ante-
cedent histories included in the files of most men. The quality
of this information is clearly variable, but there is no reason to
suppose that the broad picture they provide is seriously at odds
with reality. The last jobs held by the men at Ranby and Ashwell
prior to present conviction, classified by skill level, are presented in Table 4.9.

TABLE 4.9   Job before present sentence

Level of job	% Ranby (n = 121)	% Ashwell (n = 83)
Unskilled	54.5	31.3
Semi-skilled	24.0	22.9
Skilled	11.6	21.7
Sales/clerical	0.8	4.8
Professional	0.8	1.2
Self-employed	5.0	9.6
Unemployed	3.3	8.4

X^2 = 30.48.   df = 5.   p < .001.

The proportions reported as unemployed in this table are most probably underestimated; the jobs recorded may have been held some time prior to conviction. The differences between the two populations are marked: Ranby men were predominantly unskilled and semi-skilled workers; more of the Ashwell men had held jobs of a skilled, clerical, professional, or self-employed nature. There is some evidence too of job instability during the two years prior to current conviction. About one-third of both groups had held three or more jobs during that period.

TABLE 4.10   Number of jobs in the two years before present sentence

	Unemployed	One	Two	Three	Four or more
% Ranby (n = 130)	17.7	26.2	24.6	18.5	13.1
% Ashwell (n = 82)	3.7	36.6	30.5	18.3	11.0

X^2 = 57.47.   df = 4.   p < .001.

The differences in the percentages recorded as 'unemployed' in Tables 4.9 and 4.10 illustrate some of the imperfections of the official records of prisoners. The most likely explanation of the discrepancy is that when newly received prisoners are asked to name their occupation, they offer the title of the last job they held, which may have been a long time ago, or the one they normally do, or used to do during a previous continuous spell of employment.

During the project, intelligence and personality tests were offered to course members at both prisons who wished to know how they rated. The results of a general ability test - the AH2 - are given in Table 4.11.

The AH2 is a three-part group test comprising a verbal section (10 minutes); a numerical section (10 minutes); and a perceptual section (8 minutes). The norms used were for the Armed Forces. The table shows mean percentiles (m.p.) and standard deviations (s.d.).

TABLE 4.11   General ability (AH2)

Section	Ranby (n = 57) m.p. (s.d.)	Ashwell (n = 80) m.p. (s.d.)
Verbal	61.86 (29.63)	51.78 (32.46)
Numerical	54.73 (29.64)	52.89 (31.92)
Perceptual	55.29 (30.91)	46.59 (30.24)
Total	56.96 (29.96)	50.64 (31.64)

Differences significant p < .01

Comparisons

On a number of items, then, there were statistically significant
differences between the course members at Ranby and Ashwell, but
the similarities between them override the differences. Both populations consist largely of men in their late twenties and early
thirties, around one-third of them married, and with substantial
criminal records behind them, mostly for property offences, but with
perceptible minorities involved in violence, taking cars and traffic
offences.

If the course members at both prisons are compared with the profiles of the larger populations from which they were recruited, the
situation at Ranby was one in which there was virtually no detectable difference between the two, in terms not only of personal but
also of criminal data, except that slightly fewer of the course members had previous convictions for violence and traffic offences.

At Ashwell there were, however, some differences between the two
groups. Course members were younger than non-applicants, less
likely to be married and more often separated and divorced, and to
have held more jobs in the two years preceding their last conviction. They were also somewhat less recidivistic than the general
Ashwell population. Although some of these differences were statistically significant, they do not rest on very large numbers and
they do not portray a distinct 'type' of man who was more likely to
end up on release courses at Ashwell. Nor do they suggest that the
men who volunteered for release courses were that much 'better bets'
than their more reticent colleagues; less blessed with problems and
therefore more likely to make good on their release even without the
benefits if that is what it turned out to be, of attendance on a
course.

There was, however, one possibly relevant difference, which was
that 20 per cent of the selected course members at Ashwell had previous experience of further or higher education, compared with only
5 per cent of the unsuccessful applicants. Spread over the courses
during the project these numbers mean that there may have been one
man per course with experience of further education who would not
have been there if the membership had been entirely typical of the
general population. It may have added something to the tone of the
proceedings in a course to have a member with some experience of

going to a technical college, but it does not, on that account,
render the group unrecognisable as being drawn from the mainstream
of prisoners at Ashwell. But the fact that there were differences,
some of them statistically significant, does suggest that selection
at Ashwell was to some extent biased in favour of the more intelligent and possibly articulate prisoner, who would be more likely to
make positive contributions to group discussion and other activities.

Non-applicants

During the first two courses at Ranby, interviews were conducted
with eleven men who were eligible to apply for a course place but
had not done so. Their reactions were not necessarily typical, but
they were illuminating. One of them said that the courses were
'only suitable for the skivers and the stupid; not necessary for
an intelligent man'. One or two simply thought that they did not
have problems of the kind which a release course might tackle, such
as finding work or accommodation; others that there was no point
in thinking about release before the day of discharge. Some had
inexplicably gained from the course advertisements the idea that
they were intended for men who were going to live in the immediate
neighbourhood of the prison after release. Two or three men said
that they thought that the courses sounded interesting but that
they were unwilling to sacrifice the good prison jobs they had
secured, in order to attend something whose value could not be
estimated in advance. One man said he was so confused that he did
not feel he could have coped with a course, but thought on balance
he should have found out more about it. Some of these men were extremely rude when asked for their views and appeared to resent what
they saw as an intrusion into their privacy. If they were in any
way typical of their peers, there may be some scope for attracting
a higher proportion of men due to be released; but not that much
higher. And the effect of actually forcing men into release
courses would almost certainly put paid to their capacity to produce
commitment on the part of staff and members to the idea of working
together on common problems.

COURSE MEMBERS IN THE SHEFFIELD DAY TRAINING CENTRE

As at Ranby and Ashwell, the character of the offender groups attending the day training centre at Sheffield was a product of many
interacting factors: the nature and extent of local crime, the aims
and selection criteria of the centre itself, and the sentencing
policies and practices of the local magistrates and Crown Courts.
    Overall patterns of crime in Sheffield, according to an analysis
by Baldwin, Bottoms and Walker of offences recorded in 1966, are not
substantially different from those found in other urban areas in
England and Wales. (2)
    In some respects, however, the South Yorkshire area does have
peculiar characteristics of its own. The first of these is that,
as Baldwin et al. also show, the actual rate of crime in Sheffield

is consistently lower than that in most other major British cities, and has been so for a number of years. These authors offer a number of possible reasons for this, related to particular features of Sheffield's character and its history. Second, on the sentencing side, the South Yorkshire magistrates make less frequent use of imprisonment than do their colleagues in most other parts of the country. In 1976, for example, they sent only 5.23 per cent of convicted male adult offenders to prison, compared with a national average of 7.3 per cent, and a peak in Dorset of no less than 13.43 per cent. (3) Only four other magistrates' court areas, of which Merseyside was one, sentenced lower proportions of men to prison during that year.

For these two reasons, the choice of Sheffield as a site for an experimental alternative to prison might seem to be a somewhat odd one. It may have contributed to the difficulties the centre has occasionally had in recruiting course members; from an initial pool that was itself not large, the centre had to tease out sufficient numbers to keep itself in business.

Following a period of difficulty in 1975, however, the numbers referred and sentenced to day training gradually increased. Total numbers of men who started attending the centre in each of the four years 1974-7 were as follows: 1974, 48; 1975, 26; 1976, 57; 1977, 66. Referral is normally made by a field probation officer of an individual who has committed an offence and who runs a risk of being sent to prison. However, a small number of men either 'referred themselves' again after having attended the centre, or were referred while already on probation if their probation officer thought it might be advantageous, or simply attended voluntarily beyond the required length of their stay. For this to happen, again obviously, the officer must be to some extent acquainted with the role of the centre and have an impression of its suitability for the offender in question, who must himself express some interest in exploring the idea. If in custody, the man will then be visited by a member of staff, who will explain something of the aims and nature of the centre. If at liberty, the man may himself visit the centre, usually on a Tuesday, to find out more about it, and talk to the probation officer who will be his group leader if the court makes the appropriate order. Referrals in the 17 to 21 age range, and a few older men, for whom it is thought necessary, are also seen by a psychologist and given intelligence and personality tests. Twenty-six men aged 17-21, and eleven men older than 21 were assessed in this way during 1977.

Few offenders were rejected by centre staff. In 1977, of 121 referrals, only four were turned down - an overall acceptance rate of 97 per cent. However, acceptance by no means guarantees salvation from a custodial sentence; there are still a number of other decisions along the way. The first of these is whether a recommendation of day training is actually made to the courts. This might depend on a number of imponderables, notably the offender's own judgment of the centre (although some do not visit it), his probation officer's final decision, estimates by each of them of what sentence is likely, advice given by other parties such as solicitors, and many other forces acting on the situation. Of the 117 men accepted in 1977, 104 were subsequently recommended by probation officers for day training, a rate of 88.8 per cent.

Finally, the courts must decide. Studies of the sentencing process in English courts suggest that recommendations made by probation officers, whether for probation orders or for some other sentence, are followed by courts in seven or eight cases out of ten.
Suggestions for day training seem to be followed slightly less often
than this; just over 60 per cent were accepted during 1977. Whether
this is due to the offences or offenders involved, or, as has been
suggested, to a lack of coherence and strength in arguments made by
reports in favour of day training, or to other factors, is impossible
to say.

A finding cited by Bottomley that is borne out by the centre's
experience (and is hardly surprising in any case), is that from
amongst the recommendations made, '... in general, the rejection
rate was slightly greater in the higher courts, than in the magistrates' or juvenile courts, suggesting that lay magistrates tend to
follow sentencing advice more readily than judges or recorders.' (4)
Thus, while two-thirds of referrals were dealt with in Crown Courts,
a higher proportion of those dealt with in magistrates' courts were
sent to the centre. The result was an intake divided almost exactly
half-and-half between men sentenced from Crown and Magistrates'
courts respectively.

Finally, what happened to men who were not sent to the day training centre? Of fifty-two men known to have been otherwise dealt
with during 1977, thirty-four were sent to prison, six to Borstal,
and three to detention centre; four were given Community Service
Orders, and two suspended sentences. The average length of the
thirty-seven fixed custodial sentences was eighteen months. This
evidently reflected the larger proportion of men imprisoned by Crown
Courts, but left no doubt that the Sheffield day training centre was
functioning as a genuine 'alternative to prison'.

Two points emerge from these facts. The first is how difficult
it was to get men into the centre, dependent as it was on referrals
and the contingencies of a complex decision-making process. The
second is that so far as can be determined from the available information, if most men sent there had not been so dealt with, a
majority of them would almost certainly have ended up in custody
of some kind. In the next section we look more closely at some of
these men.

Probationers in the day training centre

Descriptive material was drawn from a number of sources in order to
build up a picture of men at the day training centre. (5)   Table
4.12 lists the numbers of men in each of the seventeen groups which
attended the centre between January 1976 and the spring of 1978.

Thus during the period of the project, 123 men were group members in the day training centre, in seventeen groups, giving an
average size of slightly more than seven per group. (6,7)

TABLE 4.12   Numbers of men attending the day training centre

Group no.	n	Group no.	n
1	7	10	10
2	7	11	6
3	4	12	11
4	5	13	7
5	7	14	5
6	4	15	9
7	10	16	8
8	10	17	7
9	6		Total no. = 123

To obtain a clearer impression of these men, we begin by review-
ing some general characteristics, before going on to look more
closely at some of the problems they brought with them.   These
impressions are based on background information about all the men
referred to the centre during 1977, a total of 120. (8)   Not all the
relevant information is available for each man, but we can construct
a broad picture nevertheless.   Where possible and useful, comparisons are made between men who were eventually sentenced to day
training, the 'DTC group', and men who, for whatever reason, were
not, the 'non-DTC group'.

Age and 'criminality'

Starting first with age, Table 4.13 presents some basic data on
these two groups.   The referrals who eventually arrived in the day
training centre were on average six years older than those who did
not.

TABLE 4.13   Mean age and age range of referrals

	n	Mean age in years	Standard deviations	Range
DTC group	65	30.2	8.9	18-55
Non-DTC group	55	24.43	7.37	17-51 (9)

Since a majority of the non-DTC group was in fact recommended for day training it would seem that the courts are, on average, sentencing slightly older men to the centre, and some younger men for whom day training had been thought suitable, most probably to some form of custody. Such a difference is not easy to explain, except possibly on the basis that the older offender was seen as being 'ready for a change' and offered the opportunity of day training to reinforce it. However a glance at the previous criminal records of the two groups suggests an alternative explanation.

This shows that, despite the differences in age, these two groups of men had approximately the same numbers of previous convictions. The small difference between the means in Table 4.14 is not statistically significant. (10)

TABLE 4.14   Mean number of previous convictions

	n	x	s.d.
DTC group	60	9.75	6.63
Non-DTC group	46	10.8	9.3

TABLE 4.15   Frequency distribution of previous convictions

	DTC group n = 60	Non-DTC group n = 46
0	−	−
1	2	3
2-5	15	6
6-10	22	23
11-15	11	6
16-20	7	3
21+	3	5

The suggestion here, in other words, is simply that the non-DTC group exhibited a higher level of 'criminality', in having notched up as many convictions as the DTC group in less time than the latter took to do so. It could be, therefore, that the courts still use the centre for, on the whole, slightly less serious cases. The non-DTC group, in addition, seem to have set out a little earlier on their 'criminal careers': while more than half (57 per cent) of this group had recorded convictions as juveniles, the corresponding figure for the DTC group was only 35 per cent. Both of these findings dovetail, of course, with another discussed earlier: the tendency of Crown Courts to reject a higher proportion of day training recommendations than do magistrates.

No doubts should be entertained, however, about the degree of recidivism of offenders who found their way to the centre: over 70 per cent of them had more than five previous convictions, and an even larger proportion, as we shall see below, had previous experience of custody.

What of the nature of the offences committed? Tables 4.16 and 4.17 classify the offences recorded, for those men on whom information is available. Table 4.16 is concerned with the present offences of those referred to the centre during 1977; Table 4.17 is concerned with the known previous offences of the same group of men. Each table records, for both DTC and non-DTC groups, the percentages of offences falling into different offence categories. Detailed offence histories were not available for some of the men in each group.

TABLE 4.16   Present offence

Offence type	DTC group n = 66 %	Non-DTC group n = 55 %
1 Violence against person	7.6	9.1
2 Burglary	28.8	41.8
3 Theft/handling	25.8	16.4
4 Fraud/deception	9.1	1.8
5 Take vehicle	10.6	20.0
6 Traffic offence	1.5	-
7 Damage	7.6	-
8 Drunkenness	1.5	-
9 Other *	4.5	7.3
10 (No offence) **	3.0	3.6

*   Including breach of the peace, loitering, possessing offensive weapon, going equipped, incest, unlawful sexual intercourse, sodomy, indecent exposure, threatening behaviour, arson, drug offences, sending threatening letter, dishonest use of electricity, disorderly conduct, neglect of wife and children, neglect of dog, hoax bomb call, false fire alarm, unlawfully wearing army uniform, and others.

** Some referrals were of individuals already on probation whose supervising officers thought they might be in danger of committing a (serious) offence, and who agreed to look at day training as a possible source of help.

TABLE 4.17   Previous offences

Offence type	DTC group n = 62 %	Non-DTC group n = 47 %
1 Violence against person	6.9	2.8
2 Burglary	25.8	27.7
3 Theft/handling	29.8	36.9
4 Fraud/deception	7.8	6.9
5 Take vehicle	7.2	8.0
6 Traffic offence	4.6	5.1
7 Damage	4.1	5.7
8 Drunkenness	6.3	3.0
9 Other	7.5	3.9

A chi-square test conducted on the raw data underlying this table was highly significant: chi-square = 42.08, df = 8, p = less than .001.

Both tables confirm that candidates for day training were predominantly property offenders, but there is a suggestion in Table 4.16 that a more serious present offence, of burglary or taking a vehicle, may be more likely to attract a prison sentence.

As a consequence of these offences, most men attending the day training centre during 1977 had been subject, over a period, to the normal range of sanctions and treatments administered by the courts, from fines and probation to detention centre, Borstal and imprisonment. Notably, of forty-six men at the centre during 1977, whose sentencing history was available, thirty-eight (82 per cent) had served prison sentences, and a further seven had at some time been in Borstal or detention centre - a considerable majority. These figures may, in fact, slightly overestimate the total number with prior experience of custody, but the proportion is undoubtedly very high.

Finally, for the bulk of the men who came to Sheffield day training centre, it was as a condition of a two-year probation order; 83 per cent had been put on probation for two years, with the remainder equally divided between one- and three-year orders.

Men sentenced to day training were on average a little older than those who were not, had in the main been found guilty of several offences, most usually of burglary or theft, and had previous experience of prison or some other form of custody.

Social background

Turning to the social background of 1977 referrals, Table 4.18 shows the marital status of men in both DTC and non-DTC groups. Almost exactly half of the DTC men were single, a large proportion amongst

men in their late twenties and early thirties, but not an uncommon
finding in groups of offenders.   Whether the higher proportion of
single men in the non-DTC group is due to their lower age, or is an
effect of greater instability of some kind is difficult to say.

TABLE 4.18   Marital status

	Married	Sep/divorced	Single
% DTC group (n = 65)	26.2	23.0	50.8
% Non-DTC group (n = 55)	16.3	12.7	71.0

The living conditions of the DTC group were varied.   Some,
whether married or single, came from very stable family homes;
others had behind them a lengthy history of drifting from place to
place, and had to be found accommodation during their period at the
centre.   Table 4.19 lists the types of accommodation in which they
dwelt and the numbers of men living in each type.   It should be emphasised that not all the family homes were stable, nor were all
those living in lodgings, hostels, or rented accommodation necessarily undergoing difficulties as a result.   A majority, in fact,

TABLE 4.19   Types of accommodation (DTC group).   n = 65

Family home (marital)	15 (23.1%)
Family home (parental or other relative)	11 (16.9%)
Hostel	16 (24.6%)
Lodgings	10 (15.4%)
Renting house/ flat/bedsit	7 (10.8%)
Staying with friends	1 (1.5%)
No fixed abode	2 (3.1%)
Insufficient information	3 (4.6%)

enjoyed fairly settled home circumstances, though a large minority
did have (sometimes very acute) problems in this area;   and a
number, originally of no fixed abode, had been placed in hostels or
lodgings with the help of centre staff and their own probation officers.   Eleven (16.9 per cent) of the men had conditions of hostel
residence attached to their probation orders.
The work records of the men presented a picture of instability

that was in general more uniform.   Though some had had periods of
regular employment at various phases in the past, the overall pattern for the past few years was one of difficulty and unsteadiness,
of intermittent or long-term unemployment.   Inevitably, the reasons
for this were very mixed, and complex enough to preclude any sorting
of these men into well-defined categories by reason for being unemployed.   Six men from the 1977 intake suffered from some kind of
lasting illness or permanent invalidity, but for the remainder,
standing as they do at the bottom end of the labour market, the
components of the syndrome included: a lack of job skills and
qualifications - for some men, of even basic literacy skills, inability to find work, inability to stay in work for very long, lack
of motivation, having a record, and of course, being in custody -
one man had spent twenty of the preceding twenty-eight years in
prison.   All of these men had work histories which debarred them
from entry to government training courses, which contributed solidly
to many other financial and social problems in their lives, and
which would add cumulatively to their difficulties in finding work
in the future.   Without a doubt, the sheer lack of a job and adequate income were often at the hub of the other problems they
brought to the day training centre.

In general, the intake does contain a large number of men who for
one reason or another may be unsettled in their lives.   In particular, all of the men recruited during 1977 had for a long period
before shown great instability in their patterns of work.

Intelligence

As in the prison, intelligence test scores were available for some
of the men referred to the day training centre during 1976 and 1977.
Table 4.20 summarises scores obtained on the Progressive and Coloured Matrices tests for a number of men, again dividing these into
those who subsequently came to the centre and those who did not.

TABLE 4.20   Mean scores on matrices tests

	DTC group			Non-DTC group		
	n	$\bar{x}$	s.d.	n	$\bar{x}$	s.d.
Progressive matrices	20	40.65	10.03	12	40.24	7.57
Coloured matrices	5	31.2	3.19	12	34.83	9.38

Though the average score of the men who took the Progressive
Matrices test is comparable with that of the adult population as a
whole, a number of men had to be given the Coloured Matrices test.
They show, in fact, a fairly wide distribution of intelligence
scores, from Grades I to V on the Progressive Matrices for example,
but in general those of below-average intelligence are likely to be
over-represented in the centre.   There are no detectable differ-

ences between DTC and non-DTC groups. Not surprisingly, many men
who come to the centre are deficient in literacy skills; the average reading age of eighteen men given the Schonnell test was 12.2
years. Though few men are totally illiterate, a proportion of every
intake group seems to have problems in this area, compounded, frequently, by a reluctance to identify them openly, and take advantage
of the centre's provision of remedial literacy teaching.

Self-reported problems

To a majority of people, the most salient characteristic of offenders in general and of prisoners in particular is the simple fact
that they have broken the law. The offence itself is of paramount
importance in any judgment of the offender that we make. To those
charged with the task of trying to ensure that the offender does
not transgress again, or does so at least less often or less severely, matters appear much more complex. A conflict between 'caring'
and 'controlling' runs through the work of all the professions to
whom the job of dealing with offenders is assigned. Those in this
position inevitably become involved, even if only to a minimal
extent, with the problems of the offender himself or herself. They
come to know something of the offender's background, and gain a
familiarity with the kinds of circumstances in which most crimes
are committed. Evidence adduced by criminologists on the relationships between crime and social class, joblessness, homelessness,
locality, or family breakdown, indicates at least part of what some
of these problems and circumstances must be. Anyone who works with
offenders on a day-to-day basis, whether prison officer, probation
officer, social worker or psychologist, could probably make a list
of them more or less without thinking.
    To design, set up and run a course intended to help offenders
with their difficulties, however, information of a more systematic
sort is needed. While social scientists have gathered a large
quantity of data on offenders, in an attempt to map out an aetiology
of deviant behaviour, it might perhaps be unwise to base the content
of a course on inferences drawn from demographic-type descriptions
of criminogenic neighbourhoods, deviant subcultures, or offence
careers. It is surely much more valuable to listen to what offenders themselves have to say; yet few attempts have been made to explore the problems of offenders from their own points of view.
    An exception to this trend is the work of Holborn (11) on the
problems articulated by men in three English prisons: Stafford,
Winson Green and Drake Hall. Using a lengthy interview schedule,
Holborn set out to appraise how prisoners saw their problems just
one or two weeks prior to their release. She divided the difficulties mentioned into three categories: 'immediate' problems,
which were a result of the prisoner's separation from society; post-
release problems; and a mixed set of difficulties associated with
prison life itself. The bulk of the problems in the first two
groups (which are the ones of concern to us here), while covering
a very wide range, clustered around two kinds of issues: the practical area, consisting of problems to do with money, jobs, debts,
rights, and accommodation, and the interpersonal area, comprising

family welfare issues and other miscellaneous anxieties centred on social and personal life. Three-quarters of the 120 men in Holborn's sample mentioned one problem or more which they would face on their release from prison, and a third mentioned problems as being connected with the offences which had brought them to prison in the first place.

Roughly similar findings were obtained in a study by Payne and Lawton (12) of the perceived problems of 178 trainees from Inner London, Sheffield and Pontypridd day training centres. Using a modified form of the Mooney Problem Checklist (a questionnaire which invites individuals to record which of a long list of problems they themselves are experiencing), (13) Payne and Lawton found thirteen problems which were mentioned by a large proportion of the respondents in each of the three centres. Six of these were concerned with money, two with employment, three with personality difficulties, one with lack of educational qualifications, and one with general confusion about future personal goals. For a number of other problems there were significant differences in frequency of reporting at each of the three centres; however, apart from the fact that problems related to accommodation and social isolation were mentioned most frequently by probationers from Inner London, no systematic pattern can be detected in these differences.

For the purposes of the work reported here, it was important to have a picture of the kinds of issues that were on prisoners' minds in the weeks prior to their discharge from prison. Although a starting-point of each of the prison and day training centre courses was to be the definition by course members of the problems that were of predominant concern to them, it nevertheless seemed worthwhile to enlarge on the picture of offenders' problems by conducting a 'survey' of our own. We therefore asked 250 men from three prisons to complete a questionnaire specifically designed to elicit their views about problems following release. This questionnaire (which is reproduced as Appendix 1), was administered by prison officers and psychologists in Ranby and Ashwell prisons, the sites of the release course project, and in Walton prison, Liverpool. The last site was included for comparative purposes: while Ranby is a 'training' prison and Ashwell an 'open' one, both of which might be expected to contain men slightly atypical of the overall prison population, Walton is a member of a different and important group of penal institutions, the closed local prisons.

All of the prisoners who responded to this questionnaire were within six months of their expected dates of release, that is, all had less than six months of their sentences left to serve. Most of the questionnaires were completed as part of an interview: in Ranby and Ashwell, as part of the selection procedure for many release course applicants; in Walton, as part of a broad-based interview concerning the prisoner's difficulties on discharge. However, a small number of the questionnaires were administered to prisoners in groups of up to ten members.

The principal item on the questionnaire was an open-ended question which invited prisoners to write a list of the problems they thought they would encounter after leaving prison. Space was allowed for the listing of up to seven problems, in approximate order of their importance to the prisoner himself. No attempt was made to gather other personal data on the same sheet, in case this should prejudice prisoners' attitudes to the exercise as a whole.

On average, four problems were listed by each of the 250 men who completed these 'release problem' questionnaires. Analysis of their replies suggested some general categories into which their problems seemed to naturally fall. Though these may provide few surprises for people who work with offenders, they are nevertheless valuable since they are the direct views of prisoners themselves. The numbers and percentages of men at each of the three prisons who mentioned problems in various categories are shown in Table 4.21.

Sorting a wide range of responses like the ones obtained from this questionnaire into a smaller set of groupings obviously involves some sacrifice of the variety that is inherent in the original replies, and can sometimes do injustice to individuals' responses if they are forced into classes which are somehow artificial or which are unsuited to them. The following quotations may help to illustrate the way in which the groupings were used in the compilation of the table. Each of the categories is roughly defined and then some examples are given of the kinds of problems that were subsumed by it. The problem types are listed in the order of frequency with which they were mentioned by members of the sample as a whole.

Work
Some kind of problem to do with obtaining a job, holding on to a job, or at work itself: 'finding work'; 'find a job'; 'employment'; 'work'; 'select different employment'; 'I should have work'; 'finding and holding employment'; 'keeping a job'; 'obtaining training in a trade'; 'timekeeping'; 'holding job down'; 'finding a job and being interviewed for it'; 'proving to employers I deserve a second chance'; 'job seeking with a record'.

Family problems
Difficulties associated with relatives or children, but excluding specifically marital problems: 'a steady home'; 'go to the courts and fight for access'; 'to pick up the pieces of the remains of a normal family life'; 'relations'; 'getting to know my sons'; 'meeting the family'; 'meeting parents'; 'bringing children up after you come out'; 'settling in with the family again'; 'find my wife and children'.

Accommodation
Housing and related problems: 'finding somewhere to live'; 'place to live'; 'going to live in a new place'; 'moving home'; 'get own house'; 'digs'; 'housing'; 'accommodation'.

People
This group includes any general mention of problems in coping with others: 'mixing with people'; 'socialising'; 'fitting back into my circle of friends'; 'meeting old friends again'; 'meeting new friends'; 'meeting people again'; 'social life'; 'meeting people who know you have been in prison'.

Money
Included here are any problems to do with general financial sur-

TABLE 4.21   Self-reported release problems of men in three prisons

Problem area	Ashwell n=43 no.	%	Ranby n=168 no.	%	Walton n=39 no.	%	Total n=250 no.	%
Work and work-related issues	35	81.4	149	88.7	23	59.0	207	82.8
Family	23	53.5	74	44.0	16	41.0	113	45.2
Accommodation	20	46.5	81	48.2	10	25.6	111	44.4
People	18	41.9	65	38.7	10	25.6	93	37.2
Money (exc. DHSS)	15	34.9	67	39.9	11	28.2	93	37.2
DHSS	10	23.2	29	17.3	4	10.2	43	17.2
Trouble/ prison etc.	11	25.6	26	15.5	2	5.1	39	15.6
Personality	2	4.6	28	16.7	2	5.1	32	12.8
Drink	1	2.3	24	14.3	6	15.4	31	12.4
Marital problems	6	13.9	16	9.5	4	10.2	26	10.4
Police	2	4.6	12	7.1	3	7.7	17	6.8
Leisure	2	4.6	10	5.9	2	5.1	14	5.6
Trust	7	16.3	5	3.0	-	-	12	4.8
Sex	-	-	5	3.0	4	10.2	9	3.6
Rights (exc. DHSS)	1	2.3	7	4.2	-	-	8	3.2
Violence	1	2.3	2	1.2	5	12.8	8	3.2
Driving	-	-	5	3.0	-	-	5	2.0
Gambling	2	4.6	2	1.2	1	2.6	5	2.0
Drugs	-	-	2	1.2	2	5.1	4	1.6
Smoking	-	-	1	0.6	-	-	1	0.4
'Settling in'	21	48.8	40	23.8	6	15.4	67	26.8
Miscellaneous	9	20.9	26	15.5	11	28.2	46	18.4

vival, excluding the specific issue of social security and other
benefits: 'money'; 'steady income'; 'debts'; 'bills'; 'rent
arrears'; 'debts all to be sorted out'; 'save some money';
'budgeting for more than one'; 'having enough money to live on';
'learning to look after my money'; 'paying off debts owed prior
to imprisonment'; 'to keep money better, balance my budget better'.

DHSS

Apart from general references to money, many men made particular
reference to the thorny issue of claiming welfare benefits: 'getting social security'; 'trying to get dole'; 'social security
payments'; 'NAB'; 'signing on'; 'dealing with officials, i.e.
social security, labour exchange'; 'dole'; 'approaching SS for
clothing grant'.

Trouble and prison

A number of men declared a problem about keeping out of trouble and
avoiding imprisonment: 'keeping out of trouble'; 'keeping away
from old haunts'; 'staying away from tricky types'; 'keeping away
from town'; 'stopping out'; 'to keep out of trouble and don't
come back'; 'resist being led astray'; 'resisting the temptation
of any easy stealing, such as unlocked cars'.

Personality

Quite a few men also mentioned problems with themselves, with their
own habits or personalities: 'hope to be able to get some confidence in myself'; 'emotional instability'; 'learning to cultivate
reliability'; 'extravagance'; 'temperament'; 'consideration to
others'; 'changing my social behaviour into a stable one'; 'fail-
ing to meet people halfway'; 'trying to be a better person than I
was'; 'loneliness'.

Drinking

Alcohol problems were reported by a number of men, though perhaps
fewer than might be expected: 'drinking'; 'booze'; 'no drinking';
'staying away from alcohol'; 'living without alcohol'; 'giving up
drinking as it has cost me a lot in cash and time'; 'cut down on
drinking'; 'a few drinks instead of too many'; 'control my drinking habits'; 'refrain from getting in depressive ruts and turning
to beer'; 'distinguishing between having a good time and getting
drunk'.

Marital problems

Family problems in which specific mention was made of marriage:
'matrimonial'; 'marriage problems'; 'marriage'; 'speaking to my
wife'; 'wife'; 'resuming a relationship with my wife'; 'dealing
with my wife's infidelity before I was sentenced'; 'reconciliation
with divorced wife'; 'making up to my wife'; 'to resolve problems
surrounding marriage'; 'sorting out my marriage situation'; 'es-
tablishing a relationship with my wife'; 'domestic problems - wife
trouble as usual'.

Police

Dealings with the police, and being a subject of their attention,

was of concern to several men: 'police'; 'police interference';
'being harassed by the police'; 'police hassle'; 'trouble with
police'; 'to stay away from the police'; 'police should leave you
alone'; 'weary of contacting police'.

Leisure time

Some men mentioned problems related to how they would spend their
spare time: 'finding suitable leisure activities'; 'rejoining old
and new activities'; 'finding things to do in my spare time'; 'to
occupy myself in different hobbies'; 'not getting bored'; 'not
being so bored'; 'discovering new interests'.

Trust

A number of men seemed to be particularly concerned with the fact
that they had lost the trust of others who were important to them,
and were worried about whether they could regain it: 'being
trusted'; 'regain people's trust'; 'getting friends and ac-
quaintances to trust me again'; 'gaining someone else's trust';
'getting to be trusted by other people'; 'going to see people who
relied on me and were let down'; 'getting confidence back to my
wife and kids'.

Sex

The thought that their sexual deprivations might not be at an end
even after they left prison seemed to worry some men; others were
concerned about their ability simply to talk to women: 'meeting
the opposite sex'; 'meeting female company'; 'sex'; 'forming a
relationship with girls'; 'meeting girls and having intercourse'.

Rights

Apart from the specific issue of welfare and social security benefits, several prisoners also listed other, or in some cases broader,
problems with the law and with officialdom; 'tax/insurance';
'county court for legal matters'; 'communicating with civil serv-
ants'; 'sorting out tax rebate'; 'dealing with government officials'; 'county courts'; 'pending court cases - civil debts';
'rights'; 'how to claim tax - your rights'.

Violence

For a few men, the problem of personal violence was a worrying one:
'temper'; 'learn in some way to control my temper'; 'resisting
temptations to get into fights'; 'learn to ignore possible inflam-
matory situations'. The proportion of men who acknowledged this as
a problem was, perhaps not unexpectedly, lower than the proportion
known to have committed acts of violence.

Driving

Being banned from driving appeared to present problems for a few
men: 'settling down to a life without cars'; 'not being able to
drive'; 'driving (banned)'; 'I am disqualified from driving, and
it might be inconvenient if I receive a job which required driving'.

Gambling

For a small number of men, the consequences of gambling were

going to present some problems: 'gambling';   'controlling gambling';   'to stop my gambling';   'staying away from gambling, mainly
betting shops'.

Drugs

A very small proportion of the men cited drug problems: 'drugs';
'problems with drugs'.

Smoking

Perhaps not surprisingly, given the alleged importance of tobacco
as a form of currency within prisons, only one man mentioned that
he had a plan for 'smoking to be cut down'.

Obviously, the categories that have been used here could be re-
arranged in a number of different ways. The 'police' category, for
example, could be grouped under the broader heading of 'people';
'marital' and 'family problems' could be lumped together; for some,
'drink' might be seen as a 'personality' problem. But since the aim
of this survey was to identify problems which could be approached in
a useful and meaningful way in release course sessions, it seemed
most sensible to draw out from the responses as many distinct categories as seemed to be possible. When a man says one of his problems, for example, is 'getting your family to have faith in you
again', this seems more of a problem to do with the general idea of
'trust', a theme which emerged in a good many replies and which
seemed a distinct category of its own, than with 'family' as such.
There were several men, of course, who mentioned events following
release which could hardly be construed as problems; into this
category could be placed 'beer - getting too little' or 'a good bit
of sexual intercourse and no bother from the old bill'. In addition, two other kinds of statement emerged from the responses, which
were difficult to classify in the above scheme:

'Settling in'

Many men replied that they would have general difficulties in adjusting to and coping with the post-prison world, sometimes referring to changes that had taken place 'outside' since the commence-
ment of their sentences, but more often just making a global comment
on the discomforts they expected to experience; 'to fit in with the
rest of society as soon as possible'; 'fitting back in'; 'resettlement'; 'adjusting to the outside'; 'community rehabilitation';
'adjusting to society'; 'adjusting to changes and cost of living';
'adapting to new environment'; 'coping in general in the outside
world again'; 'getting used to freedom'; 'settling myself to being
dedicated to the task of building a decent life and prosperous
future'.

Miscellaneous

This category was used for such statements as: 'have a rest for a
few months'; 'try to find my property'; 'decorating/gardening';
'doing the garden'; 'getting my medical treatment sorted out';
'having to face major surgery for a rotten thigh'; 'accepting once
again the role of decision-maker';   'guidance (welfare problems)';
'guidance - on release from prison';   'seeing probation officer';

'after-care'; 'to find new areas to drink in'; 'to try and help
people who have tried to help me'; 'to work hard within the community to try to wisely alter or change the prison systems in
England to the better advantage of the prisoners and taxpayer
alike'.

Casting an eye over the foregoing list of problems and the frequency with which each of them is mentioned, two possibly unexpected
findings emerge. First, not many men talk about personal damage in
any profound emotional sense, a notion which is a cornerstone of
many social work approaches to offenders' problems. Even those who
mention personality problems for the most part do so at the level
of habits and everyday behaviour. Second, the proportion of men
identifying their offending behaviour, or attempts to avoid it, as
a specific issue is not as high as might be expected given that it
is the reason for their incarceration, and not as high as might be
hoped given the aims of most attempts at 'intervention' and 'rehabilitation'. The paramount concerns of the men in these samples
at least are with the solving of everyday, practical problems to do
with employment, money and personal relations.

A final, interesting feature of these results is that, though
recruited in three different prisons, and having been given the
questionnaire at quite separate points in time, the three groups
of men are very similar in the kinds of difficulties they perceive
and in the overall frequency with which they mention them. A
Kendall's 'W' Coefficient of Concordance calculated on these data
was highly significant (eliminating the two loosely defined categories of 'Settling in' and 'Miscellaneous'; 'W' = 0.829, df = 19,
chi-square = 47.253, p < .001). Roughly the same order of 'priorities' would, therefore, seem to exist amongst groups of prisoners
about to be released, across a fair spectrum of prison establishments.

What do these findings imply about the running of courses for
offenders in such settings as prisons or day training centres?
They suggest that, amongst any group of ten or twelve individuals
taking part in such courses, almost all will have one problem connected with work, more than half will be concerned with family difficulties of some kind, a similar proportion will be beset with
financial problems of a major order, several will have accommodation
problems, a few will be problem drinkers, if not actually alcoholic,
and every group member will be likely to have at least one other
problem demanding attention. Problems of this kind have a tendency,
of course, to feed on one another: lack of a job means a shortage
of money which may lead to stealing, arrest, and subsequent failure
to find work. In addition, in any group of this kind, two or three,
and possibly more of its members will be quite difficult, awkward
individuals; and it goes almost without saying that a majority will
be initially (and perhaps constantly) suspicious of the aims of the
course and of those who are running it.

An impression of how these findings are reflected amongst the
membership of a single group can be obtained by looking at the responses of one group of Sheffield day training centre probationers
to the same question as that used in the prison survey. Each man
in the group was asked to write down the main problems on his mind

while at the centre. The pooled responses to the question are presented verbatim in Table 4.22. This group had nine members; where more than one individual named a particular problem, the number who did so is given in brackets.

TABLE 4.22   Problems specified by one group of men at Sheffield

Work (9)	Sticking at work
Money (6)	Swearing
Family and family relations (5)	Smoking
Bringing up children (5)	Confidence
Police (4)	Getting my bike back on the road
Drink and drinking (3)	Getting up in the morning
Probation officers (3)	Losing my temper and fighting
Paying debts (3)	Medical problems
Making decisions about jobs (2)	Avoiding the law
Mother (2)	Marriage
Feeling anti-authority (2)	Police record
Being unemployed	Football terraces
Can't settle down	Reading and writing
The DHSS	Budgeting

The list of difficulties given in the table spans a fairly typical cross-section of the personal problems of day trainees, and apart from the absence of accommodation problems (which most men at the centre have sorted out prior to entry), would be equally representative of the problems amongst a group of release course members. Two areas are perhaps under-emphasised in the list. First, reading and writing difficulties may be more common than appears to be the case, and second, in the day training centre at least, many men suffer from some form of ill health. Although no quantitative evidence can be adduced concerning either of these points, it may be worth noting that the centre found it necessary to set up its own remedial literacy sessions, that release courses were a major source of recruits for remedial literacy classes in the two prisons, and that in the routine medical examinations given to all Sheffield course members the amount of illness reported is very striking.

One of the significant findings of Holborn's (1975) research, (14) mentioned earlier, was that of a very strong relationship between inability to deal with everyday problems of a 'survival' nature, and degree of criminality in terms of numbers of previous sentences of imprisonment. The less socially adequate offender was also more likely to have embarked on a criminal career partly as a product of some problem which he was facing at the time. (15) Failure to overcome personal problems, then, may not only present an issue in itself, but may be closely linked to the committing of offences and to the adoption of a criminal 'way of life'.

Chapter 5

Methods and materials

The survey of offenders' problems reported in chapter 4 was carried out alongside the process of setting up and running courses in Ranby, Ashwell and Sheffield. What this means is that at the outset of this research, and even as the first prison courses were getting under way, the research team and the prison and probation staff had to make informed guesses on the basis of their own experience as to what kinds of problems would be on the minds of potential course members, without having any real assurance that these would turn out to be correct. The processes of assessing the problems of individuals and groups, and of helping them to do something about them, ran a very close parallel with each other, at least during the early phases of the research.

Nevertheless, some definite decisions had already been made about the content of the courses, dictated by the kinds of new departure which the research project was intended to make. It had been decided, for example, that they should include a number of methods which would be relatively new to work with offenders in this country, and in the case of the prisons, every effort was made to make these as unlike 'traditional' pre-release courses (which consisted in many cases of an uninspiring series of invited speakers) as possible.

In general, therefore, the content was planned so as to encourage the participation of course members, through the use of lively, activity-based methods of teaching and learning. More specifically, one of the principal aims of the project was to pilot the use of a number of techniques known collectively as 'social skills training'. The emphasis of these methods on imparting skills rather than simply giving information seemed more likely to assist the 'socially inadequate' offender than endless recitations of data pertaining to work, accommodation, or social security rights. Thus, the courses were envisaged as giving more emphasis to the development of competencies rather than the teaching of facts, or the fostering of particular attitudes or the promotion of personal insights, although these were also thought important.

At the same time, the construction of the courses in situ was to be the task of the specially trained prison and probation staff. And since the problems of their students were likely to prove more

various in practice than could be planned for in advance, an attempt
was made to approach the compilation of course content in as open a
manner as possible. Any method whatsoever was seen as a candidate
for inclusion, so long as it promised usefulness to the participants
in a course, and had enough 'face value' to engage their interest
and appear to them as a plausible means of attacking the problem to
which it was addressed. And their judgments of the methods were to
be systematically gathered so as to sort out the more from the less
useful.

As a result, the conception of the courses, as the first timetables were drawn up and materials tentatively prepared, was a very
fluid one. It combined elements of education, social work, psychotherapy, and industrial training; incorporated short lectures, discussions, role plays, simulations, films, projects, and counselling
sessions; and focused on work, rights, money management, social behaviour, and other topics which it was anticipated would be of concern to those who would be taking part.

The object of this chapter is to give an overall impression of
the way the courses were run, by outlining the rationale on which
they were based, by giving some illustrations of the content of specific sessions, and by demonstrating how these were knitted together
in the week-by-week timetables of individual courses.

COURSE RATIONALE AND THE 'SKILLS TRAINING' APPROACH

No matter what view is taken of the origins and causes of delinquent
behaviour it seems an unlikely proposition that exposure to the contents of a 'course' lasting for only a few weeks, could have any
profound or lasting impact on individuals who have been unemployed
or embroiled in trouble of all kinds for many years of their lives.
The release and day training centre courses limited themselves
therefore to two fairly humble preliminary objectives. First,
they were intended to help those who took part to find out more
about themselves and their problems. A great many course members,
afflicted with difficulties which most people would perceive as
fairly burdensome, seemed to have spent very little time reflecting
constructively on the directions in which their lives were going.
Second, once particular issues had been identified, the courses were
designed to help individuals, using all available means, to do something about the problems confronting them. One result of this was
that the eventual gains reported by course members, which are described in chapter 7, displayed a very wide range, from the detailed
and down-to-earth, like information on housing, for example, to far
less tangible and more diffuse changes, such as greater self-know-
ledge, self-confidence, or self-possession.

What is it, then, that offenders about to leave prison, or on a
course of day training, need in order to tackle their problems more
effectively? The number of possible answers to this question is
infinite, but the content of the prison and day training centre
courses can be summarised in terms of three basic ingredients.

The first of these is information. Facts, as accurate and up-to-
date as possible, need to be presented to individuals in a form
which they can easily understand; facts on work, housing, tenant-

ing, legal rights, supplementary benefits, alcohol, drugs, money and innumerable specific items subsumed by these general headings. Various means were used to impart these facts to prison and day training centre course participants. They ranged from talks given by staff or by other course members who were knowledgeable on particular themes, through films and slide shows, or the distribution of leaflets or books, to the setting of information-gathering projects and the making of visits to relevant sources. All of these methods come under what could be called the 'input' element of a course.

A second kind of need cannot however be met by the straightforward giving of information, though facts of one sort or another can occasionally satisfy it in part. This is the need of individuals for appropriate attitudes to themselves and others; attitudes which will influence whether they approach their problems in a realistic way. Some course sessions therefore looked closely at these. Primarily via the medium of group discussion, course members helped each other with emotional difficulties, appraised each other's views, argued over many issues, and provided through their reactions to each other an important mechanism of attitude change.

But facts and attitudes can take individuals only so far; to become self-reliant in solving their own problems, they need to be able to do things like find out facts for themselves, or examine their views, and put them forward convincingly to other people. A third requirement therefore is for skills. And since the solutions to many kinds of problem are often mediated by other people - policemen, friends, employers, clerks of this office or that - a crucial kind of skill is the ability to deal with others. The courses gave great emphasis to this inter-personal dimension of personal problems and considerable time and effort was devoted to developing skills of communication and self-expression, perceiving and judging other people, and handling a heterogeneous collection of social encounters, such as job interviews, courtroom appearances, visits to social security, questionings by the police, or less formal confrontations which might escalate into fights. But even if socially skilled, people with problems also need to be able to think about them in a particular way; and need, ideally, to approach them in a systematic, constructive, and purposeful fashion. Closely associated with the idea of social skills training in the courses, therefore, was the idea of training in problem-solving skills. That human predicaments and personal embroilments can be approached systematically may seem unlikely enough; but that individuals whose lives more often than not may be in a state of chaos can learn to adopt such an approach may seem to be plain wishful thinking. There is some evidence to suggest, however, that many individuals accumulate problems precisely because they lack problem-solving skills. Their stopgap solutions to one crisis often form the basis of the next; the answer to the problem of paying today's gas bill, viz. to raid the meter, creates the problem of next year's unpaid fine. Other evidence suggests that people can be trained to solve their problems in a manner more congenial both to themselves and others, and attempts to encourage thinking about problems in this way were a recurring feature of course sessions.

In practice, while some sessions were fairly clearly concerned with information, some with attitudes, and others with skills, a more common occurrence was for the three to be mixed together in an almost symbiotic fashion, to form a curriculum directed towards the solving of course members' problems.

COURSE DESIGN

On the face of it, the notion of a 'curriculum' is not one that would be expected to appeal to offenders. For many of them the experience of 'education' has been singularly unpleasant and unproductive; in their eyes any similarity to school is heavily suspect, and they might therefore have rejected, as if by reflex, any enterprise even remotely resembling it. But the school curriculum as most of us know it is only one of many possible ways in which learning can be organised. 'Curriculum', in its fuller sense, need mean nothing more than some roughly ordered sequence of learning opportunities. The topics dealt with, the specific methods used, the level of intensity, and degree of flexibility and responsiveness to participants' needs, can all be altered while the same underlying notion is maintained. It was on this broader concept of a curriculum that the developmental nature of the project ensured that no two courses on any site followed exactly the same pattern. Course content over the period of the research was constantly being modified to reflect the needs and the problems of the unique gatherings of individuals on particular courses. 'Curricula' were constructed in the prisons around two main considerations: the needs of participants, and the capabilities of the officers involved in running any one course. A pre-course questionnaire and interview (which provided the data for the survey reported in chapter 4) not only helped the officers select members for a course, but also supplied information on the kinds of problems in which that particular group would be interested, and which would therefore form the substance of the course.

As the previous chapter showed, it became clear as courses progressed that some problems continuously recurred, and had therefore always to be catered for, while others were relevant for only a proportion of the membership and some might be of concern to one man only. The various mixes of problems which arose required a constant juggling with the details of course content, not least because other and different problems were almost bound to be brought up as soon as a course had commenced. But as the courses developed and the officers became more confident, so timetables became more flexible, and they were usually designed to allow for restructuring even as a course was in progress. In most cases, the only definitely fixed events were the appearances of external speakers who had to be booked in advance (usually at two to four weeks' notice); so though each course began with an apparently rigid timetable, the reality was a fluidly organic approach adaptable to changing circumstances.

Three main themes ran through the underlying structure of the courses at all the sites. These were first of all, self-assessment, intended to discover personal strengths and weaknesses, and identify problems; second, social skills, focusing on personal and 'survival' problems in more depth, and development of the skills needed to solve them; and third, work, an exploration of job histories, skills, and employment opportunities, usually culminating in an actual search for work which was the goal most commonly expressed by those who took part in the project.

At the day training centre, an additional emphasis was placed on boosting individuals' self-confidence, on helping them to communicate more effectively, and on encouraging them to make plans for the future. A number of the shorter prison courses were geared almost entirely to employment problems. And clearly, within these very broadly conceived limits, individual course members pursued a multitude of unique aims of their own.

This chapter tries to convey the open and flexible way in which these courses were constructed; no particular format was prescribed for courses in advance. As the project progressed, however, it became apparent that courses, or the most successful ones at least, were following a similar pattern or design. This general structure or framework conformed, roughly, to the stages of a problem-solving process, consisting of:

1 Assessment: identifying and examining problems, finding out as much about them as possible.
2 Setting objectives: deciding on personal goals or any other changes that could be steps towards solution of a problem.
3 Learning procedures: achieving these goals by finding the information, adopting the attitudes, or acquiring the skills that are necessary.
4 Evaluation: checking on the results of the process.

As a framework for personal problem-solving, this process can be used to design a sequence of activities in which people might engage while dealing with a specific problem; and problem-solving 'systems' like this have been used to good effect in a number of settings, notably in industry. (1) In addition, it can be used as an organising principle for courses, regardless of their length or particular content. As a description of the curriculum which emerged the process is of course something of an abstraction; actual courses in most cases departed substantially from it and contained many other elements as well. Nevertheless the four-stage sequence provided an increasingly explicit basis for the design of successive courses.

In more concrete terms, the first two weeks of some of the earlier prison courses were devoted to assessment and self-assessment activities, including pencil and paper items, group discussion, individual interviews, and the use of video. In the day training centre this process lasted for three to four weeks, with a number of objective-setting exercises, including an interview between each probationer and his supervising probation officer, taking place in the fourth week. Later blocks of prison courses were then devoted to work, accommodation, and social skills sessions, embracing a varying number of sessions on rights, money, or whatever other topics were uppermost in the minds of that particular group. At Sheffield the divisions between social or 'survival' skills sessions and those dealing with work were more pronounced, the 'work' phase coming in the last four weeks of a course when trainees' thoughts were actually concentrated on trying to find a job to go to after their departure from the centre.

But as indicated above, the 'problem-solving' framework just outlined must be interpreted in the loosest possible sense. In setting objectives, for example, course members might be asked to do this at various points: during the second week of a course, at various points on a course where specialised topics were being dealt with, and again at the end. On some courses, personal goals were formulated twice, once fairly early on as goals to be pursued before release, and a second time at the conclusion of a course as objectives to be achieved in the world outside. The evaluation element too, might be distributed throughout a course; every week's activities were evaluated separately, as was the total content of a course seen from the perspective of the last day.

COURSE CONTENT AND SPECIFIC EXERCISES

What, then, were the particular components which went to make up release courses in prisons and the programme of the day training centre? In this section they will be described under the four headings of assessment, setting objectives, learning, and evaluation. But first it may be useful to look briefly at the relationship, on prison courses, between prison officers and the men who took part. As suggested in chapter 1, the mutual suspicions which plague this relationship could well have militated against release courses lasting any longer than their opening sessions. At the beginning, therefore, barriers had to be broken down and a climate of trust and co-operation established.

The tasks of the officers on the first day of a prison release course were to introduce the aims of the course to the new members, to outline some simple ground rules about the way in which it would operate, and to describe some of the sorts of activities involved. Officers did this in a variety of ways: by posting up sets of course objectives, by talking about previous courses, by showing video films of previous course members talking about their experiences or demonstrating some typical exercises and by distributing handouts, e.g.:

Welcome to the course. We shall be working together as a group for the next 8 weeks and it is hoped that we shall be learning about ourselves and each other in ways that will be new and rewarding. Each person joining the course will bring with him experiences and skills that he will want to share with others; he will be able to do this in a variety of ways, in group discussion and advising in role play or simulations. If you yourself have any skills or interests that other people might find useful, don't be afraid to present your ideas to the other course members.

Mr C..... and Mr N..... will be your course Instructors and, hopefully, advisors. They both have various skills to offer the group but needless to say they don't know everything - they will be learning as much from you as you from them. They are, however, there to be used as a lynch pin between yourself and society. If you have any problem, question or query, please don't be afraid to use them. If you have a problem of a personal nature they will be only too pleased to discuss it with you in private and maintain confidentiality.

The Release Unit is there to help you, don't waste the next eight weeks but use them to find out as much as you can about yourself, your strengths and abilities. You may know them already, if so, why not help others to know theirs?

> R. N . . . . .
> R. C . . . . .
> Release Course Officers

The most important of the rules or expectations governing the con-duct of the courses were those which touched on the issue of confi-dentiality. Assurances were given at the outset that all the in-formation recorded by any man about his own problems and what he intended to do about them was to remain confidential to each indi-vidual, except to the extent to which he might choose to divulge it to anyone else. This meant that he need not show anything he had collected or written to anyone; or he could show it to everyone. The men were also assured that no secret records would be kept on them by course staff, that nothing would be entered on their of-ficial files, and that no information gained through course activi-ties would be divulged to anyone else without the permission of the person concerned. It is difficult to gauge how these assurances were received at the time of their making. There is an innate sus-picion of official paperwork amongst those who have failed to re-spond to formal education and who have become enmeshed to varying degrees in the toils of the welfare state and the legal and penal systems. To many such individuals, filling in official pieces of paper is to yield hostages to fortune. There is a reluctance therefore to volunteer information which may be 'taken down and used in evidence' against them, as they see it, at some later date and in some other context. Such suspicions were most marked amongst the few men who patronised release courses who were simultaneously eligible for parole. Some of them were never able to accept that what they did or said in the course room would not somehow be used to determine their suitability or otherwise for parole. But the general experience was that after a week or so, most course members appeared to feel little reticence about responding frankly to pencil and paper exercises and saying exactly what they thought in front of other men and the officers running the courses. It also became ap-parent over time that increasing numbers of new applicants for the courses in the prisons were aware of the 'ground rules' that oper-ated within the release courses and who already felt a degree of confidence in the confidentiality exercised by the officers con-cerned. Other norms which became established in the prisons and the day training centre were that participation in any given exer-cise was voluntary, that problems dealt with were those seen and defined by group members themselves, and that all activities were

explained in language group members could understand. The overall
ethos on all the courses was the assumption that every individual
member was capable of solving at least some of his problems.

The ideas of self-assessment and of personal control over information were made concrete in the shape of a folder or file issued
to each man in which he could keep all the information he collected
about himself and his problems and ways of tackling them. For some
men these files, when filled, turned out to be significant end-
products of the course experience.

Assessment

The first use to which these folders were put was to contain the
results of a number of exercises in self-assessment. Although the
opening days of longer prison courses, and the first week of courses
in the day training centre necessarily contained much activity that
served the simple purpose of introducing members to each other and
to the course, the main aim of the early part of the proceedings was
to begin the process of self-exploration and self-assessment.

This had a number of inter-related aims: broadly it was to
define and analyse group members' difficulties, and to help them
estimate their own strengths and weaknesses. Starting from a general survey of problem areas, course members progressed gradually to
concentrating on specific items of concern to them as individuals.
The methods of assessment that were used in the prison and DTC
courses included:

1 Structured pencil and paper exercises, such as the Mooney Problem
   Checklist, (2) Lifeskills Checklist, (3) problem rating sheets,
   Rotter Internal-External Scale (4) and person perception scales.
2 Open-ended pencil and paper methods, such as sentence completion,
   brainstorming, (5) pattern notes, (6) diary forms (see below) and
   the 'Seven-point Plan'. (7)
3 Interviews: peer interviews, and interview role plays.
4 Group discussion methods. (8)
5 Self-observation and other video exercises, including 'whispers',
   (9) first impressions exercises, self-presentation, and 'ten best
   points'.
6 Group games, including 'Red Desert', (10) 'Win as much as you
   can', (11) 'Broken Squares' (12) and 'What's my Line?'. (13)

The preliminary assessment period, even in its later and more
abbreviated form, contained an introduction to pencil and paper
methods of two broad types: unstructured and structured. Structured pencil and paper tests such as questionnaires, rating scales
and checklists were introduced with the help of a simple test-
taking-and-form-filling package which explained the various kinds
of items likely to be encountered during the course and permitted
course members to practice doing them. Form-filling also gave some
men much needed experience in completing forms relevant to everyday
life, e.g. applications for driving licences, TV licences, tax
rebate and employment applications.

The simplest and most complete checklist which was found to be

useful at an early stage, either in parts or as a whole, was the
Mooney Problem Checklist (14) which contains almost 150 items
covering areas such as work, personal health and appearance, family,
money, etc. The version employed in the courses had been modified
at Glen Parva Borstal at Leicester to incorporate a simple rating
scale for each item: Not a problem/A problem/Severe problem. The
average number of 'severe problems' acknowledged by the members of
the first four courses at Ashwell was fifteen, and the number of
'problems' - thirty-five. The spread of individual scores can be
seen in the figures for the third Ashwell course.

TABLE 5.1 Problem checklist scores: Ashwell third course

| Course member | No. of items indicated as: | |
	a problem	a severe problem
A	48	27
B	49	8
C	41	56
D	30	11
E	45	8
F	53	15
G	50	36
H	46	10
I	29	7
J	46	8
K	53	24
L	39	7

The most common of the 'severe problems' was 'Afraid of being unemployed in the future', closely followed by 'Don't have enough
money', and 'Afraid I shall always be in trouble'. The range of
the items regarded as both problems and severe problems, as the
totals indicate, was very wide indeed. One man's 'severe problems'
consisted of:

    Most of my friends don't work
    Don't understand money matters
    Afraid I shall always be in trouble
    Drink heavily
    Can't stop gambling
    Have thoughts of suicide
    Most of my life spent in institutions

    Brainstorming was also used for assessment, as well as other
purposes, during the courses. At its simplest it consists of asking
participants to call out ideas related to the theme or topic under

discussion, and writing them down on a blackboard or wall-sheet. It can be used therefore to identify problem areas, to explore some of the ramifications of problems thus identified, and at a later stage to generate possible solutions to them. Considerable use was also made of 'pattern notes', a technique suggested by Buzan (15) in the BBC Book 'Use your head' and which acts as a kind of personal brainstorm. One of its virtues is that it enables individuals to work on their own, producing ideas and thoughts and feelings about any topic which happens to be under consideration, e.g. violence, drugs, depression.

Sentence completion: asking members to complete sentences such as: My biggest problem is ... also proved effective as a starter for more structured inquiry into personal problem areas. The simplicity of this method belies the illumination which accompanied the responses for some men. Sentence completion simply makes some people think more clearly. It can also be used as an aid to self-description. This is how one Ashwell man, for example, completed the sentence, 'I am the kind of driver who ...'
'... likes to speed.'
'... likes driving with other people.'
'... drives after drinking.'
'... abuses the road.'
'... does not like being told what to do.'
'... often screams at other people driving.'
The car he would 'like to have most' was a 'LABOGHINI'.

Another man, who said he was 'the kind of driver who ...' 'drives whilst disqualified', 'drives stupidly when been drinking' and who wanted a 'Ford Mustang', was killed in a chase involving a stolen car and the police not long after his release from prison.

An apparently heavy reliance on pencil and paper techniques in this description of the assessment period does not correspond with the frequency of their use in practice. It became obvious during the earlier courses that the tolerance of groups for the use of such methods was strictly limited, and care was subsequently taken to limit the time spent on them and to balance them against other activities like peer interviews, group discussion and role play. The use of a pencil and paper assessment on its own is, by any judgment, a somewhat arid pursuit; the combination of different assessment methods in a single session will always be more effective and more enjoyable; and this became standard practice.

An altogether more pervasive element of this phase was group discussion itself. While this can be started formally for a specific purpose, using a cartoon stimulus or other prepared opener for example, it was usually more animated in response to some other exercise, particularly films, or outside speakers contributing to courses, but free discussion amongst group members was a continuous feature of most courses and was found to be one of the main motors of any personal change that took place. Many of the assessment methods acted, in fact, as devices for channelling discussion in particular directions.

An illustration of the combined use of pencil and paper with both action and discussion can be found in sessions involving the 'Person Perception Rating Scale'. This consists of several (identical) sheets on which there are pairs of adjectives opposite in meaning, separated by a seven-point rating scale, for example:

Kind	1 2 3 4 5 6 7	Unkind
Honest	1 2 3 4 5 6 7	Dishonest
Reliable	1 2 3 4 5 6 7	Unreliable
Interesting	1 2 3 4 5 6 7	Boring

Each sheet consists of the same set of (twenty or so) adjective pairs. Group members asked first to go through one sheet, rating themselves on each adjective pair in terms of 'Me as I see myself', and then to join up their ratings into a profile. The exercise can then be continued in a number of ways. First, another sheet can be completed, this time in terms of 'Me as I would like to be', and comparisons made between profiles obtained here and on the first sheet; the guaranteed differences between the two pinpoint potential areas for change. Second, group members can rate each other, either in pairs (e.g. 'John as I see him', or 'Me as I think John sees me'), and then compare results; or more engagingly, each group member in turn can be rated by the whole group. This last exercise produces an 'average' or 'group' profile for each individual and yields many insights which cannot be obtained by other means. Discussion of how people are perceived by others, how judgments are formed, and what constitutes personal insight, flows naturally from it. It was not uncommon at the day training centre to find groups willing to spend several sessions preparing 'average profiles' for every member, and there were no signs that the experience was ever other than enlightening, even for those who received slightly bad news from the judgments of their colleagues.

Another exercise which was used in a number of ways and which provided a valuable stimulus for discussion was the completion of 'diary forms'. In essence these are simple blank sheets representing one week in a person's life, like the one shown below.

	Morning	Afternoon	Evening
Monday			
Tuesday			
Wednesday			
Thursday			
Friday			
Saturday			
Sunday			

Diary forms, sometimes quite spacious, can be used by individuals to record or to plan the events of a single week. For example, an individual might write down how much he spent, or drank, or worked in a given week, or note which people he met, and how often; in fact he might describe any aspect of his behaviour that was of in-

terest to him. Comparisons like these between group members, on
any dimensions of their lives, are among the most thought-provoking
self-assessment tools available. The forms can also be used to
examine crisis weeks, of an alcoholic binge, marital conflict, or
the commission of an offence, for example, in an attempt to isolate
factors that may have contributed to their occurrence. One other
particularly valuable tool was video, which was usually introduced
at an early stage in assessment, by simply panning the camera round
a group discussion and showing back the tape for subsequent comment.
On some courses the video was greeted with enthusiasm; on others
there was a degree of suspicion and hostility, and there were a few
individuals who never consented to having their picture taken at
all. One or two of them remained convinced that the cameras were
linked by secret landline to monitors in the Home Office, or the
Criminal Records Office, or both. In the vast majority of cases,
however, the use of video in self-presentation exercises and as a
feedback vehicle for role plays proved invaluable as a tool for
learning and confidence-building.

In a completely different vein was an assessment exercise that
entailed the observation of each course member's 'personal space'.
This was based on research by Kinzel (16) which suggested that
violence-prone offenders prefer to keep other people at a greater
distance from them than do non-violent offenders. By asking pairs
of prisoners to walk slowly towards each other, and to stop when
they started to feel uncomfortable, a crude measure was obtained
of the area of their 'personal space'. Discussion would then ensue
on the various factors which influenced the distance at which one
stood from others.

The end product of all these assessment methods, used both singly
and in a variety of combinations, was, for many of those who completed and discussed them, a headful of thoughts and impressions.

Objective setting

A second element in most courses, that of objective setting, was
intended to help course members make sense of all these thoughts.
In the shorter prison courses of one or two weeks, the objective
setting phase was specifically geared to achievements to be made
on release; whereas on the longer ones it was linked to objectives
to be met during the course itself as well as on release. The main
purpose of objective setting was to help individuals set personal
goals, which could be reasonably met, by drawing on what had been
looked at in the assessment period. A number of methods were used
in this process, including peer interviews, some pencil and paper
techniques, group discussion and individual counselling by course
staff.

At Sheffield, an exercise used in target setting, designed both
to help individuals sort out their own goals and supply guidelines
for subsequent course content, was the 'Checklist of aims and objectives'. This is a list of more than one hundred specimen goals
which group members might wish to set for themselves during their
stay at the centre. They were invited to work through the list,
placing ticks beside those items on which they wished to concentrate
their efforts, e.g.

    14 To learn more about my own potential work skills.
    32 To get an idea of what to look for in accommodation.
    55 To decide what needs to be done to clear up my debts.
  108 To be better able to resist pressure that others put on me.
  116 To feel more confident about speaking to others.

Space was also provided for suggestions other than those on the list. The majority of course members ticked many more items than could possibly be dealt with during a few weeks' work. Consequently some order of priorities had to be reached, and the ensuing discussion and negotiation was aimed at producing an agenda for the middle weeks of a course in which most of its members would have manifestly shared interests.

Another vital ingredient of 'target-setting' at the day training centre was a discussion session, usually taking place during the fourth week of a course, between the individual course member, the current group leader, and the supervising probation officer from the community. This session was intended to give the group member an opportunity to obtain advice from the field officer on particular problems (though he was of course free to seek this at any time); but was particularly geared to the joint setting of goals for the individual's remaining time at the centre. It proved to be an effective way of helping group members to formulate future commitments, and equally, it gave field officers a chance to pin down those areas in which course members might benefit from further work and to deal with any difficulties that had arisen.

Prison course members were also encouraged to set targets to achieve, both during the courses and after their release into the community. Many of these goals related to the obvious issues of finding jobs, but the variety and their individuality are illustrated in this man's list: 'to stop drinking', 'to look after myself better', 'to handle money carefully', 'to hold jobs down better', 'to make friends more easily and communicate', 'to control temper', 'to do more fishing', 'to gain custody of my little boy', 'to get suitable accommodation to carry out above objectives'.

LEARNING

A major part of all the courses was devoted to 'learning' in the different problem areas identified as requiring attention by course members. The aim of part of this course was simply to help individuals achieve as many as possible of the objectives they had set themselves in the preceding phase: by helping them acquire the information, examine the attitudes and feelings, or develop the skills relevant to the solution of their problems. This involved the use of a wide range of methods and materials which can be classified under four main headings:

1 Direct teaching
2 Group discussion
3 Social skills training
4 Simulations

Direct teaching

Direct teaching methods were used to provide course members with a
supply of facts relevant to the problems they had acknowledged
during the assessment part of the courses. They required, first
and foremost, information about job-finding, about vacancies, about
the services of the Department of Employment, about training and
educational courses, about accommodation, welfare and legal rights,
consumer affairs, money management, drink, drugs and gambling and
other topics.

Since neither the prison officers nor the probation officers were
trained teachers, and since the range of subject matter would in any
case have been beyond the mastery of any one person, a variety of
methods was employed to secure all this information: leaflets,
books, films, brief talks by staff members and course members, outside speakers on specialist subjects, and in some cases, visits to
places of interest in the community. The speakers who gave talks
at Sheffield included:
Crown Court judges, on the role of the judge and procedure in court;
magistrates, on legal rights, the magistrates' court, and consumer
rights; police officers, on the work of the police; probation officers, on the work of the probation service, help in job-finding,
and sex and sexual approach; lecturers from Sheffield University
and Polytechnic, on legal rights, welfare rights, criminology, and
interview techniques; a psychiatrist, on medical and social aspects
of alcoholism; a community nurse, on aspects of health education;
a member of St John's Ambulance Brigade, on first aid; a speaker
from the Abortion Advice Centre, on family planning; members of
Claimants' Unions, on welfare rights, and supplementary benefits;
speakers from the Department of Employment, on Jobcentre services
and training opportunities; and representatives of firms in the
Sheffield area.

An equivalent list for the prisons included Citizen's Advice
Bureau, St John's Ambulance Brigade, Housing Advice Centre, Child
Poverty Action Group, Police, Probation Service, Family Planning
Association, Marriage Guidance, Alcoholics Anonymous, Gambler's
Anonymous, Bank Manager, Accountant, Job Centre Manager, Leisure
Centre Manager, Community Relations Commission.

Visiting speakers are a well-known hazard for all educational
organisers; good ones are quite rare, and the bad ones, even if
they are never invited again, have to be endured the first time,
often with crossed fingers on the tutor's part lest the listeners
demonstrate their boredom or dislike.

On at least one occasion, the impact of a visitor was almost
literally explosive. The course officers at Ashwell were talking
to a detective from the Leicestershire police force, about a possible future visit to discuss offender relations. On a sudden impulse
he was invited to meet the current group unannounced. One of the
prison officers described the effect as 'rather like throwing a hand
grenade into a crowded room'. The detective beat a hasty retreat
and the officers attempted, successfully in the end, to pick up the
pieces, and restore equilibrium to their group of prisoners. The
incident underlined the importance of preparing for visiting speakers, particularly those as contentious as policemen. The planned
visit actually took place later without serious consequences.

Another method which was used to meet the information needs of course members was to encourage them to undertake projects on topics of interest on jobs, for instance, or training and educational facilities in their home areas, on leisure opportunities, and on more general issues such as contraception. Some men used the time allotted to these activities to good effect, writing numerous letters, assembling copious quantities of information, and showing the results via lively presentations to their fellow course members. One man completed a study of the mass catering arrangements at Ranby prison and used the resulting report to impress a potential employer, who offered him a job as a chef in his hotel on the strength of it. Other men wrote reports on bar work, market gardening, and ship tank cleaning.

Group discussion

As in assessment, the exchange of information could not be divorced from attitudes and feelings, and most of these 'learning' activities were valuable because they provoked discussion between course members, sometimes animated, sometimes amusing, sometimes antagonistic, but almost always engaging and thought provoking. Because discussion is not a structured exercise with a title and a cook-book prescription for doing it, it tends to disappear from the formal record. But it was the mainspring of the courses at all three sites, the forum where men aired their views and their thoughts and experiences, listened to those of others and engaged in thought and debate about issues of vital concern to them. When the prison courses were working well, discussion would continue in the course room into the meal times, and by all accounts afterwards as well, between course members and the other men in their billets.

There is some evidence that group discussion can enhance conceptual learning, and change attitudes. One small test of the latter possibility was made with three of the Ashwell groups - courses 3,4 and 5 - in relation to attitudes towards the police.

TABLE 5.2   Perceptions of police.   Average scores on 7 point scale

Dimension	Before discussion	After discussion	% change in favour of police
Good-bad	5.1	3.9	17
Like-dislike	5.3	4.3	14
Gentle-brutal	4.9	5.0	-2.5
For-against	4.2	3.8	6
Trust-mistrust	5.8	4.8	15 n = 29

(Scores from 1 to 7 (negative to positive) were assigned to each point on the scales, and summed to produce a total for the whole group.)

These, as might be expected amongst a criminally sophisticated set of prisoners, were none too complimentary. A measure derived from

the Canadian Life Skills Coaching Manual was applied before and
after group discussion of the role of the police. (17) This used a
number of seven-point rating scales on a number of evaluative dimensions; e.g. good-bad, like-dislike. The results for twenty-nine
men are given in Table 5.2.

They show a movement in favour of the police on four of the five
dimensions, the exception being 'gentle-brutal'; not definitive
evidence, but an indication, perhaps of the potential for group discussion in the modification of attitudes.

Social skills training

Social skills training, as described in chapter 2, provided one of
the major sources of methods which were employed in the courses. A
number of exercises were common to almost every course, aimed principally at imparting to group members the essential skills of communicating and interacting with others. They included:
Self-presentation: Individuals were asked to give a talk to the
rest of the group; this was recorded on video and they were then
asked to appraise their own performance as speakers, giving themselves ratings on a pre-arranged set of scales covering clarity,
fluency, and confidence of their presentation.
Simple role play exercises: In other sessions, individuals would
be asked to take parts (usually with brief instructions provided)
in role plays which depicted incidents in which they might be involved.
Street interviews: At the day training centre, where course members were in a position to do so, groups would assemble a list of
questions on some controversial topic which they would then put to
members of the public in the street, recording the resultant interviews on video. This exercise repeatedly proved to be invaluable
as a confidence-booster to the more diffident members of a group,
and provided all of them with an opportunity to express themselves
in a way that they had rarely done before.
Critical incidents analysis: In this exercise, which usually occupied a whole afternoon, course members would divide into smaller
groups, each of which was invited to produce a scripted role play,
recorded on video, of a serious incident which had happened to one
of its members. During playback, the whole group would then discuss and role play alternative ways in which the incident might
have been handled. These critical incidents frequently dealt with
police-offender encounters, and with other potentially violent situations.

Most of the methods listed above are flexible enough to be used
to look at problems of the most varied kind. But in addition,
'survival-skill' sessions were also directed at the 'cognitive'
aspect of solving problems, in other words, at such skills as in-
formation-finding, generating ideas, and making decisions. A few
sessions were customarily devoted to the quite explicit use of
'problem-solving systems', based initially on exercises in the 'Life
Skills Coaching Manual' (18) and in the book by Jackson, (19) but
more recently, in the day training centre at least, borrowing from
the ideas of de Bono. (20)

Simulations

Simulations are basically extended or elaborated role plays in which
incidents are re-created not in isolation, but within a wider and
more realistic context; as in business games and war games, where
information is supplied about extraneous events to which the role
players must respond in as lifelike a manner as possible. The simulations which were used during the project differed a great deal in
their likeness to the situations they represented, and in their
degree of dependence on prepared material, and they tended to be
composite in the sense that they usually combined an 'information-
giving' with a 'skills-training' component. The events most commonly simulated on the Sheffield courses were job search and appearances in court, but a number of ready-made simulations were also
used, including 'Shipwrecked' and 'Red Desert' and 'Radio Covingham', and 'Tenement'. 'Shipwrecked' and 'Red Desert' are part of a
series of nine simulations devised by Ken Jones for the ILEA Media
Resources Centre, (21) and are survival exercises requiring the
pooling of information and joint decision-making. 'TV Covingham'
was an adaptation of another Ken Jones simulation, this time re-
creating the making of a television news broadcast using prepared
items of news and pieces taken from current newspapers, all against
a tight deadline, and also providing experience of working in
groups, making decisions, writing and self-presentation skills.
'Tenement' is produced by Shelter and is concerned with the conditions affecting a group of tenants in a multi-occupied dwelling,
their conflicts with a grasping landlord, and their use of a number
of agencies to help resolve their difficulties. (22) Like many of
the learning materials used on the courses these simulations were
not only instructive but also fun to do. Their capacity to engage
the attention and energies of the course members was illustrated in
the sweat that ran from the face of a prisoner with more than twenty
previous convictions as he produced his TV news bulletin to a successful conclusion within two seconds of his allotted time.
   Besides filming simulated news broadcasts, video was also used in
several other ways during the 'learning' phase of the courses:

      recording of group discussion (notably, by one group for a suc-
      ceeding group's benefit)
      making tapes of outside speakers
      communication exercises, e.g. 'Whispers'
      the playback of role plays and other activity in social skills
      sessions
      self-presentation exercises ('good points' and 'bad points').

At Sheffield video was also used to prepare films about the work
of the centre to show to new recruits and to other interested groups
in the community. And at one time, video tapes were passing between
Ranby and Ashwell in the form of a video correspondence between con-
temporary groups about the problems they were tackling and about the
progress they were making in preparing themselves for release. For
many group members, an initial reluctance to have anything whatever
to do with video became transformed, after one or two exercises involving its use, into an enthusiasm bordering on addiction. Used

properly, video serves not only to enliven the process of learning, but also to broaden its impact, and can considerably enhance the self-image of those who are engaged in its use.

PROGRAMMES

As material related to each problem area was tried and modified on courses it became possible to group together exercises of different kinds in the form of 'programmes' dealing with 'work', 'accommodation', 'alcohol', etc. A typical programme contained assessment methods and learning materials whose scope was limited only by the time available to researchers and officers to collect and prepare them for use with course members.

The work programme

The most important of the programmes developed for use in release courses was the one related to 'work'. Getting a job requires quite a lot of information about oneself and about the job market, a positive motivation towards working at all and towards coping with any difficulties which might arise whilst at work, and not a few skills relevant to finding suitable vacancies and making successful applications for them.

Two examples of items which were used during the assessment stage of the work programme are the Connolly Occupational Interest Questionnaire (23) and the Canadian Life Skills Manual exercise 'Surveying marketable skills'. (24) The Connolly, a widely used instrument for school leavers, tended to be somewhat orientated towards white-collar interests. The results for sixty-seven men at Ranby, fifty-six at Ashwell, and twenty-nine at Sheffield are set out in Table 5.3.

The distribution shows a fair spread of interests amongst the three groups with a heavy concentration in the 'practical' domain; a concern with getting things done on the concrete level, working with machines, centred on activity rather than on ideas or people. But the clear exception to this pattern is the high score on the 'persuasive' dimension at Ashwell, which fits with the otherwise not very justifiable stereotype of open prisons as housing a great many 'con-men'. And although the high Ashwell scores surpass the others by a considerable margin there are still quite a few men at both Ranby and Sheffield who have interests in the area of 'persuasion'. What also surprised a number of the men who completed this test was how high they scored on 'social welfare'. The idea of working in social service jobs was not one that had usually occurred to men whose typical previous experience was that of unskilled labouring, and some of them became interested in the idea of residential work, or voluntary work, or New Careers posts. (25) It is not clear to what extent these 'welfare' scores indicated real interests, or were simply functions of the plight of the prisoner, but they suggest that there may be some scope for extending community work schemes in prison and for expanding the provision of New Careers places in agencies dealing with offenders, and others, and for training men whilst inside for such posts.

TABLE 5.3 Connolly Occupational Interest Questionnaire

Factor		Well below average	Below average	Average	Above average	Well above average
Scientific	Ranby	31.3	19.4	37.3	10.4	1.5
	Ashwell	25.0	32.1	30.4	8.9	3.6
	Sheffield	13.8	24.1	51.7	10.3	-
Social	Ranby	20.9	10.4	41.8	22.4	4.5
Welfare	Ashwell	8.9	14.3	42.9	16.1	17.9
	Sheffield	6.9	10.3	37.9	34.5	10.3
Persuasive	Ranby	20.9	7.5	41.8	13.4	16.4
	Ashwell	3.6	12.5	17.9	21.4	44.6
	Sheffield	3.4	20.7	24.1	34.5	17.2
Literary	Ranby	31.3	46.3	16.4	1.5	4.5
	Ashwell	37.5	32.1	28.6	0	1.8
	Sheffield	37.9	34.5	24.1	-	3.4
Artistic	Ranby	38.8	28.4	28.4	3.0	1.5
	Ashwell	37.5	16.1	39.3	0	7.1
	Sheffield	31.0	27.6	31.0	10.3	-
Clerical	Ranby	20.9	6.0	35.8	22.4	14.9
	Ashwell	5.4	7.1	39.3	28.6	19.6
	Sheffield	3.4	17.2	24.1	44.8	10.3
Practical	Ranby	22.7	3.0	10.6	16.7	47.0
	Ashwell	8.9	5.4	21.4	25.0	39.3
	Sheffield	-	6.9	10.3	34.5	48.2

Ranby (n = 67)   Ashwell (n = 56)   Sheffield (n = 29)
Percentage of groups scoring on each grade. Based on norms for the
general adult population

On the other hand, few men were interested in jobs associated
with science, with the written word, or with the arts or music.
Obviously, the results of the Connolly test must be influenced
to some extent by an individual's occupational history, and since
many of these men, when in employment, work as labourers on construction sites, in engineering works or factories of some kind, it
may be that the test scores are a product of this rather than being
true indications of personal choice, based on a breadth of experience, or an appreciation of possible alternatives. It may be that
for older men, these Connolly scores are more a reflection of experience than a test of aspiration.
'Surveying marketable skills' is an altogether simpler instrument
which has as its aim the analysis of apparently unskilled and uninspiring jobs into component skills. This was usually introduced by
looking at the job of barman; one which many men with varied work
records have held. This can easily be shown to involve a considerable number of skills, abilities and aptitudes, e.g. knowledge of
drinks, handling money, conversational skills, physical strength,

tact, humour, etc. Other jobs which course members had held were
then analysed in the same way on a prepared form which also had
sections on leisure pursuits, knowledge of machines and home-handy-
man skills. A summary section enabled each man to put together a
list of possible assets which he could use to sell himself to an
employer, or to choose a different kind of work which capitalised
on perceived strengths in his employment history. This was followed
by discussion, sometimes prolonged, of various jobs and what the
skills in them really are.

The job experience of a typical release course group was extensive and represented a pool of knowledge and know-how which could
be, and frequently was, tapped by its individual members. The men
on the second Ranby course were a good example.

TABLE 5.4 Jobs held by Ranby Course II members

1	capstan setter, barman, timber tally man
2	computer operator, fork lift truck driver, shop assistant, forestry, bricklayer, labourer, motor bike maintenance
3	seaman, steel erector, pile driver, rigger, lorry driver, army
4	tool maker, electronics, cooking, car driver
5	shop assistant, sewing machine mechanic, storekeeper, manager, moulding, armed forces, cooking, decorating
6	foundry work, steel rolling, seaman, gardening, maintenance
7	fishing/trawling, tyre fitting
8	bricklayer's mate, factory worker, tannery worker, window cleaner
9	decorating, dog breeding, car mechanic, scaffolder, steel erector
10	armed forces, bus conductor, demolition worker, hospital porter, laboratory technician, security officer, fireman
11	absent for this exercise, but described by course officer as having worked for approximately 1½ days since leaving school
12	never worked

By way of contrast to this impressive array of job titles, one
member of an Ashwell course summarised his 'marketable skills' as
'nothinck'.

On the basis of the information generated by these and other assessment exercises, men on courses were then encouraged to set work-
related goals for themselves which they wished to pursue and achieve
both during the remainder of the course and after their release.
One man might decide that he wished to get a specific job in a particular place. Another might want to find out about training opportunities in the catering trade. Another wished to practise and
improve his ability to write letters of application, or make telephone calls to inquire about job vacancies, or present himself more

competently in interviews with employers. Yet others might be
interested in finding ways of coping with problems such as getting
up on time in the mornings or handling the encounter with the fore-
man when they arrive late at work just once too often.

The possibilities are clearly endless, but the curriculum which
can be assembled and presented within a few weeks is not. And com-
promises had to be made constantly between the learning needs of
individuals and those of the groups to which they belonged. In
practice the 'work programme' aimed to cover as many facets of the
subject as possible in a certain amount of detail whilst leaving
open a number of sessions so that men could pursue their own objectives in their own time and at their own pace.

The sessions designed to impart information about jobs usually
included the showing of films. There are a great many commercially
produced 16 mm films on jobs, and the project itself produced some
half-hour videotapes on less skilled occupations, but neither proved
totally satisfactory since for any group of twelve men the particular job portrayed might be of interest to only three or four. Similarly, although videotapes mean that individuals can view them at
their own convenience, it would need an immense library of tapes to
cover the possible interests of even a small percentage of men
leaving prison. At Ashwell, but not at Ranby, permission was given
for groups of course members to go out on visits to factories and
to the Skill Centre at Leicester. Both were enjoyed by the men as
opportunities to put on civilian clothes and to meet people outside
the prison environment; and the Skill Centre visit in particular
was highly informative for those men who appeared to be unaware of
the existence of such places. In the community-based day training
centre, such visits were more common.

Other sessions on the work programme had to do with practising
the skills of finding out about jobs, using exercises based on the
'CODOT' (26) classification and the 'Signposts' (27) series of
cards. These were then put to practical use in project time during
which men were encouraged either on their own or in small groups to
collect information about jobs for their own use or for that of
their colleagues and when appropriate to use the information as the
basis of actual job applications. To the surprise of a number of
the men some of these efforts were rewarded with success, although
not always immediately. The record number of job application
letters written by one man on a release course was over sixty.
Without the framework of the course and the encouragement of officers, and of other members, it is unlikely that many men would have
persevered with such efforts much beyond their first two or three
rejections.

The most appreciated part of the 'work programme' was without
doubt the practising of interview skills. This began with simple
role-played situations involving pairs of group members which were
videotaped and played back individually, or sometimes more public-
ly, for critical examination by the man concerned and by his peers.
After discussion of how men have conducted themselves, further
interviews followed with different interviewers, including course
staff and whenever possible with a visiting personnel officer who
had agreed to simulate a fairly tough interview situation with as
many of the men as he could spare time to see.

Finally the whole of the job search process was simulated in
the classroom situation with men working in small groups, devising
job specifications, formulating advertisements, making applications,
phoning for appointments, being interviewed and succeeding or fail-
ing depending on their performance and the judgments of their fellow
course members acting as a selection panel.

In the whole of these procedures there was nothing which was new
or startling or difficult to administer, but the end result for the
man taking part in them was a structured opportunity for looking at
himself in relation to his future working life using a variety of
methods: pencil and paper, interviews, group discussion, simulation, role play and project work. The products of the exercises
varied from individual to individual: some achieved tangible goals
such as getting an actual job; others felt more confident about
their ability to get jobs after release; others simply aired their
views about the pros and cons of revealing their criminal records
to prospective employers. And at the very least, men learned quite
a lot about how other people tackle their problems in the outside
world.

Interaction programme

The materials assembled under this title were less structured than
those of the work programme; they were more open-ended in order to
allow individuals on courses to specify and deal with some of the
situations involving other people which they personally claimed to
find difficult. They ranged from negotiating an initial social
security payment, to coping with the most complex personal and
legal difficulties surrounding the custody of children and access
to them. Some structured exercises were used at the beginning of
the programme to elicit some preliminary problems for consideration,
including a checklist from the Saskatchewan 'Life Skills Coaching
Manual'. (28) A more specifically social skills-orientated rating
scale developed by Goldstein et al., the 'Skill Survey', also proved
useful. (29) Another measure that was used was the Rotter 'Internal-External' scale which is designed to measure the degree of control which people feel they possess over their own lives. (30)
Rotter's view would be that prisoners, and unemployed people, are
likely to see themselves as somewhat powerless. The scores from
both prisons suggest that this was not in fact the case.

TABLE 5.5 Locus of control (Rotter's I-E scale)

The table shows mean 'E' scores and standard deviations

Ranby (n = 84)	Ashwell (n = 55)
10.57 (5.13)	10.35 (3.64)

The mean 'E' or 'external' scores at both prisons proved to be similar to each other, and to general population norms, but the filling
in of the questionnaire usually stimulated considerable debate about
the extent to which individuals control their own destinies and how

far they are manipulated by forces beyond their comprehension and control. It may not be quite the use of his test envisaged by Rotter, but it illustrates nicely the principle of adapting material to the needs of the courses and their members rather than the other way about.

When course members were invited to define situations they found difficult, they quite often raised the problem of handling what they described as police harassment after release; an unwelcome interest, as they saw it, from the local constabulary in their whereabouts, circumstances and activities. One way of proceeding to look more closely at what went on in such encounters was to use the exercise already referred to, called 'Critical Incidents Analysis'. This involved small groups of course members identifying a particular incident which has been experienced by one of their number, writing a script and producing a brief video portrayal of the scene demonstrating how it had been badly handled. These scenes were then discussed by the whole group who suggested alternative ways of handling the problems, and on occasion role-played alternative ways of behaving. Or the person whose problem was under discussion went away to practise some of the alternatives himself.

One man who used this technique to good effect was Bernard J., a member of an early Ashwell course, who rehearsed a number of ways of controlling his temper when confronted by inquisitive and unpleasant police officers, ably played in these instances by course prison officers. The other course members watched and criticised his performances, and made practical suggestions about how he might emerge from these confrontations in control of himself. It is important to repeat that this was a problem which Bernard himself had raised, and that it was his own resolve to manage such situations differently in the future. These objectives were not forced on him, or even suggested to him, by the course officers; their job consisted of helping him to achieve what he had decided to do for himself.

Throughout programmes like these, whether the problem at stake was an inter-personal one, involving close associates, or a more 'public' one, concerned for example with money or rights, emphasis was consistently placed on the idea of 'problem-solving'. Men were encouraged to look at problems in a simple but systematic way, to collect as much information about them as they could, to think of as many solutions to each as possible, and to select the one they thought would be the most successful. And since this notion was also built into the basic format of every course, it was hoped that there would be an implicit teaching of the same message at the same time.

Because of the frequency with which the topics were raised by course members, separate programmes were subsequently developed on 'police' and 'violence'.

TIMETABLING

The design and specific contents of the prison and day training centre courses have now been described in some detail, starting with specific exercises and proceeding to collections of materials

Timetable for Release Course No.6 Ashwell   Week 1

Week	8.15 a.m.	9.00 a.m.	10.00 a.m.	11.30 1.00 p.m.	2.00 p.m.	3.00 p.m.	4.30 p.m.
Monday	Introduction Self and group Course general history Course details			Course rules Video Files and confidentiality Pay		Form filling programme Questions and discipline	
Tuesday	Introduction to projects	Gym	Problem checklist (assessment)	(Topics) Problem solving Broken Squares Brainstorming '5 W-H' Role play a problem		Use of video Ten best points	
Wednesday	Drink and its problems Assessment form Film Discussion Faces		Break	Lunch	Prepare present and video two minute talk	Break Evaluate and discuss two minute talk Project time	
Thursday	'Whispers'	Gym	Replay and discuss 'Whispers' role play	Rotter Internal-external scale	'Red Desert' simulation – 2 groups and video		
Friday	'Self inventory' Score and discuss		Counselling	Project time	'Crisis Inside' – film and discussion	Week 1 evaluation	

Timetable for Release Course No.6 Ashwell   Week 2

Week	8.15 a.m.	9.00 a.m.	10.00 a.m.	11.30	1.00 p.m.	2.00 p.m.	3.00 p.m.	4.30 p.m.
Monday		Interaction with police Assessment form New material Film			Job getting package	Assessment (marketable skills) Advertising etc.	Project time	
Tuesday	Job getting package (cont)	Gym Role plays Letter writing	Job getting package (cont) Use of phone Interviews		Work role plays	Video and replay		
Wednesday	Information seeking Role plays	Break	'60 Seconds of Hate' film Discuss	Lunch	St John's Ambulance	'Caretaker' role play Video and replay	Break	
Thursday	Project time	Gym	Accommodation Assessment package Tapes to replay			(continued)		
Friday	'Tenement' replay/video simulation				'Somebody Else not Me' film Discussion of film		Week 2 evaluation	

Timetable for Release Course No.6 Ashwell — Week 3

Week	8.15 a.m.	9.00 a.m.	10.00 a.m.	11.30	1.00 p.m.	2.00 p.m.	3.00 p.m.	4.30 p.m.
Monday	'Last Bus' and 'Verdict of the Court' Films		Discuss 'Think-links' films		'TV Covingham' simulation - replay and discuss		Video exercises	
Tuesday	Living alone	Gym	Introduce Man-power Service Commission	Project time	Leicester Skill Centre visit			
Wednesday	De-briefing after visit	Interaction programme	Break	Lunch		Interaction continued	Break	
Thursday	Project time	Gym	'Surgery of Violence' film + discussion		'Eat well and cheaply' Cooking for the single man			
Friday	Tape of street interviews - discuss		'Appeal to the Court' - role play		Community relations 'Shipwreck'	'Shipwreck' simulation	Week 3 evaluation	

Timetable for Release Course No.6 Ashwell   Week 4

Week	8.15 a.m.	9.00 a.m.	10.00 a.m.	11.30	1.00 p.m.	2.00 p.m.	3.00 p.m.	4.30 p.m.
Monday	Do your own thing Video Group work			Social Security	Speaker on Appointments Board			
Tuesday	Project time	Gym	Discussion on drugs. Film 'Gale is Dead'		British Steam Specialists Factory visit			
Wednesday	De-briefing on visit.	6 months objec-tives. 'Snakes & Ladders'	Project time 'Leisure and Pleasure' assessment Discuss Break	Lunch		Mr Carr Sports Council 'Win as much as you can' game	Break	
Thursday	Video tape – Gym Course evaluations				Group projects – presentations			
Friday	6 months predictions		End of whole course evaluations Details of follow-up meeting					

grouped into topic or problem-centred 'programmes'. These materials
were combined and re-combined in a variety of patterns by prison and
probation officers during the project. In the early, and longer,
prison courses, the first few weeks tended to be given over to assessment, and were somewhat overloaded with pencil and paper material. In the later courses, some of which were much shorter, these
exercises were reduced in number and scattered throughout the course
timetable. An example of a course timetable (pp.83-6), that for the
sixth Ashwell course, illustrates the way in which one team of
prison officers put together a programme which they thought would be
relevant to the release problems of their course members, and which
would stimulate and retain their interest and commitment for the
four weeks of the course.

Sheffield day training centre programme

All the day training centre courses followed a broadly similar pre-
arranged pattern and an idea of the way in which they ran can be
gained from this brief outline of a typical DTC course.

Weeks 1-4: Introductory sessions during the first few days of the
course are followed by a period dominated by self-assessment activities and exercises. These use both formal and informal methods, but
rely most importantly on a wide range of semi-structured techniques
designed to stimulate and focus reflection on particular aspects of
a man's life. This culminates during the fourth week in sessions
devoted to objective or target setting for both the remainder of the
DTC course and any suitable period thereafter. These early weeks
are usually planned by DTC staff.
Weeks 5-8: The middle weeks of most courses are concerned with what
may be broadly called learning, in diverse problem areas of interest
to group members, which might include accommodation, money, rights,
alcohol, police, violence, courts, personal relations, social
skills, family problems, sex, leisure, and many more. An assorted
selection of methods is involved, some of which were described
above. These weeks are generally planned jointly by group members
with the help of staff.
Weeks 9-12: The third month normally centred on work. Miscellaneous activities, including job search and interview simulations, work
visits, short-term periods of work inside and outside the centre,
and actually looking for a job, may all be involved. These were
most commonly planned by centre staff but allowed course members
both to look for work and to leave the DTC early should they find
it.

   Three weekly timetables are shown here, taken from courses several months apart. The first is from the   week of a course when
the emphasis was on self-assessment. The second is from the fifth
week of another course, by which time the emphasis had switched to
'learning' in this case with a mixture of both 'life skills' and
'work' sessions. The third illustration, taken from yet another
course, shows the timetable for week 9, concerned mainly with work
but with some 'survival' sessions in addition.

WEEK 1	Session 1	Session 2	Session 3	Session 4
Monday	General discussion session	'Whispers' (Video exercise)	Person perception rating scales (group ratings)	
Tuesday	Accommodation history	Good Points/ Bad Points (Video)	Outside visit: Industrial hamlet	
Wednesday	Social skills: role plays of difficult situations		Game: 'Win as much as you can'	Swimming
Thursday	Adult literacy sessions		Crafts sessions (individual choice)	
Friday	Centre meeting	'Snakes and ladders' exercise	Evaluation and planning	STAFF MEETING

WEEK 5	Session 1	Session 2	Session 3	Session 4
Monday	General discussion session	Work samples: feedback	Why work? Form and discussion	Group game 'Red Desert'
Tuesday	Session on 'Leisure and money'	Critical incidents analysis	Alcohol programme, part 1	
Wednesday	Workshop session	Outside work sessions		Gym
Thursday	Group game continued	Speaker on legal rights; discussion	Crafts sessions (individual choice)	
Friday	Centre meeting	Swimming	Evaluation and planning	STAFF MEETING

WEEK 9	Session 1	Session 2	Session 3	Session 4
Monday	Programme discussion & outline of work plan	Swimming	Connolly Vocational Interests Test and Mechanical Aptitude Test	
Tuesday	Adult literacy session	'Getting a job': introduction to job search	Health education films and talk/discussion with community nurse	
Wednesday	Personal job histories pencil and paper + peer interviews		Gym	Speaker on 'probation'
Thursday	Crafts sessions (individual choice)		Speaker from local Jobcentre; talk and role plays	
Friday	Centre meeting	Group outing		STAFF MEETING

Evaluation

At the beginning of this chapter emphasis was given to the idea that the material collected for use in release courses was to be submitted to the judgments of course members concerning its acceptability and utility. This was accomplished by the systematic use of evaluation procedures.

The evaluation element of the problem-solving process was built into the entire structure of the courses at the prisons and the day training centre. Evaluation became, in fact, an essential part of the courses and completed a cycle of activity which started with assessment and continued through the setting of personal objectives and the learning opportunities which constituted the bulk of the curriculum. Every week, every course member filled in a simple evaluation sheet on which he rated the usefulness of every course activity during the week. He also rated his own level of confidence regarding the finding of work and accommodation, and handling social situations. Individual course activities were evaluated in two ways: first, by rating them for 'usefulness' on a five-point scale, and second, by nominating 'three things you liked this week' and 'three things you disliked'. A number of activities did not appear on more than one or two programmes, or were changed substantially between presentations and cannot properly be treated as the same session for comparative purposes. However, there were a number of sessions which retained a constant format. The mean rankings for these in the prisons are given in Table 5.6.

The feedback obtained from evaluation material was used exten-

TABLE 5.6   Evaluations of course activities

	Ranby n = 54		Ashwell n = 46	
Rank order	Session or activity	Mean rating	Session or activity	Mean rating
1	Use of video	4.37	First aid (St John's Ambulance)	4.60
2	Gym	4.10	Gym	4.22
3	Job interviews	4.07	Use of video	4.11
4	Tests (IQ, personality, etc.)	4.04	Visit to Skillcentre	4.09
5	Discussions	4.03	Self-presentation	3.96
6	Project work	4.00	Interaction programme	3.91
7	Form-filling programme	3.97	Discussions	3.88
8	Films	3.96	Films	3.85
9	Role-playing	3.86	Job interviews	3.84
10	Self-presentation	3.74	Tests (IQ, personality, etc.)	3.82
11	Accommodation programme	3.69	Simulations & games	3.77
12	Money programme	3.61	Role-playing	3.75
13	Interaction programme	3.56	Accommodation programme	3.68
14	Simulations & games	3.46	'Whispers'	3.61
15	Letter writing	3.24	Form-filling programme	3.56
16	Alcohol programme	3.06	Project work	3.56
17			Problem-solving methods	3.52
18			Letter writing	3.51
19			Money programme	3.16
20			Alcohol programme	3.11
21			'Broken Squares'	2.91

Note   Maximum possible mean rating = 5.00
       Minimum possible mean rating = 1.00

sively in the modification and improvement of course content. It
can be seen from the table that the means are all above the halfway point on a five-point scale and that only one point separates
the top item from the sixteenth in the Ranby ratings and the twenty-
first on the Ashwell list. The use of video too should not be
divorced from its context which in most cases is that of recording
role plays, improving interview technique and helping men assess
their self-presentation abilities. And the weekly sessions in the
gym provided an opportunity to let off steam for men unused to
spending such long periods of time in any sort of classroom situation. Likewise the relative unpopularity of the alcohol programme
at both prisons does not necessarily reflect on its quality so much
as on its relevance to more than a minority of any one course group
at any one time.

Another index of the popularity of particular pieces of course
content was provided by the responses of men to the open-ended
questions asking them to name three things they liked and three
things they disliked during the week. These corresponded roughly
with the ratings in the table above, but it is interesting that at
Ashwell, the three worst-rated activities were the police programme, a race relations speaker and an exercise based on Maslow's
hierarchy of human needs. (31) Police and race are both issues
which arouse strong feelings in prisoner groups; and in both instances representatives of the police and of the immigrant population paid visits to the courses during these programmes. It may
also be significant that at Ranby there were no immigrant members
of release courses and at Ashwell only one West Indian and one
Asian member during the two years of the project. It is also interesting that the gym period showed up quite frequently in the 'dislikes' section of the evaluation form. Its high overall rating dis-
guises, in other words, quite different reactions; some individuals
find it the best thing they can think of, others hate it with all
the passion of unathletic schoolboys.

Over the period of the project more than enough material was
developed to fill courses lasting up to eight weeks full-time. By
processes of trial and error items were retained or rejected; those
which remained were held to have passed the double test of feasibility and acceptability.

Chapter 6

The conduct of the courses

The separate elements of the project have now been described: the ideas behind the development of the curriculum, the training of the staff, the course members and their problems, and some of the methods and materials which were assembled to help them cope better with some of them. The aim of this chapter is to look at how these elements were knitted together in the actual conduct of the nineteen separate prison courses that took place during 1976 and 1977, eleven of them at Ranby, and eight at Ashwell; and at the integration of some of the course content into the programme of the day training centre at Sheffield.

RANBY AND ASHWELL

The original target length of the prison courses had been twelve weeks. This was curtailed to eight weeks to fit the quantity of prepared material available at the beginning of 1976. Subsequent courses were systematically shortened so that some impression could be formed of the viability of different lengths of timetable. With hindsight, it would have made more sense to start with the shorter courses and work up to the longer ones to allow for a gradual build-up of materials and staff skills.

The durations and dates of the courses at the two prisons are given in Table 6.1.

During January 1976 the officers at both prisons were engaged in planning their first courses, recruiting course members and locating training and teaching resources both inside and outside the prisons. They were also involved in efforts to create an organisational structure which would enable them to devote their time and attention to the job in hand.

Both courses began on 9 February 1976 and lasted for eight weeks. It soon became clear that there was not enough prepared material for even this length of course and the officers became engaged in a hectic and sometimes desperate struggle to devise new course content as they went along. The second courses, when other pairs of officers took over, also lasted for eight weeks, and were just as strenuous. For, besides attempting to master a complicated set of

TABLE 6.1

Ranby courses			Ashwell courses		
Course no.	Length (weeks)	Dates	Course no.	Length (weeks)	Dates
		1976			1976
1	8	Feb. - March	1	8	Feb. - March
2	8	April - June	2	8	May - July
3	8	June - July			1977
4	6	Sept. - Oct.	3	6	Jan. - Feb.
		1977	4	6	March - April
5	6	Jan. - Feb.	5	6	May - June
6	4	July	6	4	August
7	2	August	7	4	Sept. - Oct.
8	1	September	8	2	November
9	1	September			
10	2	October			
11	4	Nov. - Dec.			

new skills, in addition to devising new materials, the officers also found themselves engaged in a running battle with the administrations of their establishments to get the conditions they thought necessary to do the job properly. The battle was over the allocation of hours to the project and it became an issue which was never to be resolved, and which brought the whole project almost to the point of collapse on a number of occasions.

The combination of all these factors took its toll of both the individual officers, and of the project as a whole. It is difficult, looking back, to see why the enterprise did not founder completely during this period.

One officer took sick leave for most of his first course and played no effective part in the project from then on. Another decided that he did not really like the work and began to look for a different posting in the prison. Two officers were promoted to senior posts, and another asked for a transfer to another establishment. At Ashwell these moves meant that after only two courses it was no longer possible to continue, and the courses ceased until the following year. At Ranby, the third course was struck by further ill health amongst the officers and was not completed properly; nor was it fully documented, due to the resignation of a researcher at the same time. These casualties suggest that the officers had been pitched into their roles with inadequate preparation by the project team and with insufficient institutional support. The fact that any courses were completed at all, and that the results were not disastrous, speaks volumes for the determination of the officers not to be defeated by the challenge they had undertaken.

In the first year of the project therefore, four courses were run at Ranby and two at Ashwell, involving seventy-two men altogether. Detailed results for these and subsequent courses are presented in chapter 7, but leaving on one side for the moment the effects on the officers, the responses of the men who attended the courses varied from the ecstatic to the almost totally disparaging. The most noticeable feature of the first eight-week courses was the variability in mood of the course members. These were immediately obvious to officers and research staff as ups and downs of mood which appeared to have little if any discernible relationship to the course content, or to conflicts within the group between individual members. But when the 'downs' came they disrupted the entire programme and caused despondency amongst the staff.

One officer decided to make a direct challenge to the members of the second Ashwell course about this aspect of their behaviour. 'The day started with an agonised confrontation,' he recorded in the diary he kept. 'I accused the group of malingering and shirking its responsibilities. This shook them rigid, and after making my caustic comments, I left the group to debate its reactions.' Confrontation, in release courses as in other contexts, is a risky business, and the ensuing period was not without anxiety for this officer and his partner. However, 'an hour and a half later I was summoned back and they admitted that a lot of what I said was true.' His challenge paid off in a renewed level of commitment to the objectives of the course, and to active involvement in its activities. One or two incidents of this sort also show up as troughs in the weekly evaluation scales related to 'enjoyment', 'usefulness' and 'confidence'. Our first thought was that these were group phenomena of 'fight or flight', and that the training of the officers had been defective in not preparing them for the possibility that they would occur, and in not providing them with the tools to deal with them when they did arise.

Later release courses were contracted to six weeks and to even shorter lengths. It may be that the officer training was better; it may have been the amount of material available by then; it may have been the greater experience of the officers still in post after a year of working on release courses; but for whatever reason, the mood swings did not recur during the thirteen courses which were completed during the remainder of the project. There were, of course, problems, and there were good days and bad days, but there were no recurrent major crises of the sort which plagued officers in the early days.

In order to illustrate the working of the project in the prisons, the fourth Ranby course will be described in some detail. It has been chosen because it was neither the best nor the worst that took place in the two establishments and because it demonstrates some of the positives and negatives that characterised many other courses.

Ranby course four: September-October 1977

The members of this course were not selected at all. 'Because of
staff sickness,' wrote one of the two course officers, 'we had very
little time for preparation or the selection of inmates;   consequently we started off with twelve inmates to choose from, and two
of those were totally unsuitable. Therefore, we press-ganged two
others whose EDRs [earliest dates of release] suited our purpose.
I am sure you will agree this was a fine start!' They also added
the cleaner from the educational block who expressed an interest in
the course. The group thus assembled comprised a mixed group, not
untypical of other Ranby men, but less committed and amenable than
some groups chosen from larger numbers of applicants.

Alec J.
    Single man aged 22, serving twelve months for arson and burglary.
    First time in prison. 'Works as a fork lift truck driver and can
    go back to his job on release.' 'Leisure time taken up with
    tinkering with cars, motor sport, drinking and dancing.' De-
    scribed by one course officer as 'a quiet lad who is easily led,
    with insufficient strength of character to stand up for his
    rights or himself ... not over-blessed with intelligence.'

Carl W.
    Aged 26, no fixed abode, serving twelve months for theft.
    Third time in prison, also been in Borstal; 'an experienced
    criminal' according to the officer who interviewed him, 'and
    shows no regrets.' Volunteered for the course to get away from
    his civilian work supervisor in the prison.

Bill E.
    Aged 48, a married man serving six years for fraud, the longest
    serving man to take part in any of the courses at either prison,
    who 'produced a tale of successful business ventures, wise in-
    vestments, and the establishment of a secure future. Unfortu-
    nately he seemed remarkably poor in remembering details and his
    sense of time appears distorted - unless he is a well-preserved
    90-year-old!' Bill was an extrovert, and because of the length
    of his sentence, and his gift of the gab, he was listened to by
    the other course members. In the opinion of the officer who
    interviewed him for the course, he applied principally 'for a
    change from prison routine'.

Roger M.
    A 29-year-old ex-Merchant Navy man, separated from his wife, and
    a veteran of 'considerable treatment for alcoholism'. Serving
    twelve months for robbery. 'His spare time for a number of years
    has been taken up with drink, ten-pin bowling and fighting.'
    Officer's summary from his assessment interview: 'I can't make
    up my mind about this one.'

Ken D.
    Aged 23, unmarried but living with common-law wife and three
    children. Serving twelve months for wounding. Described by of-
    ficer as 'presentable youth who has an employment problem'. Also

'generally quiet and well-spoken but ... suffers from an uncontrollable temper.

John K.
Aged 26, married and divorced, three children. Twelve months for burglary. Fragmented work record. Four 'O' levels, talented guitarist, 'his main consideration is money. Attempted suicide, but has got over a lot of his problems.'

Alan T.
Married, two children, aged 27. Doing twelve months for burglary and taking a vehicle. In and out of work. 'Strikes me as a good bet,' wrote the officer on his assessment interview report.

Terry Q.
No fixed abode. Divorced, three children. Aged 31. In and out of prison. Doing nine months for theft and actual bodily harm. 'A man who has joined the course for a genuine reason.'

Bob W.
A single man of 24 whose 'work record is non-existent.' 'He seems to suffer from an inferiority complex partly due to his small stature and partly due to his low education and intelligence levels.' 'He claims has licked the drug habit and screwing but he has no intention of working. I can't believe this.' Serving twelve months for assault and possession of drugs. Thirteen previous convictions.

Kevin P.
Aged 28. Good work record, mostly in painting and decorating. 'Most of his trouble has come from drink brought on by domestic crises.' 'During his current sentence he has lost his father and his wife has left him.' Kevin won one officer's vote as 'most likely to succeed' amongst these course members. Eighteen months for theft, TDA, burglary.

Mick S.
Another man on bad terms with his wife. 'His wife says she doesn't want him back, but as it is his house she can't keep him out.' One child. Aged 26. Various unskilled jobs. Serving eighteen months for a variety of property offences.

Neil M.
Aged 23. Listed his previous jobs as lathe operator, investment counsellor, and labourer. Described by officer as 'typical immature inadequate'. 'His parents have disowned him.' Serving twelve months for burglary.

'Buzz' B.
Buzz was a singular course member. Aged 30. Convicted of burglary. Previous convictions for dishonesty and assault. Claimed to be a Hell's Angel. According to his course officer, 'although he is only semi-literate he is quite intelligent ... his main problem is believing in himself.' Previous work in the building trades.

These men had put down their names for a release course for mixed
and various motives. Some of them were not able to specify release
problems, others wanted help with re-adjusting after a period of
captivity, yet others wanted to do something about preparing to find
work, and one man designated 'himself' as his biggest release problem. Among the reasons they gave for applying for the course were:
'It's better than the kitchen.' 'Learn something.' 'I think I need
this course.' 'A good idea - something different.' 'For help.'
'Was advised to.' 'Sounds interesting.'

When asked what they thought they would get from attending the
sessions, their answers were equally diverse: 'Learn more about
life.' 'To talk to people and have help in re-adjusting.' 'Learn
to cope.' 'No idea.' 'Insight into what's going to happen when I
get out and to prepare myself.' 'Practice for interviewing.'

They were also asked if they wanted to stay out of prison, and
why? 'Doesn't matter' said one man - Alec J. Others were more
positive: 'In a rut and getting older.' 'Happier without.' 'To
look after wife and kids.' 'To look after family.'

The timetable for the first week contained a mixture of activities which introduced most of the methods to be used during the remainder of the course, and started the process of self-assessment,
as well as beginning to look at specific aspects of work and job
search. It was not an easy week. 'We had all the usual problems
of people getting used to each other,' said one of the officers.
'Personality clashes were fairly frequent, but by Friday we were
beginning to look something like a group.' Course members also
referred to these problems in their end-of-week evaluations. One
man disliked 'ignorant people spoiling the course for others,' and
suggested that the officers should 'sort wheat from chaff within
first week ... enabling genuine pupils to get on with it.' Course
members were also not a little critical of the course organisation.
One man, Mick S., complained about 'waiting around' and 'boredom'
between course activities and several men suggested that the officers 'fill spare time with doing more tests or films'.

However, most of the actual course activities were positively
evaluated by the men; nine of them specifically said that they had
liked the use of films; seven specified the role plays, and seven
the group discussions.

There was another undercurrent to the week which was that 'some
of the group voiced suspicions about prison officers in uniforms
running courses like this whilst still performing normal prison
duties.' Despite this, the work of the officers received high
ratings on a six-point scale at the end of the week.

The second week continued the twin themes of social skills and
work-related activity. 'Good group formation' reported one of the
officers, although 'with one exception.' The individual activities
received much more fragmented evaluations from the group members;
the films, this time on drugs and violence, were first favourites
again, followed by 'job applications', and by 'first impressions',
an exercise which looked at how judgments of other people are formed
on first meeting. Letter-writing and form-filling attracted most of
the 'dislikes' of the week, even though seven members rated letter-
writing on the top two points of a six-point scale of usefulness.

It is an example of the splits which often occurred in groups between those with particular needs and those without; one rough measure of group cohesion was the tolerance which the latter extended towards activities of benefit to the former. There still appeared to be some problems with course organisation during week two; one man wanted to 'occupy the spare time more', and Bill E. still thought a 'weeding out' process was needed.

The programme for the third week introduced some material on leisure and drink alongside the work and social skills exercises. The speaker from the Fisherman's Mission split the group again - four men thought he was 'very helpful' and four that he was 'not at all helpful'. Similarly there were two men who complained about the session on drink, presumably because it was not something that caused them personally any difficulty. One officer's view of the third week was that, 'the novelty has just about worn off and boredom is creeping in.' 'Apart from that,' he thought, 'they are still working pretty well.' But there was an additional source of frustration: 'The course administration and preparation is suffering tremendously because of the shortage of time and the management policy of no overtime whatsoever.' One of the consequences of this lack of time was that 'personal interviewing had to go by the board.'

Week four of the fourth Ranby course contained a number of distinctive features; in addition to the continuing emphasis on work and work-related activity, which included 'own projects' - a period during which several men made efforts to find jobs for themselves, there were sessions on self-catering and violence, which in the event lasted for the whole of the Thursday, displacing accommodation search. Films again featured highly in members' ratings of the week's activities. The 'violence' programme, however, polarised opinion in the ratings to an extent unmatched by any other item of content in the entire course; seven men rated it very highly and six thought it was not at all useful. One of the officers thought it one of the 'highlights' of the week together with 'catering' and the use of intelligence and other tests administered by a visiting member of the research team. 'The catering was extremely well received,' he reported and one of the reasons was 'that female participation always makes for a more attentive group, as was borne out by the presence of Mrs X..... in the violence discussion.' (Mrs X..... was a member of the Ranby Board of Visitors.) A final point about the week: 'Video was only used once, this being on Thursday, and perhaps the short break from it re-created interest, for the role-playing was the best yet.'

Weeks five and six concentrated on social skills more than on work, and concluded with an opportunity for course members to formulate goals to be achieved during the first six months of their freedom.

The session on the police went down badly with the group; it was the lowest-rated activity of the whole course. It sometimes seems that prisoners so dislike the forces of law and order that any discussion of them arouses negative feelings in them, although as we saw with the discussions at Ashwell, there may be slight changes of attitude taking place. Some members of the group were interested in the results of the intelligence and personality tests which they re-

ceived during week five;   'Very pleased with results of tests,' said
one man at the end of the week. The objectives the men set for
themselves at the end of the course also varied enormously, e.g.
Alec J.: 'to keep out of prison ... I hope within five years to
become a famous rally driver as I've already done some.'
Carl W.: 'to find a flat first and then to get me a job ... I am
sick of prison.'
Bill E.: 'the second thing I shall do is put my suitcase down ...
start by trying to adjust to my family and friends. I will need to
work hard at my business.'
Roger M.: 'to have operations on both hands ... seven days continuous ten-pin bowling to get back to my previous professional standard.'
Terry Q.: 'I intend to work hard and play hard, i.e. wine, plenty
of women and song.'
Bob W.: 'to find a job ... buy a car, and wear nice clothes and
then some day have a family and a nice wife.'

The most common objectives were to stay out of prison and to get
work of some kind, but one or two were rather more exotic - rally
driving and ten-pin bowling - than was normal for men leaving release courses.

When the two officers who ran the course evaluated the whole
proceedings one of them described it as 'something of a shambles'.
This was partly due to lack of time for preparation, and to the
absence of one of the planned complement of two officers on two days
of each week. The other major problem lay in the unselected compo-
sition of the group which led him to 'speak confidentially to four
of the members who would not enter into any of the group activities.' Things were easier during the second week, but it became
obvious by the third week that at least two of the members were just
there 'for the skive' and another two were 'trying to be disruptive'. His colleague, who had become disenchanted with the release
course project, and had been accepted for a different posting in the
prison, was of the opinion that 'the rubbish on the course tended to
stifle the good intentions of some of the weaker characters and to
modify the course content by non-cooperation.' It is probable that
his disenchantment was not too well concealed from the course members and may have contributed to some of the problems which he and
his colleague faced from a difficult group of men. His last word
on the project was that 'within the prison environment it is virtually impossible to run a course with sufficient freedom of movement
and free from red tape.'

The other officer, in his concluding remarks, noted that there
had been good things on the course as well. He had found it 'a
fairly easy course to run'. 'Another thing that surprised me about
the group was how well they took to the violence programme on which
we spent a whole day.' He too thought that the unselected nature
of the group had caused difficulties but finished by saying, 'let
us remember that these are the types of people for which a course
of this sort was designed and if we only pick the best, then of
course it would be easy to run the courses, but how are we going
to prove that they will help the recidivist to stay out of prison?'

The final evaluations of the members were, as might be expected,
of mixed quality. Eleven of them said that, if they could choose

again, they would still opt to attend a release course. One man,
Carl W., said he would not: 'The course has learned me nothing
personally; I think it's a waste of money.' He also rated his enjoyment of the course at the extreme negative end of the scale and
criticised one of the two course officers who, he said, 'if nothing
went his way ... he went back to being an officer and showing
authority when we were told that on the course he would not act as
an officer ...'

Despite all the tensions there had been, both between some of the
members of the course, and between some of them and one of the officers, the overall enjoyment ratings from the group were positive:

Have you enjoyed the course?

A lot   2   6   1   1   1   A little

As were many of their open-ended responses:
'Pleased at results of personality and IQ tests.'
'Have learned a great deal about myself and other people.'
'I now think before I do or say anything.'
'Have learned to stop and think before acting unrationally.'
There were mixed comments about the ability of uniformed officers
to run release courses: 'Would be more beneficial without uniformed
officers as there is a barrier.' 'Useless for officers to be on
course.' 'Under circumstances I feel they cope quite well.' 'The
officers have been very good.' All the course members also recorded
their views of the course on videotape. Buzz B., whose written
evaluation was not all that negative, took this opportunity to
record his view that 'It was shit.'

Problems in running courses

This account of the fourth Ranby course raises some of the difficulties faced by the officers in their attempts to run successful
release courses. These were of two main sorts; firstly those internal to the courses themselves - problems of recruitment and
selection, sustaining the motivation of some quite difficult men,
balancing the needs of individuals against those of the group,
coping with disruptive members, and getting the pace of the activity
right; and secondly problems to do with the administration and management of the prisons in which the project was located.

Officers felt happier when there were sufficient applicants to
allow a personal choice on their part of those they wished to include in a course group. They did this on the basis of a single
interview in which they looked at occupational history, family circumstances, perception of release problems, and made some estimate
of the individuals' level of motivation to undertake and profit from
the course. Officers were also influenced by their previous knowledge of prisoners gained during their disciplinary duties prior to
the project, and during the periods between courses; and by the
recommendations and suggestions of fellow officers, particularly

those associated with the work parties from which the applicants
came. There were no objective criteria laid down to guide the officers in this task, and the selection process was necessarily a
hit-and-miss affair. Some men who were positively chosen by officers from a pool of applicants turned out to be poor choices, lacking in motivation and antagonistic to other course members. No
doubt much better candidates were turned down. On one occasion, an
officer refused point blank to entertain an application from one
prisoner, widely known in the establishment as a 'spoiler' and a
trouble-maker and with whom he had had previous difficulties. He
was prevailed upon to see how the man behaved as a course member,
agreed, and was surprised, and delighted, to find him a co-operative
and enthusiastic member of a good group.

Another factor which affected recruitment was the length of the
courses. These were progressively shortened to test the effectiveness of the materials over different periods of time. But the
shorter the courses, the fewer were the men who applied for them.
Barely enough men applied for the two one-week courses held at Ranby
in September 1977, and a planned one-week course at Ashwell was
abandoned altogether for lack of potential members. It seems likely
that men are prepared to sacrifice good prison jobs for a substantial course from which they expect tangible benefits, but not for a
more transitory experience.

Once having secured a viable group, the next problem faced by the
officers was that of sustaining their interest and motivation for
the duration of the course. This was not always easy. 'Two men
elected to leave on the first day,' according to one course officer,
'when we had to tell them that the pay on the course was dropped by
the Home Office to only 88p per week.' Another man 'for reasons of
his own, was adamant that he could not continue with the course' at
Ashwell. 'A great deal of time was spent,' reports the officer, 'in
trying to get him to change his mind, without success.' And another
man absconded from the prison at the beginning of his course 'due to
wife having a baby and not hearing from her.' The officers at Ranby
persuaded another would-be resigner from a course who felt that he
would be 'a disruptive influence' because of his self-confessed
'radical anarchist' views, to stay on.

In other cases, it was not the men who resigned, but the officers
who removed them. For one officer, 'The week was marred by the fact
that I had to remove one member of the course due to his truculent,
oppressive behaviour.' Difficult members were more often persevered
with, sometimes to the detriment of fellow students. Dominant or
aggressive men were, on occasions, banished from the room for a
session or an afternoon to allow things to calm down. One group
itself confronted an un-cooperative colleague with his behaviour and
came to an agreement with him that he should leave, but things were
not always resolved so amicably. A disruptive member on a Ranby
course was moved by the officer from his chair next to a friend,
whereupon 'he became abusive, demanded his seat back, threatened to
resign, and when he couldn't get his own way he adopted the classic
pose of most inmates who are playing "I'm not here, and I'm not
paying attention" - hands in pockets, legs straight but crossed,
head resting on back of chair, eyes closed.'

These were of course extreme cases, but there were some groups that never 'gelled' and were extremely difficult to interest and work with constructively. Pacing the materials and mixing the activities into a convincing pattern was also something that the officers learned to do by experience, and which proved to be easier in the mid-length courses, than either the longer eight-week or the shorter two- and one-week ones. 'The two-week course feels to be over before it begins,' complained one of the most experienced of the officers. 'I wish we had another week,' said another, 'barriers down, but too late.' And another thought, 'My own feeling is that the course is unfinished, and the fact that we are still involved daily with members coming to the office with queries, would suggest that they feel the same way.'

The final consensus was that courses somewhere between four and six weeks were the best ones to run; short enough to pack with material, but not so long that members started to become bored with it and with each other, and long enough for the officers to retain one of the casualties of the shorter courses - personal work with each member on his release problems.

The final set of problems which beset the project in the prisons stemmed from the relationship of the courses to the institutions in which they were based, and in particular to the lower and middle reaches of their management structures. In order to grasp better what these were and how they were experienced by the course officers it is necessary to return to the origins of the whole project.

The research proposal arose, not within the prison department itself, but in discussion between researchers and the Home Office Research Unit, as it then was. The prison department was represented in these negotiations by its 'P2' Division, the division with responsibility for 'treatment and training' throughout the prison system; for the implementation of Prison Rule Number One in other words.

The search for establishments in which the research could be carried out was conducted between researchers and governors, and senior uniformed staffs of individual prisons in the western region; the south-eastern region; and the Midlands region. Fortuitously, both Ranby and Ashwell turned out to be in the same region, but no contact was ever established formally with Midlands regional staff responsible for the prisons.

The inducement for the prisons to take part in the project was that their officer establishments would be increased by the equivalent of two full-time officers so that, apart from physical accommodation, no direct costs for the project would fall on the prisons giving house-room to release courses. The intention was to train four basic grade officers from each prison, and for them to work in teams of two, running alternate courses; the 'instructors' from one team returning to discipline duties whilst their colleagues ran their course. The resulting work pattern was not ideal from an officer's point of view since it divided his time between quite different functions, and although it was thought impracticable for an officer to continue running courses without a break, it would have been better if he could have spent the time between them preparing for the next course, writing new materials, recruiting new members and helping his recent graduates to complete the work they may have started on job applications and other specific plans for their release.

One of the problems with all these initial arrangements was that they were made in principle but never committed to writing; or if they were, they were not communicated in that form to either of the two prisons taking part in the experiment.

There were two consequences of this omission: one merely curious, the other potentially fatal to the future survival of the project as a working entity. The curiosity is that four full-time prison posts were, in effect, allocated to the project for two and a half years, without any written authorisation whatsoever; an expenditure in excess of £50,000 on the strength of unrecorded telephone calls. From an administrator's point of view, such an arrangement has obvious advantages; no one can be called to task or held to commitments when none of them have been written down.

A more serious consequence of the absence of written terms of reference was that it left the release course officers at the mercy of the Chief Officer and the Detail Principal Officer (Detail PO) at each prison; all of them busy men with other priorities to attend to, and not necessarily sympathetic to the aims of Release Units. It is not clear whether any or all of the men who filled these posts during the currency of the project were for or against the project, but the evidence is that they treated it primarily as an administrative chore rather than with any deep sympathy for what was being attempted. Nor could they be at all identified with the content of the courses since it resembled nothing in the repertoire of discipline duties with which they were familiar. It is this remoteness from other discipline tasks which offered to release courses both the freedom they needed to develop and grow without hindrance, and also the threat of uncomprehending attacks on the conditions required to carry out an arduous programme of educational and training activities.

Since the primary business of the prison is that of keeping men in secure conditions and policing the internal activity of the place, the overriding preoccupation of the chief officer and of the Detail PO is with 'manning', the allocation of officers in sufficient numbers to control and supervise 'parties' of men at work, at meals, whilst asleep, and at play. Although neither Ranby nor Ashwell is a high security establishment, there are, in common with other prisons, minimum staffing requirements which have conventionally been met by the working of overtime, sometimes in large quantities. Apart from a few 'fixed' posts such as censor officer or gate officer, most of these discipline duties are seen as interchangeable; supervising the bathing party is not very different from supervising the meal queue or the cleaning party. In theory any officer can do any or all of them with equal ease. They require no preparation, no special skill and can be competently executed by anyone wearing the prison officer's uniform. It is not surprising, therefore, that release course work should tend to be classed in the same way: something to be done interchangeably by whichever of the trained officers was available on the day in question, and independently of the need for continuity and preparation.

Chiefs and Detail POs accordingly removed release course officers at short notice to cover discipline duties where they judged the need to be greater; on one occasion a course officer was taken from the classroom in order to drive the prison bus. They also restrict-

ed the amount of time available for preparation both between and
during actual courses. This was already the case before the introduction of budgetary controls in the prison service in April 1976.
As part of the restrictions on public spending the prison department
allocated a fixed budget of staff hours to each prison, which acted
as a ceiling for expenditure within the financial year. This was
based on average past figures, but it restricted severely the amount
of overtime which could be worked. Its effects on the prison
service at large were profound; for release units it almost spelled
a sentence of death.

Before undertaking training for release course work, all the officers had been assured, at both local and national levels, that:
(a) their careers in the service would not be jeopardised by taking
    part in the project; and
(b) that they would not suffer financially by undertaking the work.
These assurances were, of course, verbal ones; but they were so
firmly impressed on the officers that, when they were repudiated in
practice, their response was one of disbelief, dismay and anger.
One officer estimated that his wages were more than £20 a week lower
when working on the release courses than when on discipline duties
because the administration interpreted the allocation of two full-
time staff to the institution in the most literal sense possible:
that of two staff on flat hours, with no overtime allowed. This
immediately placed the course officers at a disadvantage in relation
to their colleagues in the rest of the prison, and meant that, if
they were to maintain their wages at previous levels they must
undertake discipline duties either before or after strenuous work
with a group of men in an educational situation. This might involve an officer coming in with the early shift and patrolling the
boundaries from 6.30 a.m., running a release course from 8.00 a.m.
until 5.00 p.m., and resuming boundary duties until 9.00 p.m. It
could be argued that other prison officers work similarly long hours
in order to earn their wages. The point about release course officers was that their work was emotionally and intellectually demanding in a way not true of other duties, and to be done properly it
required considerable preparation of course material. Sufficient
time for this was never provided, and the result was that officers,
particularly during the early stages of the project, took work home
to do in their own time.

Budgetary control exacerbated the restrictions on time for release course work, and during the life of the project virtually all
the officers involved were driven, at one time or another, to the
point of resignation by what they considered to be unfair treatment.
Despite appeals to regional and head office, the unwritten ambigui-
ties about this position were never resolved. Then early in 1976 a
body called the Manpower Review Team visited Ranby prison and decided, without consulting either the release course officers or the
research staff or the 'P2' Division of the Prison Department, that
release units could be run with a 20 per cent saving of staff time.
Officers were not henceforth to be replaced on days off, leaving
the courses staffed by only one officer on two days each week.
Again, repeated protests to region and headquarters failed to have
any effect on this decision.

The best way to convey the reaction of the officers to these events and constraints is to use the word 'betrayal'. Practical effectiveness suffered and so did morale, and the turnover of officers was such that the average life expectancy of a release unit officer was less than twelve months, which, following initial training costing more than £2,000 per officer, did not constitute particularly good value for money. Some of the casualties amongst the officers were due to the demands of the work itself, but in other instances good officers moved to other duties earlier than they might have done, out of frustration and disillusionment.

The strain of running an innovative course as well as battling against the system is graphically captured in this extract from an officer's diary, kept during his first experience of running a course:

> This group is not gelling. Today I had a feeling of hopelessness and came home feeling very depressed. I have tried to look objectively at what is going on. Two things come to mind:
> (a) We have about four members of the group who seem to be along for the ride. They appear to have little interest in anything we do and contribute very little to the course. This could indicate our lack of expertise when selecting course members. Sometimes I feel like belting them in the ear.
> (b) We have been messed about by the management; they refuse to put a relief into the unit when either one or the other of us is absent. They have gone back on everything they have promised us and consequently we have little or no time to prepare a curriculum as the course develops. I have stopped taking work home because I am getting no respite from the gruelling pressure of this course.
> The plans we had for the course from day one have not been allowed to materialise as fully as we had hoped, and the course is suffering. I know this must sound paranoid, but I don't think I am trying to excuse my own shortcomings. If we could have had our head with this course I know we would have been far in advance of where we are today. We will have failed these twelve men by the end of the course because I know I personally could have operated at a higher level of efficiency if the stumbling blocks set by management had been non-existent. Perhaps I am too easily depressed at having to overcome adversity. If we had the time we could overcome; but we don't and we can't.

Opposition to the work of the release unit also came from departments of the prison not in the direct chain of command over the officers. The most frequent conflicts early on were with the works departments and industrial managers who resented losing their key workers to what they saw as an irrelevant activity. Skilled tradesmen, for instance, employed on the work party from Ashwell which had been building the Borstal complex at Glen Parva near Leicester, were all but excluded from applying for release courses. And the same was true, although to a lesser extent, of men holding positions of responsibility in the industrial workshops at Ranby. Even arranging to interview some men before selection for courses sometimes proved to be fraught with difficulty: 'Went to town on interviews. Felt drained; needing to fight people just to interview men. Wonder how hard we have to fight once they have been chosen, i.e. works, gardens, etc. Depressive day.'

From their peers in the ranks of the uniformed grades, the officers also faced reactions which varied from indifference to outright hostility. 'We've had no co-operation as such,' said another officer. 'When we came back (from training) no one wanted to know, no one came to see us, no one offered us advice. As regards staff, we published frequent invitations but very few came near.' He thought that other staff adopted this attitude because, 'A lot of people don't want to know; don't want to get mixed up with other people's lives at all. They're quite content just to turn the key.'

The most commonly encountered criticisms of course officers were from uniformed colleagues that they were on a 'skive', or that they were 'soft' on prisoners. 'Generally speaking the majority of the staff regard it with caution and 25 per cent are openly hostile. They say "When we look after victims then we might do something for this lot."'

The final entry in one officer's course diary can serve as an epitaph to this discussion of the difficulties which beset all of them. 'Christ knows what is going to happen to this bleeding project.'

PROBLEMS OF TRANSITION IN THE DAY TRAINING CENTRE

Sheffield day training centre is an organisation of a wholly different scale and character to the Prison Department, but there were difficulties to be overcome in importing and implementing novel methods and materials within an existing framework. The agreement by which Sheffield and the release course project decided to work together had suited the purposes of both parties. For the research project, it afforded the opportunity to test the materials it was developing in a setting outside prison, and added an extra dimension to the work that was to be done. For the day training centre it promised new methods and resources that could bolster the centre's programme, and, potentially, a way of re-organising that programme in its entirety if this seemed desirable. The research was to develop a package in work, survival, and social skills; and this was exactly what the centre was looking for. Inevitably, however, there were problems involved in putting all this into effect. One group of these came from the nature of the release course project itself. The bulk of the methods and materials were still not in a form in which they could be easily assimilated elsewhere and nor, at that time, was there any straightforward way of describing what some of these methods and materials were. The only source approximating.a form in which it could be used by the centre was the Saskatchewan Newstart 'Life Skills Coaching Manual'; although there was a great quantity of material available, it needed a lot of work to be cast into a useful form. In addition, however, there was enough of the new material in existence to indicate that it was in some respects a substantial departure from the day training centre's earlier manner of working; and this raised other questions for the centre itself.

A second set of problems were those which accompany any change

engendered in an institutional setting, and which occur on several
levels. First, even the most willing partners to change retain some
residual attachment to established patterns of working - to the
orthodoxy of the workplace as they have experienced it. Second, any
agency working with people acquires a certain 'image' in their eyes,
and in those of other workers; standard opinions and expectations
crystallise out; change is impossible without some adjustments and
misunderstandings. Third, members of staff are unlikely to have
uniform perceptions of the direction and value of change, and internal stresses and strains are unavoidable. Fourth, and with particular reference to the Sheffield centre, the amount and distribution of resources has to be re-assessed, and a large number of
decisions made on the practical level. All of these problems and
more were to occupy staff at the centre for many months.

A third knot of problems derived from the partial nature of the
centre's involvement in the research project. Unlike the prison
courses, for which the officers were trained in a group and began
work together from scratch (which of course has its own difficulties), only one staff member was trained initially to import the
'new' methods into the day training centre, and had to work in relative isolation. This, coupled with the arrival of new members of
staff unfamiliar with either method of working, added to a prevailing confusion over the centre's purpose, the whole being transmitted
in anxiety to the group members in the centre, conspired to make
this a very uncomfortable time for all concerned.

The combination of these factors meant that the adoption of
methods from outside was a lengthy process. In what follows a crude
distinction is made between three phases of involvement of the
centre in the use of newer methods of working. It should be added
that these represent a particular view of the course of events and
that others might perceive them differently, and arrive at other
judgments. The aim is simply to characterise the working of the
day training centre at various stages during the period of the research project.

Three phases of involvement

The identification of three phases in the centre's history between
January 1976 and early 1978 should not be taken as implying that
these were somehow unrelated epochs, sharply differentiated from
each other, and separated by periods of discussion, advance planning, or other distinctive markers. They were merely phases in an
overall uniform trend, which merged easily into each other, and all
discussion and decision-making vis-à-vis the centre's programme took
place alongside its day-to-day working. The main points of difference are simply, first, the amounts of time in an average week which
were spent using the 'new' material, and second, the numbers of
staff involved in - and feeling committed to - the adoption of imported methods.

Using this framework, the earliest phase which can be identified
was the first five months of 1976. The first two groups of probationers to proceed under the 'block intake' system - the requirement
that all men sentenced to day training within a given period should

start on the same day and remain together for twelve weeks - arrived within one week of each other towards the beginning of the year. (This was on Monday 26 January and Monday 2 February. The interval between intake of new groups is of course usually longer than this, but has been adjusted a number of times for various reasons, between four, five and six weeks.) This period could be described as an exploratory one - a number of new exercises were sampled, and imported on a purely sessional basis into the programme. In many respects, the overall structure of the preceding years was retained - daily centre meetings, staff review session, and a wide range of the earlier activities timetabled much as before. Assessment and selection of those referred to the centre were also conducted as outlined previously.

During this period, only one staff member, who had attended the first of the staff training courses, was familiar with methods and materials from the release course project, and was inevitably somewhat isolated and under certain pressures as a result. There were additional internal problems arising from uneven levels of understanding and support given to the slow influx of new material; and the staff group as a whole wrestled with fundamental issues in the role of the centre, e.g. the relative importance to be given to its retributive or helping functions, the problems of motivation, and the dubious meaning of 'voluntarism' in the context of a probation order with a requirement of attendance. Such problems could only be exacerbated by the willingness of groups of men to pounce on any evidence of uncertainty in the centre's purpose, and take a ride on the anxieties of the staff.

Nevertheless, the first group produced some remarkable successes, and a lot was learned from this early period about what would be acceptable to men in the centre. A two-day seminar with centre staff and three members of the prison project team helped to iron out some of the difficulties, though leaving others untouched. Notably, various modes of staff organisation were explored, including the allocation of different sections of the programme to different members of staff, and the division of staff into pairs which would each be responsible for one group in everything it experienced in the centre. In the end, however, the model chosen was as follows: each group would have a leader (a staff probation officer), who would stay with a group for the whole of its time in the centre, and organise its activity overall. Groups would arrive every six weeks, thus leaving one officer (from the three available) 'floating' and at different stages of the sixty-day programme, ancillary staff with various specialisations would join the group leader in running the course. The 'floating' staff officer would carry out assessments of those referred, evaluate his last course, plan his next, and generally be on hand as a back-up in the event of illness or other unforeseen event. With minor alterations, this general pattern still prevails within the DTC until the end of the project.

The hybrid nature of the timetable at that time undoubtedly kept tension at an unsatisfactory level within the centre, and this was to persist for several months as the amount of new material included in the programme steadily grew.

A second phase that can be identified in the gradual re-structuring of the centre's activity would be, broadly speaking, the second

half of 1976. This period was characterised by more extensive borrowing and testing of materials from the prison project and elsewhere, by greater staff interest and involvement in the development
of a centre 'curriculum', by more frequent attempts to plan whole
courses, and timetable whole weeks in advance. This phase too was
not unaccompanied by problems of its own.

Chief amongst these was a decline in the numbers of men referred
to the centre, particularly in the summer months. One reason given
for this was a reluctance of field probation officers to refer men
whom they thought might be turned down by the centre - a consequence
of its past policy of rigorous selection, which may itself have been
a consequence of the tendency of some field officers to use the
centre as a 'dumping ground' for their most intractable cases.
Equally plausible as an explanation was the tendency, remarked upon
by staff in all day training centres, for numbers of referrals to
exhibit marked seasonal fluctuations, with a trough in the summer
holiday period. Whatever the case, morale in the centre was certainly affected, and the viability of the 'newer' approach with
small groups was called into question.

A key decision to emerge from this period, partly as a consequence of the above problem, was a major shift in the centre's
referral and selection policies. The age limit for those eligible
was lowered to 17 years, and the selection procedure for those over
21 was abolished: henceforth the centre would accept any adult offender channelled in its direction by a field probation officer.
This decision was taken for a number of reasons. First, it would
help boost the numbers of men on their way, and show increased
willingness - in the eyes of outside probation officers - to take
the widest possible range of clients. Second, it recognised that
the only real way the centre could identify suitable target groups
would be to work with a variety of offender types. And third, it
helped to open up the centre as a probation facility in a broader
sense - to take for example those on probation who were judged to
be 'at risk' - and so explore potential future avenues for working.

Throughout this period as a whole, a series of decisions were
taken which helped make the day training centre more capable of sustaining a sixty-day programme with larger, more mixed groups of
probationers. The stresses and strains of the borrowing process,
of introducing new methods of working into the timetable in bits and
pieces, were finally resolved by the decision to train another staff
member on the second training course in November-December 1976, and
from the beginning of the new year to operate as fully as possible
along 'release course' lines, tailored to fit the needs of the
centre.

It is this period of fuller adoption and development of such
methods that constitutes 'phase three' as it is conceptualised here,
a period lasting from the start of 1977 into 1978. Needless to say
many problems had still to be solved, there were further staff
changes to come, including the advent of New Careerists in the
centre; there were numerous areas of programme requiring attention,
and a growing background anxiety over the future of day training
centres as a whole. But in the organisation of its programme
throughout, and in the content of individual weeks and sessions, the
centre had departed considerably from its modus operandi prior to

1976.   Methods of assessment and problem-solving, course content, usage of resource, organisation of staff, all were developed - and continue to be developed - by the day training centre in a framework of its own devising, which would be almost unrecognisable to a returning visitor who had last seen the centre in 1975 or before.

Chapter 7

The results of the courses

ASSESSING THE RESULTS OF THE COURSES

The principal aim of the research reported in this book was to develop and test some methods and materials for equipping offenders
with skills relevant to keeping them out of trouble. It was also
concerned with assessing the capacity of serving, basic grade prison
officers to use the materials effectively with serving prisoners.
These are large undertakings, and they lack, by their very nature,
the kind of hard-edged definition which lends itself to proofs of a
straightforward statistical kind. Evidence was therefore collected
in a number of ways. These included the collation of 'hard' data,
but greater weight was given than is usual in evaluative research
to the so-called 'subjective' views of the people most directly affected by the work of the project: the prisoners and probationers
who took part in the courses, and the prison and probation officers
who acted as their tutors.

Their views were gathered in a variety of ways: in answers to
rating scales and other 'closed' evaluation questions, in interviews, in videotape recordings of self-presented views and peer
interviews on reactions to courses, in follow-up forms, interviews
and meetings, in group discussions, from letters and telephone
calls, from observation, and from the comments of third parties such
as relatives and field probation officers. Much of this material is
of the type sometimes dismissively referred to as 'anecdotal'. But
any method for describing human responses, no matter how 'scientific' its pretensions, depends in the end on the report of the subject, or that of the observer. Both of them are fallible witnesses
at the best of times, and at their worst, positively misleading.
This research made no breakthrough in the search for a solution to
this methodological conundrum, but a multiplicity of methods for
collecting data did permit some comparison to be made between sets
of results obtained in different ways. If they turned out to be
contradictory or in conflict, then it would have been difficult to
say anything with any certainty about the subject being studied.
But if they pointed broadly in the same direction, then statements
could be made which are perhaps slightly more valid than those derived from the application of only one kind of measurement.

So far as the prison course members were concerned, we were
interested firstly in their responses to courses whilst they were
still on them, and when they ended, in any gains they might claim
to have made, and in any criticisms they might have; and following
release, whether they still saw the experience as relevant and
useful. Finally, but not most importantly, we proposed to look at
whether membership of courses had any perceptible effects on subsequent re-conviction rates.

RANBY AND ASHWELL

At the beginning of the research it was far from clear that ordinary
prison officers would be able to acquire the knowledge and master
the skills demanded by the course design which was to be tested.
And even if they were to prove capable of doing those things, there
was still no guarantee that they would be able to break through the
barriers of mistrust and hostility which have historically marked
the relationship between prison officers and serving prisoners.

Our initial insistence on the voluntary nature of release course
membership promised to provide an instant and rather brutal form of
evaluation in this respect. If men failed to apply at all for
places on courses, or if, having applied they were to quit them
in substantial numbers, they would presumably be voting with their
feet either against the whole concept of officer involvement in pre-
release training, or against particular officers' execution of it.
In the event, 132 men at Ranby, and 92 at Ashwell enrolled on
courses between January 1976 and December 1977, a total of 224. At
Ranby, two men were asked by officers to leave courses because of
their disruptive behaviour and two others left when they were told
that their prison pay was to be reduced for the duration of the
course to the average for the prison. One man at Ashwell was also
asked to leave, and two left of their own accord following the development of personal antagonisms within the course group. There
was also a man at Ashwell who absconded during a course, one man at
Ranby who was transferred to another prison, and one who left a
course early because his fine had been paid. So from nineteen
courses, run by a dozen or so different combinations of officers,
the total losses of members were small.

At the ends of courses, their members were asked, 'If you could
choose again, would you apply to come on the release course again?'
Their replies were emphatic, as Table 7.1 illustrates:

TABLE 7.1

	Ranby (n = 109)	Ashwell (n = 62)
Yes	91 (83.5%)	58 (93.5%)
No	8 (7.3%)	1 (1.6%)
Uncertain	10 (9.2%)	3 (4.8%)

It could be argued of course that these figures reveal little that is significant, since any diversion from the dull daily routine is likely to be welcome to prisoners, even one that involves quite close contact with prison officers. And given the nature of much of the work that men have to do in prison, it is not too difficult to devise activities which appear attractive by comparison.

Reasons for volunteering

Many of the men admitted later that their motives for applying in the first place had been less than pure: 'To be honest,' said one man, 'I came on it for a doss.' Or, 'I came on it through boredom.' It is not easy to estimate with any great accuracy what proportion of each course was recruited on the strength of these or similar motives, but an informed guess would be that the average was around a third, and on some courses the figure may have been as high as a half; hardly a promising start for a venture which was to rely heavily on self-motivation for success.

But other men applied because they thought the course could indeed help them: 'I came on the course to sort myself out.' 'I'd made a real mess of my life.' 'I lost all my confidence in making my own decisions.' 'I'd lost the ability to cope.' 'What it boils down to is I'd forgotten about the world outside and any difficulties I did have.' 'I've been in prison a couple of years and I've gone out and just bamboozled into things and ended up in prison, so I came on this course to get the information where I've gone wrong.'

Many of these men gave only general reasons for volunteering for a course, but some were more specific: 'I had a bit of trouble communicating with people; getting on with people.' 'I wanted to gain more confidence in myself and go home and not be afraid of pointing fingers.' 'I thought you could help me with marriage, housing and jobs.' And some expressed an interest because the idea of the courses seemed to be in such contrast to their previous experience of imprisonment: 'I've been in prison several times and during those imprisonments no attempt has ever been made of trying to sort out what makes me as an individual tick.'

A recurring theme in these replies is the loss of confidence which accompanies imprisonment of even modest duration, and the feeling of being out of practice at everyday activities.

Expectation of courses

It is of a piece with their mixed motives that many of the men had quite unclear expectations of what it was they were letting themselves in for when they applied for places on release courses. Some had no idea at all what to expect; others had derogatory views: 'I expected a typical type of release course, telling us how we are and why we'll be back.' 'I thought it was going to be a right load of rubbish; I was very pessimistic.'

But whatever they thought at the beginning, many members reported that they thought differently by the end of courses: 'After the

first week,' said one man, 'I realised that I'd become very interested and that I could learn something from it.' 'I came in cyni-
cal,' was the comment of another, 'but over the six weeks I've
changed my view completely.'

The atmosphere

One of the first things to strike course members, especially on
courses which were going well, was the nature of the prevailing
atmosphere, e.g.: 'On the course it's been a right friendly atmosphere, far more friendly than in the prison itself. When I came
into the course I felt I could talk freely to any of the lads and
bring any problems out without anybody laughing or making jokes and
that; and being sympathetic towards everybody else, you know, which
I find is a very good thing.' 'A very relaxed atmosphere.'
  On some courses this atmosphere took a little time to develop but
when it did, the results could be unexpected; to the man, for instance, who said that what he had liked about his course was 'seeing
a group of people form a degree of trust - a thing that I didn't
think happens in prison.'
  There were of course individuals who never overcame their innate
suspicions of what was going on despite all the explanations and assurances which became a standard feature of course introductions.
In the middle of one course an officer reported: 'Noticeable change
in Martin J.: beginning to accept other people's views, *but still
thinks the room is bugged.*'

Enjoyment

Having got over their initial reservations and grown more relaxed in
the company of their peers, the most common reaction of course members was one of enjoyment: 'It's been ever so good.' 'I've enjoyed
every minute.' 'The release course - fantastic.' 'It was absolute-
ly better than I expected.'
  Several course graduates remarked how quickly the time had gone
whilst they were on the course: 'Time has passed quickly - too
quickly in fact.' 'It's been a good four weeks, and a quick four
weeks. About the quickest since I've been here.'
  Two men identified possible reasons for their interest and enjoyment and for the swift passage of time during the course: 'It gave
me great enjoyment to be a human being again.' 'It was just like
being outside again, being in here.'
  The net effects of being treated in this way were usually positive: 'I can honestly say that I never thought I would find anything in a prison that would hold my attention as much as this
course has done this week.'
  It may be thought that these statements have been specially
selected so as to create an impression of enjoyment which cannot be
substantiated in other ways, but in the final written evaluations
all the men were asked to rate, on a five-point scale, their enjoyment of the courses they had just completed. 92 per cent of the
Ashwell men and 88.9 per cent of the Ranby ones rated their enjoyment of the courses on the top two points of the scale.

There were, of course, dissenting voices to be heard amongst this chorus of delight: 'I was bored,' said one man. And several more agreed with the man who said: 'The course has not done anything for me.' 'The course has learned me nothing personally; I think it's a waste of money.'

The overall impression however is that men had been agreeably surprised by the nature of the courses, had enjoyed them, and considered them to be 'a good thing'. But something more than having 'a good time' is necessary to justify the effort and expense of running release courses and this must be sought in the more tangible gains which men claim to have made.

Self-assessment

Non-prisoners could be forgiven for thinking that the uneventful nature of life inside would provide both the opportunity and the motivation for prisoners to examine their lives past, present and future in as much detail as they desired. But although this sometimes happens, a more common strategy is for men to avoid serious thought altogether because of its unsettling effect on their capacity to serve their time. Release courses, which were directly concerned with the problems that men faced after release, did create an opportunity for constructive self-examination and reflection, and some men referred to this in positive terms: 'This course has given me a while, even if only a short while, to stop and think and create something by the effort of my own mind. It has given me the opportunity to absorb and analyse different approaches to life and different opportunities.' 'It made me think more than I used to.'

Sometimes the unaccustomed mental activity which this entailed caused men to say at the end of the first week or fortnight of a course that their 'brains were hurting' or that they had not been able to get to sleep because 'thoughts were going round and round' in their heads. They were not, however, complaining about what was happening to them, just describing it: 'It's opened up a lot of avenues in my head,' is how one man expressed it, 'thoughts I've never considered before.' And the results of this introspection were generally welcome: 'I've had six weeks now learning about myself and I've learned more about myself in the last six weeks than I'd learned in the past couple of years.' 'I found the course to be very deep in self-assessment, something I found I really needed, and a learning of my faults, being shown how to put them right, and shown how much help I can get and how easy it really can be. I can't say more than brilliant, perfect, can't praise it enough. Thank you.' 'In all honesty it's made me see myself as I really am.' 'It's showed me some of my problems, showed me where they've stemmed from.' 'It's helped me to realise things about myself that I'd never even dreamed of.'

A lot of the credit for all this thinking was given by some men to the pencil and paper assessment exercises they completed: 'They bring out what's in your mind' was how one man put it, and another thought that, 'It's given me a picture of myself.'

Others, like this man, were more suspicious: 'When I started the course I was very apprehensive of them analysing us.' But in time he came to the view that, 'The whole course is based on a self-analysis programme, and to make this work you must be completely honest with yourself.' Sometimes the fruits of honest self-appraisal were mixed: 'I have realised a few things about myself this week which mostly I didn't like. A couple of things I did like.' But in most cases an appreciation of personal weakness led to a desire to change or improve it: 'Some things I've liked about myself. Other things I've realised need polishing up or changing completely.' 'It's made me more aware of my downfalls - and ways I could overcome them in the future.'

And, useful as it was, this learning about self was not achieved at the expense of others on the course; in fact many men claimed to have learned as much, if not more, about other people than about themselves. 'It's shown me things about myself and other people I never knew before.' 'I've found out a lot about other people - not to judge them from first impressions.'

And they say they have benefited from doing so: 'It has broadened my outlook as concerns people. If you can understand other people - it helps you to understand yourself.' 'There's two people on the group that I really disliked when I came on, and I've found with getting to know them, and the problems they have with their wives and their families outside, I can quite understand them being the person they are; aggressive and just don't want to know people.'

Self-confidence

Lack of confidence often acts as the adhesive that binds together an assortment of the anxieties and practical problems facing prisoners immediately before and after release from captivity. Self-confidence is a subjective and elusive state of mind not normally amenable to precise measurement, and the evaluations relied to a large extent on the testimony of the men concerned for evidence that it had improved or not over time. But if there is one word that can be used to characterise what men said they had gained during release courses it is 'confidence'. 'I feel a lot more confident than I ever have for a long time.' 'I was scared stiff of going out but now I've got some self-confidence.'

These general statements were reinforced by the ratings made by each course member at the end of each week in relation to his confidence in three areas of possible release problems: work, accommodation and social situations. The ratings in Table 7.2, taken from the sixth Ranby course, are typical.

The confidence ratings can also be presented as a percentage of the maximum score possible on each scale, and in these terms the results for the Ashwell third course are as shown in Table 7.3.

There are fluctuations in these ratings but the upward trend of the figures is unmistakable, and they confirm the comments made by men in writing and on video about their feelings of increased confidence.

Until they are released, however, such results must be treated as no more than subjective claims by the men concerned, except where they can be related to behaviour in the prison situation itself. This was possible in those cases where men had begun to tackle their own shyness: 'It's helping me to mix and talk to other people.'

TABLE 7.2   Mean confidence ratings for Ranby Course 6

| | Week number | | | |
Confidence re:	1	2	3	4
Social situations	5.18	5.46	5.82	5.82
Accommodation	5.09	5.27	5.27	5.27
Work	4.82	5.36	5.64	5.55

Maximum rating = 6
Minimum rating = 1

TABLE 7.3   Confidence ratings - Ashwell Course 3

| | Week number | | | | | |
Confidence re:	1	2	3	4	5	6
Social situations	72%	77%	86%	91%	91%	94%
Accommodation	69%	90%	80%	91%	95%	91%
Work	65%	71%	92%	94%	96%	91%

'I'm not shy no more; I can talk naturally.' 'Once I used to sit on the bed and I wouldn't talk to hardly anyone but now I talk to the whole lot. I wouldn't do that before.

One or two of the men ascribed these changes to the use of video: 'The first week of the course I was quiet and would not appear on the video. Now I am not quiet and I am not afraid to appear on the camera.' Others thought it had to do with their membership of the course group: 'I have surprised myself by having enough confidence to do things like talking in front of a group.' 'The group work has helped me to come out of my shell and given me a bit more confidence than I had before.' 'I've benefited from the course by listening to other people talking and learning how to express myself better.'

And for yet other men the effects of their increased self-confidence during the course made themselves felt in their contacts with people at home: 'My girlfriend says that the letters she's been getting for the past eight weeks have altered from the letters she was getting before; so the course is doing me some good.' 'I couldn't talk to my father; he came up two weeks ago and it went really smooth, the best visit I've ever had.'

Increasing confidence was, in a number of cases, accompanied by changes in attitude of various kinds, ranging from the modest: 'I'm looking at things in a different way' to the more far-reaching: 'I've got an entirely new outlook on life.'

Problem-solving
Earlier in this chapter one man was quoted as saying that previously he had left prison, and just 'bamboozled into things'. The 'skills' approach adopted by the project stressed the importance of

acquiring rational and self-conscious methods for solving problems
and coping with difficult inter-personal situations. It attempted
to teach, amongst other things, what amounts to 'reflectiveness' -
the ability to think before acting, and to make informed choices
about what to do next. This was not seen as a philosophic form of
reflection but much more the ability to think on one's feet. And
one of its effects in practice may be to provide alternative forms
of behaviour to the kind of violence which appears to come naturally
to some of the men who are in constant conflict with the law and who
spend time in prisons, whether for violent offences or not.

Several men did say they thought they were better equipped to
deal in a more considered way with some of the situations they were
likely to encounter after release: 'I believe I have benefited from
the course as far as tackling problems is concerned instead of going
bull-headed into them.' 'Problems - before, I just went straight
into them shouting and bawling, but now I've been on the course it's
made me stop and think before going into it.' 'It's learned me to
slow down and think things out in the sense that there's five or six
ways round a problem instead of just blundering into it.'

These were not, of course, seen as magic solutions, but rather as
one man put it: 'I've been given the key to these problems and it's
up to me to use that key.'

Self-control

Parts of many courses, particularly at Ranby, were specifically devoted to the problem of violence, and particularly to the ways in
which potentially violent contacts with policemen might be handled.
For some men both of these topics were boring non-starters; they
were neither violent nor in constant conflict with the police; but
other men had problems with both, and some of them, at least, found
these parts of the curriculum helpful: 'The best part of the course
was showing you how to handle the police; before I used to fly off
the handle, but now I can cope with them.' Or another man: 'I've
learned a few things like holding your temper and not just getting
stuck in.'

Work

During the courses, as much as one-third of the time was devoted to
the subject of work. This was partly related to an assessment of
personal job strengths and weaknesses, and partly to the whole business of job search procedures. Time was also put aside for men to
write to outside employers, if they wished, inquiring about jobs.
The emphasis placed on this activity varied from course to course
and depended on its duration, the nature of the membership, and the
dispositions of the officers. On one or two courses as many as two-
thirds of the members received offers of jobs or training places
before they left prison. These tended to be the longer courses of
six or eight weeks; shorter courses did not permit the officers to
pursue an interest in the progress of particular applications.

For men who were successful in this way the results of the job
search programme were self-evident: 'My main chance of a job has
come through this course.' 'I've got a skill centre training
place.' But even if jobs were not fixed before release, many of the
course members thought that they had derived some benefit from those

parts of the course devoted to work: 'I have learned a lot about jobs and job-getting.'

And some men's thoughts were turned in new directions: 'The visit to the skill centre helped me to look at other fields.' 'I've decided to change my trade and get a job in welfare.' 'It broadened my outlook, like investing in a small business which I'd never thought of before.' 'Business-wise I think I'll put into practice everything I've learned on this course.'

But by far the most popular and helpful activity in the work programme was the preparation for finding work, and in particular for being interviewed: 'It has learned me how to apply for jobs.' 'Before I came on the course, interviews were one of my weak points. I now feel I could handle the interview situation.' 'The personnel officer was useful. I'll feel less nervous in interviews in future.'

One man thought that what he had gained from interview practice had spin-offs in other directions too: 'In fact the course has helped me to have more confidence in myself, not just in interviews but in all aspects, such as talking to people, working in groups, making decisions, and putting ideas forward and discussing them.'

It should be remembered that all the results in this chapter refer to the gains which men thought they had made whilst on the courses, and that perceptions of increased self-confidence might not survive the trauma of release into the 'real' world outside the prison gates. And there is always a danger that increased self-confidence is simply a nice name for the arousal of unrealistic expectations in some men about their prospects. The next chapter will look at how things turned out in practice for some of the release course graduates.

Drink, drugs and gambling

Drink was usually admitted as a big problem by only one or two, or at the most three or four members, of each release course, although it was apparent from group discussion that perhaps twice that number were often heavy drinkers to the point where their everyday lives were affected to some degree. Prior to the start of the experiment, some thought had been given to the suitability of release courses for men with alcohol problems, but a decision had been reached not to exclude them. It had been thought that alcoholics and problem drinkers in the dry, or almost dry atmosphere of the prison might respond well to the course content but find it difficult to apply it in practice after release. One spectacular example of this is given in the next chapter. And another man, not a self-confessed alcoholic, came close to assaulting several members of the research team who encountered him in a drunken state some months after his release. In one or two other cases, however, and it must be emphasised they were not numerous, the outcome seems to have been more hopeful. At the ends of courses some of these men said that they had recognised an addiction problem with drink or drugs or gambling and were resolved to do something about it after their release: 'I've definitely given up drinking.' 'I had a drink problem. I spoke to Larry (course officer) about it and it's a lot better. It's gone out of my mind.' 'Drugs - I think I might stop taking them.' 'As regards gambling on the whole, I think I've cracked it.'

Other reported gains

Finally there were a number of idiosyncratic gains reported by individual group members which range from the concrete: 'I learned about accommodation and social security.' 'I have learned myself to type on the typewriter, and it has helped me a lot.' 'I was never very good at filling in forms; I always got someone else to do that. But now I've learned how to do that' to the more intangible: 'My marriage problem's virtually sorted out.'

And despite the low rating given to getting into further trouble as a significant release problem there were even one or two men who thought that what they had done on the course would affect their future criminality: 'I have learned from the course that I can say with confidence, I SHALL NOT BE COMING BACK TO PRISON. I'm not claiming that it is the course that enables me to say that - I would have said it before, but now I know it is true.' 'If I stick by what I've learned it will help keep me out of prison.'

One last statement from a course member will gladden the hearts of those who attach great importance to reducing the rate of re-conviction amongst ex-prisoners: 'During my imprisonment I have organised three criminal endeavours to undertake when I get out. They would have brought me a lot of cash. I feel now that I would be stupid to carry them out.'

Criticisms

Against the accumulated weight of the good things men have said about courses it is possible to quote only a much smaller quantity of criticisms. No course member ever claimed to have been harmed by his experience, although proponents of the 'therapeutic damage' viewpoint might well expect such an outcome from the employment of 'untrained' and inexperienced prison officers in something which superficially, at any rate, resembles a 'treatment' situation. The most telling of the criticisms made by course members were about the irrelevance of the curriculum materials to their own problems and to the poor organisation which marked the operation of some of the courses. In some cases men dismissed the whole of the course content as irrelevant to their own post-release life: 'It didn't help me at all, although it might help someone with problems.' 'I haven't got a great deal from it because I don't have the same problems as them.' This suggests that the selection procedures for course members could be significantly improved, and that individuals who do not perceive themselves as having real problems after release could be screened out at an earlier stage.

In other cases the dislikes were more personal, and not necessarily an indication that a course member had been wasting his time: 'The work period was wasted on me.' 'Role plays were a bit boring; I don't see what people get out of them.' 'I disliked the talk on gambling; only because I do not have this problem.' For some topics the balance between interest and boredom was a fine one; alcohol, for instance, was interminably absorbing for alcoholics and near-alcoholics. For men without this problem, more than two or three sessions on the subject became boring. Satisfying the needs of the one group without losing the interest of the other proved to be a curriculum problem to which no wholly satisfactory solution was ever found.

The most prevalent of the criticisms made by men in their evaluations of courses was of pencil and paper methods of assessment and
self-assessment: 'Although I believe they are important, I don't
like filling in questionnaires.' 'A lot of the forms have been a
total waste of time.' 'There were too many questionnaires.' 'Certain of the tests seemed to me personally spurious.' These stric-
tures stemmed in part from the way that early courses concentrated
a lot of the assessment procedures in a two-week block at the beginning. Later courses which distributed pencil and paper exercises
more evenly throughout their length evoked fewer complaints. But
it remains the case that for a minority of men, anything which involved using a pen or pencil is an intolerable way of passing the
time, and for them it is important to provide alternative means for
achieving the same ends.

The second serious criticism of the courses by their members concerned boredom and disinterest due to a different cause, that of
poor course organisation and administration. 'It dragged a lot,'
said one man. Another disliked 'the amount of wasted time', and
another said, 'I suggest that we do more practical things to avoid
the group falling apart from boredom.' It is not difficult to find
reasonable excuses for failures of this sort; the officers were
inexperienced, they were not given sufficient time for preparation,
not enough material was available at the beginning of the project,
speakers did not turn up on time or turned out to be unsuitable, and
so on. All of which are true, but they do not fully explain the
boredom reported by some men. The fact is that on some courses, and
for a mixture of reasons, including those discussed in chapter 6,
the officers' motivation and enthusiasm was at a low ebb. The
existence of bad evaluations is, however, reassuring in one sense,
since it confirms that the good results obtained at other times were
not just the product of releasing men from their ordinary prison
routines; they had to be produced by hard work, thorough preparation and imaginative administration.

Prisoners themselves were alive to some of the difficulties which
their course officers were experiencing with the managements of
their establishments. One member's verdict on this course was that,
'It's not worked as well as I thought it would - trouble with the
authorities; if that had been better it would have been fantastic.'
Another man said that he had not liked 'the way the prison has
knocked the unit'. And a course member from the other prison complained that, 'The prison doesn't seem to be prepared to help the
prison officers to do the job properly.'

One final source of friction was provided by fellow group members: 'Disliked the incredible opinions and outlooks of some
others; and the non-participation of some others.' 'Some members
were not participating as much as I felt they might have done.'

'Screws' and 'cons'
The hinge on which this part of the project turned was the nature of
the relationship which it might prove possible to create and sustain
between groups of serving prisoners and the two-man teams of specially trained prison officers who acted as their release course
tutors. Enough has already been said to suggest that the courses
succeeded to some extent in breaching the traditional barriers be-

tween officers and men; otherwise the expression of enjoyment and
satisfaction would have been less frequent and less convincing than
was in fact the case. But in their final evaluation forms course
members were also asked to comment directly on the desirability of
having prison officers involved in the project at all, and on the
performance of their particular course officers. 'I was a bit worried about the fact that the instructors were going to be screws,'
said one man, 'because I've done a bit of time in the past and I've
been in several prisons, and somehow or other there's always been a
wall or division between screws and cons.' 'Well I've found out
since then,' he continued, 'that there simply isn't one, that a wall
doesn't exist at all, certainly not on the course. After the first
hour on the course that wall that was going to divide me and those
screws ceased to exist. They ceased to be screws at all, in fact
they became part of the group for me.'

This reversal of the normal state of affairs was symbolised on
the courses by the reciprocal use of first names between officers
and men. It may seem only a small step forward to achieve what is
commonplace in many other working situations but the divisions which
have riven the social organisation of prisons since the reforms of
the early nineteenth century owe less to feelings of status or even
of class than to something which most closely resembles a caste
system. The delicacy of the whole topic was made clear by the officers on the first staff training course who devoted an entire
afternoon of anxious debate to the question of how to address the
men on their courses. The first name friendliness which emerged
spontaneously on the first courses was however subject to strict but
tacit limits of time and place. Neither the men nor the officers
felt free to address each other other than formally when they met
outside the course classroom, for fear, on the one hand, of under-
mining the authority of the officer, and on the other so as to avoid
any suspicion that a man might be a 'grass'. But within the con-
fines of the course there was created an environment in which the
ordinary rules and conventions of the establishment were 'inoper-
ative': 'The officers we had on the course; we had a relationship
between all the group and the two officers. It was a friendly one.
All through the six weeks everyone felt comfortable. Discipline -
we don't find any. It would damage more than help. The cons on
the course and the officers training them are friends, but outside
they've got a job to do. In here you can say what you want. You
can actually interrupt the officers when they're speaking and they
won't say "I'm going to book you." There's an actual friendship
there.'

Other men were less sure of the relationship and saw the situ-
ational nature of the name-calling as not very desirable: 'They've
still been prison officers. You call them by their first names but
you can't call them that in front of other inmates.' And there
were a few men who could never bring themselves to fraternise so
openly with the enemy and who continued to address the officers as
'boss' or as 'Mr So-and-so'. One such man said: 'I don't trust
them for a start; but it's not just them, I don't trust anybody.'
Another tactic was to treat the officers concerned as special cases,
singular exceptions to the general run of screws: 'I hated screws;
I still hate screws, but Mr ..., he's fantastic. He's like a second

dad to you.' Some men also thought it would be better if the officers were to work in civilian clothes, to emphasise the different
nature of their release course roles: 'The group would react to
them more without their uniform. If they wore ordinary clothes
they would break the barrier.' Others disagreed: 'It's not the
uniform, it's the man underneath.'

The extent to which the officers were able to create an atmosphere in which the distinction between the 'men in blue' and the
'men in grey' ceased to matter for all practical purposes is evident
in these two comments: 'After a week or two they're just one of us,
just another human being, not prison officers and prisoners.'
'We've been treated on this course on a par with them (officers).'

One result of being treated in this way was a set of tributes to
the work of the course officers: 'The officers do a great job and
run the course very well.' 'The officers who ran the course conducted themselves admirably, which in itself was a lesson.'

And in some cases it led to an altered perception of prison officers as a group: 'My opinion of prison officers has changed.' 'It
has given me a completely different outlook on them. I think that
without them the course would not have been the fantastic, unbeliev-
able success it has been.' There were also a number of men who
pointed out that release courses could bring benefits to the officers involved and to the prison system generally as well as to the
men attending them. 'I'm pleased to see that prison officers are
taking an active part in this course, as at one time I thought they
just didn't care, and being a prison officer was just a job, and
there was no sense of duty. I feel very differently now and hope
that more officers will show an interest in this type of course in
the future.' One of the questions on the final evaluation forms
asked men to comment on the fitness of prison officers to act as
release course tutors compared to specialists or outsiders. The
overwhelming consensus of opinion amongst the men who answered this
question was in favour of prison officers doing the job rather than
anyone else. The most common reason for preferring prison officers
as instructors was because of their familiarity with prisoners and
their problems: 'I think the best people are the officers. They're
the people who've been with the convicts and really know them.' But
there was also a note of caution in one of the evaluations: 'Screws
should do it, but not all screws, because some of them are right
bastards who don't care about you.'

What the officers said

With exceptions and abstentions, the men who completed release
courses at Ranby and Ashwell said that they enjoyed them and found
them useful in a variety of ways which conformed with the aims of
the research project. Follow-up data suggests that these claims of
benefit were not just transitory phenomena, forgotten the minute the
men were released into the outside world. Their evaluations also
clearly and explicitly paid tribute to the work and energy and
imagination of the officers who had been running the courses. But
what did the officers themselves have to say about their experience?

For a start they said what hard work it was: 'I was tireder at

nights when I got home, and I was hungrier at dinner times. It is
a strain making sure that the materials are good enough to put over
well.' This strain was particularly noticeable on the first two
courses at each prison when the officers were inexperienced and the
quantity of adequately prepared material was too limited for the
duration of an eight-week course. One officer, referring to his
colleagues who were in this position, said: 'I could see they were
under pressure. They had to take a lot of work home; to be critical, it was ill-prepared. They were so embroiled in it, putting
everything they'd got into it. It got pretty exhausting.' And an
officer in another prison said of his first course that it was
'harder than I expected. In normal circumstances in this job, no
one ever makes demands on you in any way, whereas on the course the
cons' demands are constant - for information, to be taught something
about themselves, to be helped morally - so it's very demanding.'
Or, as his colleague, a man of fewer words, put it: 'I went home
knackered.'

In order to keep up with the men's demands and to run a course to
his own satisfaction, the first of these officers found that, 'I was
doing more and more work in my own time, partly creating new materials, partly planning the next day or the next week, writing it as we
went along. If the course members expect results then you have to
do it in your own time because there's no way you can score anything
or write up interviews.' As time went by and they gained more experience and the material became more plentiful and familiar, the
strain on the officers lessened appreciably, but did not disappear
completely: 'It was extremely hard to start off. I'd never been
in a classroom situation. I didn't realise the stresses and strains
of changing people's ways of thinking or trying to change their ways
of thinking. That's basically what we were trying to do. After the
first twelve months it's easier. But it's still a great strain.'
Coping with these demands was made more difficult by the officers'
feelings of isolation and non-cooperation within the prison: 'I
worked harder than I've ever worked in the service and I got less
money than I've ever had in the service. We were on bare wages -
no overtime at all, even before the cuts came. I was about £20 a
week down; I'm earning £20 a week more now I'm not on the course.'

The amount of time available for preparing and carrying out release course work, the effects of budgetary controls and the attitude of other staff members in the institutions clearly affected the
ability of the officers to do their course work as well as they
thought they should. These difficulties were offset in part at
least, for some though not all of them, by the rewards they received
from doing the work itself: 'I've had more job satisfaction in the
last six weeks than in the last six years in the service.' 'Everything we've done in the last six weeks has been a success to one
degree or another.' 'Well, to me, it's what the job should be about
really.' 'Instead of just being a number, looking after them and
then turning them out at the end of their sentence, at least you're
trying to find out why they're here, and correcting whatever faults
they've got, or helping them to correct them. I got a great deal of
satisfaction from that.' 'There's much more job satisfaction.
You've only got to come to the end of a course to find out the job
satisfaction. All the work you've put into it during the course

seems to come out in satisfaction right at the very end. You get
the evaluations and feel the course has gone down really well. It
makes it all worthwhile.'
     The causes of the satisfaction varied from officer to officer.
One thought it derived from the fact that, 'Each day is different.
It's getting over things to other people; getting the satisfaction
of them being able to learn something directly from me.' Another
officer quoted the case of a particular man whose post-prison performance had pleased him: 'Alec M. has been out for the longest
time in his life. That gives me a lot of pleasure.' Or another:
'It might sound a bit cloy, but I really do get a terrific kick out
of seeing a man suddenly see the light. It's a pat phrase, but it's
there. I couldn't help but get that reaction.' For this officer,
it was the ability to provide an experience which promoted this kind
of change in men which was the most rewarding part of working on release courses: 'It's a very fatalistic attitude that prisoners have
got. They've shook tomorrow out of their minds, and this sudden
awareness of what could happen, and when they realise it doesn't
need an awful lot of effort on their part to put it right, then they
see it and latch on to it and get excited about it. It was amazing
to see this sudden self-awareness develop and to think I had helped
them to achieve it, I think it's the most fantastic experience
that's ever happened to me.'
     Not all the officers involved in the project were enthused to
this extent. One or two treated their work on the courses in a very
matter-of-fact way, declining to take work home in the evening, and
permitting the programme to sag if there had not been enough time
allocated by the administration for them to prepare their material
adequately. Interestingly, the results obtained by these officers,
whilst lacking something of the immediate personal warmth achieved
by some of the others, were certainly not inferior in terms of the
changes reported by men both during and after the completion of
courses. And an unlooked-for bonus was that a number of the officers reported that they too had benefited from their training and
the experience of running courses, in terms which are not too dis-
similar from those used by the graduates of their own efforts: 'One
of my main problems,' said one of them, 'has always been under-
rating myself until the last twelve to eighteen months.' Others
thought they had gained in a variety of ways: 'It's brought me out
of my shell and I feel more confident of handling anything that
comes up now than I did before.' 'It helped me to understand
people better.' 'I didn't know whether I'd have the ability to
stand up in front of twelve prisoners. Time has proved that I can.'
'The officers are being affected as much as the inmates. They're
learning an awful lot as each day passes.' 'I think if I'd had the
experience of the release course before I sat the Assistant Governor's exam I'd be an AG by now. Just meeting people in the community, going out, talking to them, I've got an awful lot of confidence
in that respect.' 'It helps you to rationalise your thinking when
you're giving a talk or leading a group discussion you find that
you're beginning to put yourself over in such a way that people are
stopping to listen to you. That's been a great benefit to me.'
     Changes in the confidence and competence of the officers in their

management of release courses was evident not just to themselves but to external observers of their performance as well. There were noticeable developments too in the abilities of officers to relax in their course work; to work flexibly rather than to a rigidly pre-arranged schedule; and to respond imaginatively to some of the problems of their group members, both on the courses and outside. The best example of this was the officer who started an experimental one week course at Ranby with the question, 'What is the problem?' and developed the programme from there without previous preparation.

SHEFFIELD DAY TRAINING CENTRE

The objectives of the research at Sheffield day training centre focused on the feasibility of the methods and materials, and the possible effects of their use on trainees. Similar methods to those of the release courses were used to gather information for this pur-pose: the weekly attendance records of the course members, weekly evaluation sheets, and 'exit' interviews.

Attendance

A difficulty faced by all the day training centres, indeed by any agency whose concern is to help problem groups in the community, is simply that of 'holding on' to members of its target population, sustaining their interest in such a way that they will be more likely to attend. This in fact is a double-edged problem: for the offender who should of course attend to fulfil the requirements of the court, and for the centre which stands little chance of benefit-ing its consumers if they simply absent themselves.

Regular attendance is therefore a fairly crucial issue. But for course members, distractions and pressures of many kinds relentless-ly take their toll. Too many absences can lead to the return of a course member to court for breach of his probation order. For this and a variety of other reasons, a number of men may fail to complete their sixty days' attendance. In 1976-7 twenty-nine men failed to complete courses at Sheffield. A straightforward breakdown of the reasons is given in Table 7.4.

TABLE 7.4 Reasons for not completing courses

Reason	No. of men
Committed further offence during course	17
Terminated, due to illness, wife's illness, unsuitability	5
Breached	5
Took own case back to court	2
Total	29

Given that it is not easy to ensure that men complete their sixty days, one fundamental test of a programme's acceptability might be whether or not it seemed to help more men complete centre courses. Figure 7.1 charts the percentages of group members, in each of seventeen groups, who completed the Sheffield course.

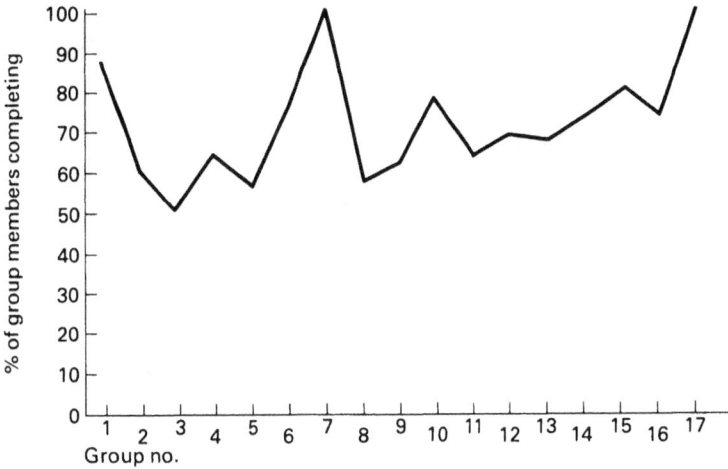

Figure 7.1   Percentages of group members completing their course

Although these figures are inevitably somewhat erratic, they do manifest a slow upward trend. While the average proportion of 'completions' for groups 1-4 is 63.5 per cent, that for groups 14-17 is 85.75 per cent, a substantial rise. More men now manage to complete courses at the day training centre. A more striking illustration of improved attendance emerges, however, from Figure 7.2. This shows

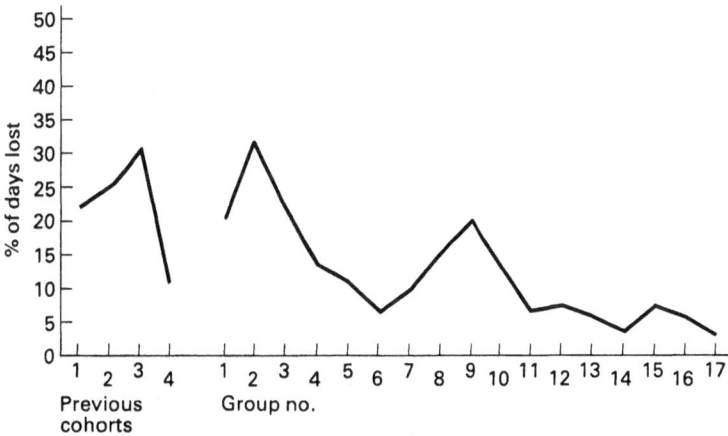

Figure 7.2   Unexplained absence

the number of days of 'unexplained absence' (i.e. excluding sickness, interviews, court appearances and so on) recorded in the centre's register for each group, as a percentage of the total number of days' attendance expected (measuring sixty days from each man's date of arrival). For comparative purposes, attendance records for 1975 are included, sorting men into four 'cohorts' of seven members each (average group size during 1976-7). That there was a considerable improvement in day-to-day attendance at the centre cannot be doubted; increasing numbers of men were able to leave the centre after fifty-five days, and this trend seemed to be continuing into 1978. Both this and the previous measure are of course of an extremely rough-and-ready nature, and provide only the most global impression of the centre's apparently increased ability to maintain the interest of its course members. For a fuller picture of why this might be happening, we must turn to the views of group members themselves.

Responses to the course

One way of gauging these views is to look at course members' ratings as recorded on the centre's weekly evaluation sheets. Apart from individual scales on the usefulness of specific activities, there were also more general scales on enjoyment of the week, learning about self and others, and confidence about finding work and coping with social situations after leaving the centre. Though these are incomplete for some courses, particularly in their later weeks, those available show fairly positive results. Figure 7.3 presents

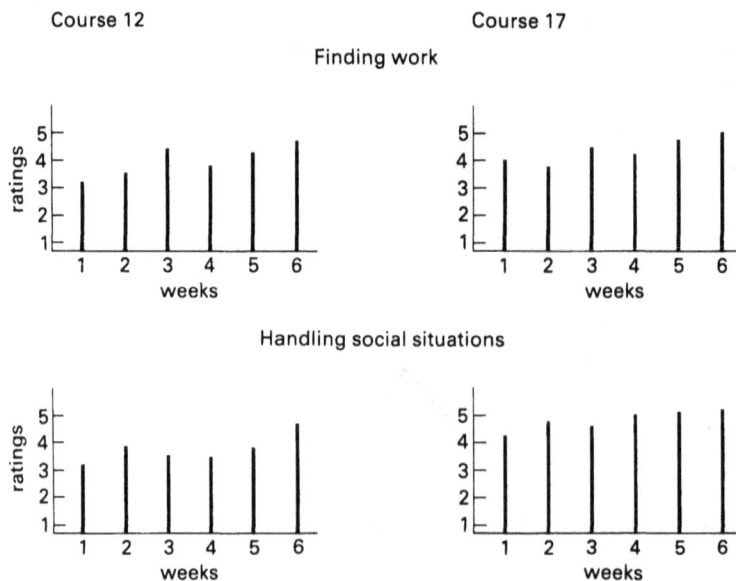

Figure 7.3 Confidence ratings

confidence ratings for the first six weeks of courses 12 and 17, averaged over all group members, on a five-point scale where five means 'very confident'.

An alternative way of expressing these results is in terms of percentages of the maximum ratings possible. Thus the 'work' and 'social' confidence ratings for the first seven weeks of course 15 would be as follows:

TABLE 7.5

Week	1	2	3	4	5	6	7
Finding work	78.8	76.6	86.6	91.6	90.0	90.0	95.0
Handling social situations	70.0	72.2	80.0	86.0	74.0	80.0	88.2

The emergence of these findings from figures collected over several months and from different groups in different situations is fairly encouraging, for three reasons. First, these ratings and others, lean on average towards the positive end of the scale; second, most, though by no means all, tend to show slight increases over succeeding weeks; and third, there is also a slow improvement from one course to the next.

The sources of these changes in confidence may perhaps be found in the kinds of help men feel that they have received. Some of these have been identified by men during 'exit' interviews in the last week of their courses. The commonest kinds of statement they make refer loosely to general changes in motivation and self-confidence: 'It got me out of the rut.' 'It's changed my outlook.' 'It's given me a lot of things, I know that - self-confidence.' 'It's helped me a helluva lot. It's brought me out - I'm more confident - and kept me out of trouble. I've learnt now.' 'When I came I didn't talk much but I do now.' 'I was very quiet and it's brought me out a bit.' 'It's built my confidence up.' 'I feel there's something going for me now. I was despondent when I came here - always looking on the bad side of things.'

However, a large number of specific gains were also reported, of both a practical and an inter-personal nature: 'Yes, I know a bit more ... a lot more, about rights, social security, work rights.' 'It's helped me with accommodation - I'm better off now.' 'It's helped me with reading and writing and talking to people; filling in forms; and to get a job.' 'It's helped me a lot financially and otherwise. And I think I've got to know myself better. I had a wrong idea of the type of person I was.' 'I've sorted my finances out - the main thing that brought me here. I've come to terms with all my debts and I'm well on the way to sorting them out.' 'I've cut down on drinking, but I'm smoking more, so it's not helping my money ... but I've got an idea of what I'm capable of and not capable of ... and realise what I'm looking for in life. I can manage money better, and get on with people better.' 'I couldn't read at all, now I can a little bit. It's learned me about other people, to fill in forms, and go for interviews.' 'Normally I'm shy about speaking to other people. Being in groups has altered that.' 'It's helped me with my wife. She didn't like the idea at the start. Now I can go and get a job - before I couldn't - she wanted me at home all day.'

And in relation to work, men attributed job market success to help received in the centre: 'I've got back into a work routine, getting up early. And I've made new friends.' 'It's learned me how to look for better jobs.' 'When I went for my last job I took two hours to build up the courage to go in and ask. Yesterday I walked straight in.' 'I'm leaving here with a job. I was out of work for eighteen months before coming here.' 'I've found a job; and I'd feel confident if I had to find other jobs.'

Both during a course and at the end of it, men were also asked to name things they liked and disliked about the programme. The former generally fell into four broad categories. First, leisure activities that form part of the centre programme, such as outings, gym and crafts, were, perhaps not surprisingly, named more often than anything else. Second, several aspects of the centre's way of working were mentioned, for example, 'the informal atmosphere'; 'not calling anybody "sir"'; 'having to use my brain'; 'what the DTC stands for'; 'doing a lot of things I've not done before'. Third, personal relations in the centre were looked upon favourably; staff were seen as 'easy to get on with' and course members also enjoyed, in the words of one man, 'the comradeship of the group'. Finally, many specific course activities were named by individual men - though it is not unlikely that for each of these, someone could be found who had an entirely opposed view of the activity in question.

Only positively toned comments have been relayed so far. But there are adverse ones too, in some cases pointedly critical, in other cases downright dismissive of the whole enterprise. Two fre- quently heard complaints from members of earlier courses seem now to be made much less often. The first of these concerns the amount of pencil and paper work in courses - especially in their opening weeks - which was clearly too much for most of the men. This was subsequently reduced to what, judging by the number of criticisms, was a more tolerable level, and only pencil and paper items that had been generally well received were incorporated into the assessment procedures. The second complaint related to the sometimes intense feelings of boredom men felt, particularly during the later weeks of courses. Once again, while the programme still contained some empty spaces during these weeks, and men occasionally felt that not enough had been planned for them, the second half of the course later became much better organised, and this criticism too was heard with decreasing frequency.

Two other problems identified by course members in exit inter- views may, unlike the ones just cited, be ineluctable features of a day training sentence. First, in the eyes of some men (and of some probation officers), the centre can create greater dependency amongst course members, and make them less able to cope with an un- friendly world after their departure: 'I've enjoyed it - but some- times too much ... I might be relying on it ... you can either reject it or get to rely on it.' It goes without saying that this is the opposite of the centre's intentions, and while it could be objected that this man, and others like him, might come to depend

on others in any situation, the effects of a sixty-day course in
which group members are given a great deal of attention are bound
to be worrying in some cases. Some field probation officers have
found men too demanding after they have completed their courses.

Second, although most men who come to the centre bring practical
problems which must be (and are) dealt with immediately, a number
complain that insufficient time is allocated to them as individuals
during parts of the centre course: that is, they may be less likely
to be seen by staff on a one-to-one basis. As some course members
have suggested: 'Try not to involve the group too much in some
people's problems. It puts the dampers on you.' 'Get the staff
onto one person at a time - and just work in groups for one period
a day. Have more work with individuals.' 'The lads in the group
have opened their hearts to me (an older course member) more than to
a probation officer ... I don't know if you couldn't help individuals more with personal problems that don't come to light ... especially in the younger ones.'

Certainly the amount of time staff spend with individual course
members could be increased, but the inevitable limits would still
leave some course members dissatisfied. In a sense this and the
problem of dependence work in opposite directions, with the day
training centre permanently caught between them: a certain amount
of tension - between giving people help and making them dependent
on it, between working with individuals or working in groups - may
be intrinsic to the centre's programme no matter how it is organised. At the moment these two kinds of problem remain, for some
course members at least, unresolved.

Naturally, many other items - from course content, to staff decisions, to assorted happenings within the lifespan of a group -
become targets for comment and criticism by course members during
their stay. Many men come to the centre to avoid imprisonment, and
others resent having to attend rather than take up work. Some
measure of discontentment is ever-present and no undertaking (designed as a genuine alternative to prison) could hope to escape a
share of the protest which results.

THE VALUE OF EVALUATIONS

Lest it be thought that this chapter is nothing more than an essay
in self-congratulation, it is worth posing two questions at this
point: How typical are the quoted judgments of course members? and,
What do they really mean? Sceptics would argue that they are probably selective and not necessarily indicative either of what men
really thought of the courses, or related to their subsequent behaviour in any relevant way.

Individual remarks cannot, of course, be taken as typical of
anything other than themselves. Those which have been selected for
quotation have obviously been chosen to convey as vividly as possible the verbal responses of men to the courses they attended. But
they are not on that basis alone to be dismissed as unrepresenta-
tive. At least half the graduates of the courses are represented
in the selection of comments given above and many others have been
excluded because they were merely repetitive of sentiments already

expressed. And taken together they tell a roughly similar story. There does not exist anywhere any evidence which could be used to contradict or even substantially to qualify the message of enjoyment and utility which has emerged unforcedly from a range of evaluative measures taken over a period of time. But are they genuine? A cynic might say that favourable replies can be obtained from an experimental group by numerous devices: by phrasing questions in a loaded way so that they elicit positive rather than negative views, by conveying, even implicitly, an expectation that only 'good' evaluations are being sought and that 'bad' ones will be harmful to the future health of the project, by insinuating that criticism will be construed as woundingly personal by course staff or researchers, by appealing to the innate sycophancy of inmates, probationers and other dependent populations, by engineering situations in which outright untruths are uttered by respondents for various reasons. And finally there is the chance of infection by the elusive 'Hawthorne' effect, which has haunted the efforts of social scientists to measure accurately the effects of their interventions in human affairs. The dangers that any or all of these will influence what people say are multiplied when evaluations are conducted, not by disinterested third parties, but by those directly concerned with proving that a particular approach is a success; in this case, the prison and probation officers and researchers concerned with the project. And when the respondents are all convicted offenders - thieves and con-men for the most part with a sprinkling of violence cases amongst them - many observers would counsel caution in accepting as true anything they may say, as opposed to what they actually do, preferably as measured 'objectively' by entries on the Criminal Records Office computer.

Most of these objections can be reduced to a single proposition: that there is established between researchers and researched a covert conspiracy to produce results which exaggerate in subtle but significant ways any favourable features of the work in hand, whilst de-emphasising or discounting some of its bad points. Conspiracies, and especially covert ones, are much easier to suspect and allege than they are to refute and disprove. In the end, the disbelieving are unlikely to be convinced by even the most sophisticated standards of proof of which the social 'sciences' are capable. There are, however, some factors which ought to be weighed against the idea that the results reported in this chapter are seriously misrepresenting reality in any systematic fashion.

In the first place, it was not anticipated that the research would yield especially good results. Nothing in the reported results of social work innovation and criminology research over the past twenty years would lead anyone to believe that anything startling could be achieved in this field, especially with a design which included prison officers acting as teachers, counsellors and group leaders to numbers of serving prisoners. On any rational view the expected outcome of such an experiment might well be to replicate the findings reported from the Dover Borstal experiment, (1) or the IMPACT project in probation, (2) where low-key and unspectacular failures were the order of the day. The nature of the responses made by offenders who have patronised this project were therefore unexpected. When they first made an appearance during

the staff training course placements at Leicester and Nottingham
prisons they were thought to represent the effects of a 'holiday
syndrome' amongst men suddenly released from the boring and restricted routines of ordinary prison life into an atmosphere of
novelty and new people. Similarly, the responses of the men to the
first two courses at Ranby and Ashwell were not regarded as definitive. They were followed in both places by courses which appeared
to be less successful and the probability was that evaluations
during the remainder of the experimental period would describe a
declining curve as the initial energy and enthusiasm of the staff
waned. In fact the reverse has been the case and later courses both
in the prisons and the DTC have produced even better evaluations
than the earlier ones.

Equally, the positive comments were not restricted to any one research site, to only one or two courses, or to one or two particularly successful teams of staff members. They have been remarkably
uniform throughout in their content and tone, referring in similar
ways to the same features of courses and to the same kinds of personal perceptions, even though the responses of earlier course
graduates could not have been known to those who came later. They
display, in other words, a high degree of internal consistency. And
the offenders who have passed judgment in this way on the programme
are themselves an assorted lot; from first offenders with pretensions to gentility to professional criminals; from borderline sub-
normals to men with long records of violence and dishonesty and with
personal histories disfigured by the most severe indices of depriva-
tion and disorder.

In the prisons, a second, and even stronger check against the
possibility that what the men said was unreliable was provided by
the previous working experience of the prison officers taking part
in the experiment. All of them had done ordinary disciplinary
duties in more than one type of prison establishment. One or two
of them enjoyed previous reputations in their prisons for strictly
disciplinarian attitudes. And collectively they shared all the wary
cynicism of their calling about the men with whom they spend the
greater part of their waking hours. They were well used in other
words to measuring the words of inmates with generous pinches of
salt. This is the considered judgment of one of the longer serving
officers on the notion that men were dissembling in their responses
to courses: 'You can hold a prisoner's attention until he gets
bored, and then there's no way you can get him back. It would be
easier for him to go and lie in his cell or go on the garden party
than stay with you being bored. They would explode. They would
tell you "What a load of balls", "It's out of the window." Once
they're aware they can criticise without repercussions you watch
them go. They're critical in the normal prison situation anyway.
They'll exhaust all avenues to voice their dissent. There's no way
you could take twelve men and hold them for a week unless they
wanted to be there, unless they're interested.' His colleagues
agreed that so far as they could tell the men were, in the main,
filling in their evaluations as honestly as they could; and that
there would be little point in serving prisoners inventing flatter-
ing untruths about the excellence of something being done by their
traditional enemies.

It is also curious, if such positive evaluations are thought so easy to collect from captive and semi-captive populations of offenders, why it is that the literature is not already filled with glowing accounts of similar experiments. So perhaps, the final word in this chapter can rest with three prison course graduates: 'It's the best thing I've seen in a prison sentence.' 'It's one of the best things that ever happened in prison.' 'Someone's come up with a good idea and it's working.'

Chapter 8

Afterwards

What happened during the courses in the prisons was of vital concern
to a research project which was to a large extent a feasibility
study of how the prison officer's role might be extended into the
area of rehabilitation. But since the focus of the courses which
they were running was on preparing prisoners to cope better with
the problems they face after release it was also essential to make
some attempt to find out how the men had fared in the outside world.

The original research design was not based on a strictly experimental model with 'treatment' and 'control' groups. It would in any
case have proved difficult, if not impossible, to compose properly
matched groups of this kind from the numbers of men who applied for
courses. And there would have been undoubted difficulties in following up the post-release activities of any control group members.
Thirty-five randomly selected men at Ranby were asked if they would
be prepared to take part in follow-up procedures. Seventeen of
them said that they would be willing to return written follow-up
forms to the prison after release, but only seven said that they
would consider making themselves available for interview.

These reactions are not surprising; the natural feeling of most
ex-prisoners is to forget as speedily as possible the experience
they have just completed, and to avoid all contact with both
other ex-prisoners and with prison staff.

For illustrative purposes, however, it was important to keep in
touch with as many ex-course members as possible and this was
tackled in the following ways.

Methods

The purpose of the follow-up procedures and the uses to be made of
information gathered in this way was carefully explained to every
course member. Each man was asked to leave with the release course
staff an address, not necessarily his own, where he could be con-
tacted. Contact was to be maintained through the periodic return
of follow-up forms issued to men before their release, through let-

ters or telephone calls and personal interviews, and by invitations
to attend follow-up meetings to be convened at intervals during the
project.

Although men were not asked to make a specific undertaking to
keep in touch with the project, most of them appeared to be willing
to do so. In practice some of the men most expected to remain in
touch failed to do so, and some surprising individuals made strenuous efforts to report their progress from time to time.

The numbers and percentages of men from the first seven courses
at the two prisons who kept in touch with the project by any means
at all up to 1 April 1978 are set out in Table 8.1.

TABLE 8.1

Course no.	Length	Ranby No. of members	Kept in contact	Length	Ashwell No. of members	Kept in contact
1	8 weeks	12	9	8 weeks	9	6
2	8 weeks	12	7	8 weeks	12	9
3	(unfinished	12	O)	6 weeks	12	5
4	6 weeks	13	7	6 weeks	12	8
5	6 weeks	12	5	6 weeks	12	7
6	4 weeks	12	6	4 weeks	12	9
7	2 weeks	12	8	4 weeks	11	5
Total		73	42 (57%)		80	49 (61%)

Excluding the men on Ranby Course 3, which was not properly completed, the figures are comparable for both prisons; around 60 per
cent of the men have kept in touch in some way. Since this has
meant, in most cases, writing to or telephoning the prison officers
running the courses it may be taken also as a measure of the extent
to which it is possible for officers and prisoners to work together
successfully and to breach the traditional barriers which exist between them.

It must be said, however, that these contacts did not take a form
which could easily be quantified for evaluation purposes. Although
returns of the first-week forms were encouraging, hardly any men
sent in those designed to look at their first two months of freedom.
Telephone calls and informal letters were quite often substituted
for the more formal measures. This meant that men were able to
report fully on those things they personally thought were important,
and in some cases there was protracted correspondence with officers
lasting for periods of more than a year. Telephone calls tended to
be accompanied by pleas for information or advice concerning employment and other release problems, which suggests that some thought
could be given to the provision of a reverse-charge switchboard
service for ex-prisoners manned by selected officers at each establishment, and extending their growing involvement in 'welfare' and
after-care matters.

In addition to the forms which men took with them when they were
released, all ex-course members were sent a follow-up questionnaire
during the last few months of the project and this yielded some
material from men from whom nothing had previously been heard.

Attempts to interview course graduates, who lived in an area
which stretched from the Isle of Wight to the Shetland Isles, but
with heavy concentrations in the Nottinghamshire/Leicestershire
area, were not too successful. Although a number of interviews were
completed and have provided useful illustrative data, researchers
spent a number of fruitless hours waiting for ex-prisoners who did
not turn up, or who were found not to live where they were thought
to be. It was decided therefore to abandon the idea of systematically interviewing even a small sample of ex-course members.

The final source of follow-up data was the two meetings held for
former course members and prison officers in Nottingham in December
1976 and December 1977. Fourteen men attended the first meeting:
six from Ranby and eight from Ashwell. Twenty-seven men came to the
second of them: sixteen from Ashwell and eleven from Ranby. The
fact that both these meetings were held on Saturdays, and involved
considerable travelling for some individuals indicates the effect
that courses had had on some men. Several of them brought their
wives or girlfriends to the meetings; one or two clearly came to
make sure that their men did not get into mischief at this meeting
of ex-prisoners. Others came to say what a deep impression the
courses appeared to have had on the attitudes and behaviour of their
husbands or boyfriends.

Each meeting provided opportunities for discussion in small and
large groups, for filling in follow-up forms, for individual conversations, and for the recording of video comments.

The experiences of course members after release which are reported here are drawn from these varied communications. Together they
describe what happened to some men during the first few days and
weeks and months of their freedom.

The first day

For the single, homeless man, the first day out of prison is a race
against time to register as unemployed, to find lodgings and to draw
supplementary benefits if any are due. The scale of discharge
grants now makes all these things easier than was the case until
comparatively recently. But, homeless or not, single or not, many
men's agendas for their first day of freedom reflect interests not
normally featured in the official itinerary: 'I spent most of the
day walking around the town inspecting changes and window-shopping.
I went to my friend's girlfriend's 21st on the night and had an enjoyable time.' 'I went water skiing, swimming and got slightly
inebriated.' 'Stayed in bed till the pub opened. Then went back
to bed in the afternoon to recover from the Sunday lunch time session. Stayed in rest of day with wench and little girl.' 'My
friends come round to my house and we had a party.' 'I just had
walks around to familiarise myself with my surroundings.' 'I was
met at the station by my mother and we went for a drink, and later
to visit my grandmother. At night I went for a drink in town and

got myself drunk.' 'Got drunk and the usual.' 'After the usual
homecoming which I will not go into, I went to the unemployment
office, jobcentre and social security.' 'Signed on at D of E. Rest
of day personal.' 'Met girlfriend; can't give details.' One man
spoke for a whole constituency of the newly released when he said:
'Can't get enough sex.'

Other men had less pleasant experiences on their first day out:
'Got stopped by the squad: CID. Done nothing wrong, just aggrava-
tion.' 'Within fifteen minutes of getting off train I bumped into a
guy I knew had just been released from Winson Green four days earlier; offered me some pills. Went to collect clothes from friend;
same thing happened. Glad to say it didn't bother me.'

There were also reports from one or two men of the classic ex-
prisoner's nightmare: 'People look upon me as dirt, I think.' 'I
had a very strange feeling that people were looking at me all the
time as if they knew I had just been released from prison. I found
that I couldn't communicate with people very easily.'

But the feeling did not last long for a man who had had similar
sensations: 'I am settling down to being out of prison and I don't
feel that people are looking at me any more.' There is still, however, the problem of explaining away a recent absence: 'On the
course we covered reaction from other people and friends but I have
found it difficult to explain to people who I meet for the first
time where I have been for six months. This often seemed to occur
in conversation.' Others had precisely opposite reactions: 'Everyone has been great and it is not true about people spitting and
throwing stones when you come out.'

Achieving personal objectives

When the first flush of freedom had passed many men turned their attention to the sterner tasks of re-establishing themselves in civilian life. As the release courses developed, increasing emphasis was
placed on encouraging members to formulate personal objectives which
they wished to achieve after release. This helped to summarise the
findings of the assessment activities, and crystallised for each
individual the concrete steps he needed to take if he was to survive
successfully outside. The actual objectives varied from the minute-
ly particular, e.g. 'to dig the garden', to the almost cosmic goal
of 'finding personal happiness'. Most of them, however, were
finite, realistic and attainable and were kept in personal files for
future reference. In some cases the objectives were the outcome of
joint conversations between men and officers, but mostly they were
conceived and expressed by the men themselves. A typical set of
first month's objectives was:
1 Re-settle with family and friends;
2 Find suitable accommodation;
3 Keep out of trouble;
4 Generally fit back in at my own pace.
This man wrote later to say: 'All in all my first month's objectives are going OK although I didn't set myself too stiff a task.
I do use my info from my folder if I think it is necessary and will
continue to do so.' Another man had set himself more detailed objectives to be achieved over a six-month period:

First Six Months Objectives
1st week: Hoping accommodation to be secured before release,
will obtain employment and try to pick up the pieces of old
friends' relationships. Spend weekends helping friend to get
his car business on firm ground. Sort out social security for
clothes and benefit if necessary and make inroads into getting
a tax rebate.
1st month: Having got employment and accommodation sorted out,
will see ex-wife for access to my two children. Will try to
make weekly visits to Mansfield to renew relationships. Save
money for future at £10/week. Have the odd drink and have a few
ladies to keep me company.
3rd month: Saving money still. May buy a car off friend if
cheap enough. Should be having children for the day by now - may
even be reconciled with ex-wife, depends on both attitudes.
Job situations should be settled down enough to take time off for
a holiday.
5th month: Accommodation should be settled for next few years.
Holiday should be coming up. Ex-wife and children situation will
be very clear. Should have a decent sum in the bank. Will start
taking long-term view of placing finances in a building society.
Prison will only be thought of when writing letter to course,
having no intentions of ever returning.'

Later this man reported: 'I've been out a fortnight now. It's
been pretty hectic going but I'm finally settled. The hostel is
great, good food, good atmosphere, and nice and easy-going. I'm
going back into mining. I see the training officer tomorrow. I've
got a good work record, so I should be OK. The money's good which
is just as well because I'm looking forward to buying a house and
putting down a deposit around Christmas. I wouldn't have done normally but my ex-wife wants to come back to me and I know I want her,
so that's the way it's going to be. I achieved all my objectives
for the first two weeks (just) so I'm on schedule. You've got no
chance of getting me back.'
It has not proved possible to match objectives like these with
achievements in as methodical a manner as had been hoped, but the
flavour of the post-release experience can best be conveyed by
looking at some of the specific problems men faced and how they
claim to have coped with them.

Work
Prior to coming on release courses, very few men in either prison
were certain of going out to a specific job at the end of their
sentence and the survey of release problems showed that four out of
five serving prisoners saw getting a job as a problem; it was the
single largest difficulty they foresaw for themselves. More time on
the courses was accordingly devoted to this topic than to any other,
and a lot of the follow-up feedback was correspondingly concerned
with the business of finding and keeping jobs.
During the longer courses a number of men set themselves the
target of actually finding work before leaving prison and on some
courses a high proportion of the members was successful in securing
offers of jobs to go out to. On shorter courses there was not

usually enough time to pursue applications to any kind of conclusion, but most men felt confident that they could get a job without
too much difficulty. One or two found work without any effort whatsoever, e.g.: 'I phoned for a taxi home and the owner recognised my
name and picked me up himself. He asked me if I wanted work and we
arranged that I should start work the next night. I have since been
working very hard but am really enjoying the work.' Or the man who
said that he had decided 'to have a week at home, but on the Wednes-
day an employer came to see me whose driver had let him down and
asked me to start immediately, which pleased the wife no end.'
Cases where men found work with previous employers were quite frequent and it may be a good strategy for men with reasonable previous
work records to try former employers as a matter of course.

There were also those who were less motivated to look for work in
the first place: 'Well Bill, I must be honest with you, I have not
looked for a job at all.' But another man found a degree of motivation which he had not had for a long time: 'Well, when I come out
of prison I went looking for a job but I could not get one as I had
been out of work since 1965; but on 15 January 1978 I was walking
past a firm where I had worked in 1965, so out of the blue I just
went in and now I am working after all this time on the dole. As
thirteen years on the dole is a long time and if any of the lads
think that dole is better than work then they can keep it, as all
I want is to work for my family.'

In other cases however, motivation was not enough, and jobs were
scarce: 'I did have a slight problem at first in finding work but
I feel that this was due to Christmas being so near at hand at the
time of my release.' 'I have been busy looking for a job and I
still can't find one so till I get one I am doing people's gardens
for them.'

When there are vacancies available the ex-prisoner is immediately
confronted with a fundamental dilemma: should he reveal his criminal record and his recent imprisonment to the prospective employer
or should he attempt to conceal it? Many hours of course time were
given over to discussion of this perennial chestnut, to which, of
course, there is no easy answer. Sometimes it pays a man to conceal where he has been, sometimes he pays for such deception by
losing a job he is doing perfectly well: 'I had a job in a hotel
for a few weeks but they checked up and found out that I had a
criminal record, so they sacked me on the spot.' How this employer
found out about this man's criminal record is an interesting question. There is no official way in which a criminal record can be
divulged to employers by police or court officials, but ex-prisoners
refer so often to occasions when this is what appears to have happened that it must be assumed to be true. One man who found work as
a salesman with a firm which knew of his criminal record reported
that whilst driving a car belonging to his boss, he was stopped by
the police for a traffic infringement. At first he was interviewed
politely enough by the patrolmen, but when they checked his name
with Criminal Records and it came back positive, he was, he says,
abruptly ordered, 'Out the fucking car', and a call was made to his
employer to tell him of his employee's criminal record.

In other cases it is not the police who are guilty of divulging
people's pasts to employers: 'I got myself a part-time job at night

to earn extra money to keep my business going, but an anonymous girl phoned up and told them that I had been to prison, so I was dismissed.'

An alternative strategy is to tell prospective employers immediately about convictions so that complications of this sort cannot possibly arise, but this is not always a good way of actually getting a job in the first place: 'I have gone to them being straight, and telling them that I have been in prison but I don't think that is why I got knocked back - at least some of them were willing to give me a chance, but two of them nearly blew a fuse when I told them - anybody would think I was Jack the Ripper.' 'The main difficulty in obtaining work is due to the fact that I have a prison record and quite a few firms who have found this out have not bothered to reply to application letters. In fact I have found it more helpful not to tell employers.'

As might be expected, it is the technically skilled and the verbally confident who have least difficulty in finding work. 'One of the biggest surprises is that employers in this area don't seem to be bothered about the fact that I have only just come out of prison. They are more bothered about the fact that I am a fully skilled toolmaker.'

It is difficult in most of these instances, and in others not recorded here, to say whether the experience of the release course was directly helpful when men were looking for jobs. In some, where employers had offered men their old jobs back there was clearly no effect; but some men do refer directly to the course as a factor in finding work. 'Have found employment at my first attempt. I found the interview situations that were used on the course gave me added confidence. By the way I decided not to tell them I'd just come out of prison, so I'll just have to keep my fingers crossed; I told them I'd been in South Africa.' And eighteen months after his release from one of the prisons, one of the Ranby Course 4 members wrote to the course officers on the headed notepaper of a leisure firm saying, 'I am now the manager of this establishment and I owe that to you both and the release course in giving me confidence in myself.'

One of the aims of the job search part of the programme at both prisons was to enable men to look at a wider range of occupations than would ordinarily occur to them, and to help them where appropriate to seek out and secure training for new kinds of work. A considerable proportion of the men at both Ranby and Ashwell scored high on the people/welfare dimension of the Connolly Occupational Interests Questionnaire and some of them took seriously the idea that they could have talents in social work rather than the manual or technical trades they had pursued hitherto. The transition between the two is far from easy, the most direct way being via a New Careerist post. Two or three men applied for such jobs at the Barbican centre, a day centre run by the probation service in Gloucester, and the New Careers project in Bristol, but none was successful: 'I heard from that New Careers project today and got a knock-back, which I was half expecting to be honest.'

One man did write to the course officers to say that he had found work in a residential establishment for young offenders and that he proposed to organise a release course for the boys there before they left. When researchers rang the establishment to offer help in this exciting venture, it transpired that the man had briefly held a post there as a gardener and then left under some sort of cloud. But his mind was clearly on higher things.

The jobs, or to be more accurate the titles of the jobs, reportedly obtained by course graduates are listed in Table 8.2; some of these were pursued by more than one man, some by one only.

TABLE 8.2

Ranby	Ashwell
Painting and decorating	Kitchen porter
Assistant garage manager	Bricklayer
Barman	Labourer
Driver	Cook
Toolsetter	Sales manager
Factory floor inspector	Carpenter
Steelworker	Foundry work
Labourer	Pigman
Hotel chef	Car seat maker
Upholsterer	Driver
Stock controller	Sewing machine mechanic
Die caster	Country park worker
Scaffolder	Catering
TV Sales and Rentals	Clerk
Cone grinder	Hosiery technician
Foundry work	Factory work
Window cleaner	Machine operator
Paint sprayer	Forester
Welder	Doorman
Dyer	Plasterer
Plant hire	Taxi driver
Night porter	
Miner	
Stone dressing	

These titles cannot be compared in any useful way with the known jobs of course members before their prison sentences because of the vagueness of many of the jobs they describe, and also because we can only speak of the experience of men who kept in contact with the project. The numbers from each course keeping in touch, and the

numbers of those who reported successfully finding work shortly
after their release are recorded in Table 8.3.

TABLE 8.3

Course	Ranby		Ashwell	
Course no.	No. in contact	No. finding job quickly	No. in contact	No. finding job quickly
1	9	7	6	5
2	7	5	9	9
3	-	-	5	5
4	7	6	8	5
5	5	3	7	5
6	6	5	9	6
7	8	3	5	3
Total	42	29 (68%)	49	38 (77%)

It is possible that having good news to report about finding work
may be one of the factors which distinguishes men who keep in touch
from those who do not, but the proportions finding work quickly
amongst those who did report on their progress was encouragingly
high.

Social security
After work, it is the difficulty of negotiating social security payments which dominates the reports of some course graduates. Some of
these are abusive, e.g. 'Social Security are a pain in the brain',
or 'Social Security have led me up the garden path - they are a pack
of liars. They promise the moon and never make good.' Others refer
to specific difficulties, e.g. 'The Social Security wouldn't give me
an appointment until Friday.' 'SS said they would send someone to
see me within a few days but they haven't been to see yet.' 'Humil-
iation caused by SS insensitivity to private details, e.g. mention
of prison and general inquiry into what, where and why.' 'Waited
three and a half hours at the SS (on 14 October) to be told they
couldn't find my file.' A more common complaint was about the absence of money altogether, or the smallness of the grant received:
'Social Security - they say you can get this and that. No way. A
lot of what they say is just propaganda. I've just got a week's
money - £7.62 - yes, for a week.' 'They expect me to live on £9.70
a week, so I am in the middle of a big argument with them.' 'Was
very upset with Social Security stopping wife's payments on day of
release. I had to spend two hours in office on morning of release.'
'Social Security refused to pay anything to myself or wife and
child.'
One man solved his cash problem in a time honoured way: 'Have
had to pawn my two rings to get over this week.'
But being without cash is something that naturally turns the

thoughts of many ex-prisoners to illicit ways of getting their hands on some: 'Received not one penny from the social and if I wasn't in a good position as regards money I would definitely have to obtain cash in some way.' Or another: 'I've thought of stealing for a living.'

And in the face of frustrations like these, tempers sometimes began to fray: 'Blowed my top at the SS because I tried it the sweet way first but no good.' Another man persevered with better results: 'SS gave me a mixed reception; my first visit ended in my walking out. My wife tells me it was my belligerent attitude which caused the officials to refuse my demands. Went back two days later feeling much better owing to my accommodation problem being resolved, was very polite and got complete satisfaction.'

Requests for discretionary grants for clothing and other purposes also met with mixed fortunes. Some were refused point blank: 'I went to the Social Security and asked for a clothing grant but it seems I haven't received that either.' Some were more successful: 'SS pay me £17.10 a week (£13 rent) and they've just granted me £37 for a clothing grant.' 'Saw Social Security by appointment; received voucher for clothing.' One course member visited his local benefits office armed with a list provided by a Child Poverty Action Group lecturer on his course. 'When I showed it to the bloke behind the desk, the poor bugger looked sick,' he said. He came away with £140 worth of discretionary benefits.

It should also be recorded that one man had a good experience at the Supplementary Benefits Office: 'I have also been to Social Security where I found all concerned most helpful.' But when men mention the DHSS in their follow-up forms, letters and statements, it is, as often as not, to complain about them and to ask, as this man does, for more information concerning his rights: 'Well I went to the Social Security and I have had no luck with them. They give you nothing to live on. I wish I knew more about my rights about the SS; not only how much money I will get, but so I am told there is a lot more that I am entitled to.' After 'longer courses', 'more on Social Security benefits' is the most frequently suggested improvement made by ex-course members. Another suggestion made by one or two men for getting a better service from Supplementary Benefits was to ask the local probation officer to intervene, and the researchers also stumbled upon an effective but little known method for stimulating the system into rapid action.

Some months after his release one ex-course member in Nottingham was unemployed and drawing supplementary benefits which were suddenly stopped without explanation. He was summoned to appear at a central office for interview several days later, which in certain circumstances could have been fatal to his hitherto good intentions. He described this difficulty to members of the research team who decided to follow him to the DHSS in order to make a video film of his efforts to have the grant restored. The presence of video equipment on the pavement outside the office provoked a visit from the deputy manager who said that he would close the office down and call the police if any attempt were made to bring the camera into the building. The man himself was ushered into the manager's office and told that a mistake had been made, and he was paid before leaving the office.

Accommodation

Of the men who were polled about their release problems, 44 per cent
said that they anticipated some kind of problem with accommodation
when they left prison. Quite a lot of course time and effort was
therefore given over to the subject. 'Problems pretty much as anticipated, primarily accommodation. Answer lay with the Citizens'
Advice Bureau. They could not have been more helpful, or successful,
and were completely non-patronising, a thing I hate. Bottom of the
list were the probation service who clucked and cooed, but did precisely nix.' Another was equally successful in the search for a
suitable place to live: 'I have found myself a lovely home with a
friend. It was very worrying at first. I had to stay with my
girlfriend's parents for the first two nights. However, everything
has turned out well on the accommodation side.' It appeared to
have turned out well for many other men too because four out of
five of those who remained in contact after release said that they
had had no problem with accommodation. And of the remainder the
most typical complaint seems to be the high price of reasonable
flats: 'I am still looking for a place of my own, but the only
places that looked habitable cost £20 per week so I can only hope
that I will be able to get a break.'

The fact that so few of the follow-up forms mention housing as
a problem may reflect a genuine lack of difficulty, or more probably that the men who are single and homeless are much less
likely to keep in touch than their more settled colleagues.

Drink

Despite its lowly ranking in the problem survey results, drink
was the most frequently mentioned difficulty in the follow-up
material. It is not necessarily on that account the most serious
of the problems faced by former course members, but the gap between
the two figures indicates that more attention could profitably be
paid to the topic during pre-release preparation in prison. We
have seen that the first day's programme for a number of men consisted of drinking with all and sundry in celebration of their new-
found freedom. For some men this was merely an enjoyable interlude
before the real business of re-integration began. For others it was
the beginning of a regular pattern, perhaps even the resumption of a
cycle which might lead directly back to prison: 'Got pissed on four
pints.' 'I'm drinking every chance I get a few quid.' Several
other men clearly saw their drinking behaviour as something over
which they wished to establish a greater degree of control and their
letters and forms refer to efforts in this direction, sometimes successful, sometimes less so: 'Cut down on drink.' 'Haven't been
getting drunk.' 'I'm still drinking but not to the extent as
before. I find I can drink more socially now, and having a really
nice bird has certainly helped.' 'I'm not working at the moment,
but I'm off the drink. I don't mean that I don't drink at all because I do, but not half as much as before.'

Occasionally, failure was costly: 'Got done for drunk and disorderly. £10 fine for singing outside my own house.' 'Got drunk
one night just after my release and then broke my leg.'

As with all this evaluative data, it is not possible to make
simple, causal connections between a man's having completed a re-

lease course and his subsequent behaviour. If someone says he is not drinking as much as before, is that simply his perception? A way of saying pleasing things to project staff? Or is it real? And if it is, how has it come about? There is no way of answering these and similar questions in any convincing way for any individual. All it is possible to do is to lay as many of these individual cases alongside each other as possible, and to permit the reader to draw his or her own conclusions. We have assumed that when men refer to changes in their drinking behaviour they are implying that they have achieved a greater measure of control over it in part because of the activities they engaged in during release courses. Here is one man who makes the connection explicitly: 'As you know I had a bad drinking problem. Well on Saturday I learned that my mother had died whilst I was inside and I was very upset and greatly shocked. So I immediately turned to the drink for some sort of comfort. You can imagine how I felt at the time, very depressed and in rather a dangerous mood. I went out to the pub with the intention of getting completely drunk and intending to harm someone else for the loss that I suffered. Well, through my own willpower and what the re-lease course on "knowing myself" taught me, I was able to walk out of the pub completely sober and looking at things from another angle.'

It would be presumptuous, however, to suggest that release cour-ses have turned out to be any more successful with the general prob-lem of alcoholism than any other approach, a point which is well il-lustrated in the following case history of Pete K.

Pete, 33, was serving his tenth prison sentence, eighteen months for stealing a bottle of whisky from a supermarket. He thought the sentence severe in view of a preceding period of four trouble-free years, when he had been living with a woman and doing part-time work as a probation volunteer. He was separated from his wife and two children. He left school at 16 and had held a variety of jobs, labouring, machine work, clerking. Some of these jobs he lost through drinking and for a time he only worked as a barman. In 1965 he spent twelve weeks in an Alcoholic Addiction Unit. He came on the course to see if it would help him to settle down and to break his drink habit which he was already tackling through attendance at meetings of Alcoholics Anonymous in the prison. He quickly emerged as an outstanding course member: intelligent, perceptive, and re-sponsive, but not uncritical of the course and the way it was being run. And he had some constructive suggestions about how it could be improved. In one of his weekly evaluations he said: 'Since coming on the course I die at 4.30 each day until 9 a.m. the next day.'

In fact, far from dying in the evening, he ran informal sessions in his billet, repeating the course content of the day for his fellow inmates. He also put together a brief programme on alcohol problems and presented it to the release course. He scored high on people/persuasive and clerical/computational on the Connolly Occupa-tional Interests Questionnaire and after some abortive attempts to find a job in residential work or social work he was accepted by a Further Education college to take a course on wages structure and industrial relations. During the release course he taught himself to type in preparation for this. In their end-of-course comments the officers described the assets he might offer to an employer as

follows: 'Intelligent, versatile, quick-thinking, excellent worker,
dependable, good appearance, gets on well with workmates, fair
typist, willing to learn, speaks well, neat at writing and figures.'
   Pete's own summary of the course was: 'A combination of AA
meetings plus the release course and self-awareness have given me
200 per cent more hope than pre-course days, which if you know my
past is MAGIC.'
   The magic, alas, did not last very long:

Ranby Release Course 1
'After the course was over'
A commentary by Peter K.

Leaving any prison is always a traumatic experience and one
really never gets used to it.
   Before I left my last prison I had been fortunate enough to
be accepted on a full time pre-release course which was run on
an experimental basis by the Industrial Training and Research
Unit based at a Cambridge office.
   The course was conducted at the prison by trained prison staff
and a visiting psychologist. The twelve men selected would work
as a team in a mainly classroom situation. I showed great promise and indeed felt it was helping me a great deal. I began to
dwell less on the past and looked forward to a better future.
   My future, I felt, was assured by a promise of a place on a
Government training course (wages structures and industrial re-
lations) at a Nottingham college. I attended the course but as
a result of the events to follow I was to regret ever even
leaving the prison camp!
   My first day out of prison is a typical well-known pattern.
On my person I had £20.10 and booked into the Musters Hotel,
Nottingham, until the Friday, £18.40 Bed, Breakfast and E. Meal.
   As I didn't have to attend the college for thirteen days I
didn't really know what I was going to do. It was then the
Easter holidays, so I went for long country walks arriving back
at the Hotel and going to bed. On the Friday of that same week
I became aware of the reality of my situation. I approached the
manager of the hotel and explained my dilemma. He was sympathetic - but sorry he couldn't help. Hotel policy, etc. Despite
my offer to work, he still said no. So much for honesty, I
thought.
   For many months a friend whom I had known in Leicester prison
had been writing to me at Ranby and had on many occasions said I
could come and share his flat. I was reluctant to do this as he
was currently having a homosexual affair with another guy and I
would have felt embarrassed. Despite my respect for him I found
the prospect rather distasteful.
   On the Saturday I was forced to contact him in the club where
he works. He was delighted to hear from me and invited me to
dinner that evening. He had a large room which he and Stephen
shared and a small kitchen and he had obtained a spare mattress
in anticipation of my calling there - so I slept on the floor.
It was an intolerable situation which began to play on my
nerves. I have always been the sort of person to grin and bear

it, so I had to accept it as it was though I often felt that
drunk it wouldn't have mattered - but I had resolved not to go
back to my old ways of thinking.

One of my other bad points is that I find it pretty difficult
to ask people for money and it was my reluctance to do this that
led to things going so desperately wrong in the week that followed.

1   My expenses to the college were £1.60 per day.
2   My friend had given up his room and moved back to Derby.
3   I found it difficult to get to MOSS as it was a crammed course
    and they frowned on bad timekeepers.

So this left me in a pretty bad state.   I was homeless, money-
less, and bloody hungry.   For two days I attended the college
with no food inside me and nowhere to sleep.   Eventually I got
contact with the P.O. Services in Derby Road, Mansfield, who said
they knew of an address I could stay at, but felt they didn't
know enough about me to give me some money for a meal as they had
been instructed not to help transients financially.

I took the next day off from college to go to the DHSS who
gave me a voucher and £2.20 to stay at the probation address.
Never in all my life had I been to a more cheerless, scruffy and
depressing place.   My suspicions about its hygiene were confirmed
the next day when I discovered a type of lice in my pubic hair
(known as the crabs).   Then to top it all my glasses fell off on
the way to college and, as I've worn them for more than 26 years,
I was like a man who had suddenly lost his legs, without them, my
glasses, I am as blind as a bat!   One of the worst experiences
I've ever had has been in this prison in my cell not being able
to read.   Even large print is beyond me.

On the morning that I broke my glasses I was as depressed as
a man could possibly be.   I asked an optician to fix them but the
mercenary bastard wouldn't unless I layed bread on him.

Well I just started walking and hitching not really caring
where I ended up.   I found myself in London on a bleak cold
morning, dirty and unshaven with my only possessions on my back -
which wasn't much - and about 90p in my pocket.   On the second
day in London and after having slept rough I lay on the grass
outside a church complete exhausted, my feet blistered and lacer-
ated, the hunger grinding acid in my guts.

When I awoke, my shoes had disappeared.

Imagine how I felt.   I just felt like curling up and dying.   I
went to see the rector.   His wife said he was out.   I showed her
my feet and explained about my shoes, my bad experience.   She
replied, 'Oh yes, I know.   One of our chaps had his brief case
stolen on the tube.'   She told me to go to the Methodist church
2 miles away.   'They,' she said, 'will help you.'

The police said the same, only this time they directed me to
a hostel five miles further on.   This went on for two days, getting sent from one place to another.   Nobody really caring what
the result was - I often prayed that I would meet a Trueman and
his policy 'THE BUCK STOPS HERE'.

I headed out of the city of apathy.   Before going I phoned the
central probation office in 1a Frederick Street.   After spending
my last 10p on a phone call I was told to go to the Borough High

Street. This seemed daft to me as I gave the YMCA address which
was just a short way from la Frederick Street. The conclusion I
came to was that if you are NFA you are not entitled to any of
your civil rights or benefits. Even the P & AC Service didn't
want to know you. After my experience in London and Brighton,
not to mention Nottingham, I will never again see the Probation
Service in a good light. Of all the people I expected to see
hypocrisy from they were furthest from my mind. They proved me
utterly wrong.

Anyone reading this would assume that I was on the make when
I called to see the POs in the various towns. Indeed this was
the impression I got - they were always on the defensive making
sure I knew in advance that I would not receive any material help
or help in finding an address. Not once did I come across anyone
kind enough to listen without suspicions and impatient glances at
their watches. I left their offices as I came in - depressed,
confused and on the verge of tears, indeed, suicide.

On the second day in Brighton I tried to kill myself. All I
did was make myself very ill. The last straw was when I called
at the Brighton office of the Probation Service and the officer
there told me frankly he didn't believe a word I said - that he
had a friend who was an alcoholic and he had said we were all
liars. I had not had a drink for eighteen months. After a short
time he cut our talk off, making it clear he wouldn't have much
time after. Rather than be humiliated any more, I left.

Had the people in Brighton, like London, become so hardened
and callous that they didn't trust anyone any more? All they
had to do was pick up the phone and confirm my story with the
release officers at Ranby.

Peter's saga came to an end under the Brighton pier where he
drank cocktails of surgical spirits and orange juice. He was ar-
rested for shoplifting and given a suspended sentence. The following week he was re-arrested for a similar offence and sent to prison
for eighteen months after just three and a half months at liberty.

No firm conclusions can be drawn on the basis of so few cases and
such anecdotal accounts but it does appear that at least some parts
of the course approach have helped some men to do something about
their drinking, or at least to feel that they are doing something
about it, and that a more comprehensive 'drink' programme could be
developed and tested more systematically with populations of self-
confessed problem drinkers.

Getting on with other people
During the courses themselves it was a noticeable feature of the
weekly and final evaluations, both written and on videotape, that
men referred to a growing appreciation of the problems of other
people, and in some cases, to increased confidence in handling contacts with them. 'Other people' is a very large category and for
most men, the most difficult, although sometimes also the most
rewarding relationships they have are those with wives and children,
or with girlfriends. Sometimes these were effortlessly resumed
after release: 'Everything at home has worked out just fine and I
have a good relationship with my wife and children so I'm very

happy.' Others though, found it less easy: 'Spending a lot of time with my children trying hard to make up for lost time.' 'I've spent a lot of time gardening but basically I have endeavoured to convince my wife that I have reached the end of the road as far as criminal activity is concerned.' And one man who had spent longer than most other course members in prison described the problem like this: 'I took for granted that my wife and children would act and accept me as though nothing had happened. One needs to realise, particularly after a long period that one has to accept you are a stranger to your wife and family. You must re-court your wife and adjust with your children, not take it for granted they will accept you. I wonder how often children wonder who the strange man is sharing mummy's bed.'

Yet other men found that their relationships with women had deteriorated beyond all hope of repair: 'I am trying to get things sorted out with my girlfriend at the moment because when I came out she told me that she didn't want me any more. It was a great shock to me and it still hurts.' This man told us that he had stood in the garden of the house where his girl was now living with another man and had thrown stones through all the windows to register his disapproval. The police were called, but as they often do in matters they deem to be 'domestic', went away again without taking action against him.

Perhaps the saddest cases were those involving separated or divorced couples who were in dispute over access to children. One man wrote back to say that his biggest difficulty in the outside world was 'not knowing where my daughter is'. And several men in similar positions asked that more time on future courses be allocated to this problem area.

In some cases, however, getting started with a woman seemed to be the problem rather than managing effectively the ends of affairs and relationships: 'I am still having fun, but have not found a woman friend yet; will try to find one,' wrote one young ex-prisoner on one of his follow-up forms. Another former course member was quicker off the mark; the week after his release he and a friend picked up two girl hitch-hikers with whom they spent the night in a hotel. Unfortunately the girls turned out to have escaped from a women's prison and both the men were subsequently charged with aiding and abetting their escape.

On a less dramatic note there were continuing claims of improvement in the ability to get on with other people in a variety of situations: 'Relationships at home improved.' 'Getting on better with parents.' 'I get along with people more freely.' 'Have got on better with people.' 'I am living at home and thanks to the release course I am not as shy as I was. I go out more and I enjoy myself dancing.'

The police

Handling contacts with policemen is a special category of getting on with other people which affects a proportion of men who have recently left prison. The case of the salesman and the rude policeman has already been recounted, but he was not the only ex-course member to encounter such problems with the constabulary: 'Owing to the train being so dear I decided to hitch! Before I even reached the motorway I was stopped by Nottingham CID and they were bolshy: made me open my case in the middle of the street and generally wanted to know all my business. As I wasn't sure if I could tell them to get stuffed I had to get everything out and repack. I helped them as I thought fit to although I was really fuming at their attitude.' This man anticipating precisely this kind of encounter had spent some time during the release course rehearsing alternative ways of coping with police 'harassment'. He had not foreseen the exact nature of what transpired but he said afterwards that making video films of role-play incidents involving less than civil policemen had helped him to control his temper when it happened for real.

Violence

Incidents of potentially violent behaviour towards other people do not occur more than once or twice in the follow-up material but there is one man who claimed that his attendance on a two-week course had had a profound effect on his life.

Alan B. is 30 years old, but looks older. He is married, but has no children. He has fifteen previous convictions, most of them for violence, and has been in approved school and detention centre, and in prison four times, including a sentence of five years for battering his wife into unconsciousness. Prior to his present sentence he had been undergoing psychiatric treatment. The officers running the course for which he applied were reluctant to accept him as a member because of his reputation and because they feared he would disrupt the group. To begin with his behaviour in the group fulfilled their worst fears, but it was the other group members who took him to task about this and who made it clear to him that he was not only bad-tempered and violent but thoroughly un-likeable as a person as well. These plainspeaking comments had a profound effect on Alan who later said about the experience: 'I've been turned inside out. That's how I look on it now. I looked at myself for what I am. And I don't like what I see.' As the course progressed his outbursts of temper in group discussions decreased in frequency and virulence and his changed behaviour was noticed throughout the prison by both staff and prisoners. At the end of the two-week course, during which Alan took a particular interest in the parts of the programme devoted to violence, he wrote to one of the officers: 'Not only has this course taught me a lot about myself, but it has taught me how to understand other people and their problems. I now understand my own problems and how to deal with them and no way without this course could I have ever got any-where near the help and advice I have received. If a course of this kind had been set up on one of my earlier sentences, I honestly believe in my own mind that I would not have the record I have today.'

A cynic might say that whatever happened during the course could not be translated into changed behaviour after release, but at the second follow-up meeting which took place several weeks after his discharge, Alan made a long personal statement on video film in which he said: 'I've got a reputation. But if anybody wants my reputation I'll sign it over to them. I'd never walk away from any kind of trouble. I've been in two bits of trouble and I've walked away. I'm fighting a lot of people out here legally - I'm not hit-

ting them.' He obviously thought that because of the course he is
better able to defuse situations in which he would previously have
resorted to violent behaviour. He was still of the same opinion
when he was last heard from, some nine months after his release,
and up to August 1978 - the time that data from the CRO was available - had not been reconvicted.

Solving problems

Social skills training aims to equip people with the ability to
solve some of their problems more effectively. There was evidence
from evaluations of courses that some at least of their members
were beginning to feel more confident about doing this. The real
test of what they had learned, however, lay in what happened after
their release. Testimony from the follow-up material suggests that
permanent gains had been made in some cases: 'It showed me how to
handle situations better.' 'I feel better equipped to manage problems.' And even more explicitly: 'I think now before I act.
Before, I just used to react and worry about the consequences when
it was too late. I don't think I am as selfish as I was. I think
about others as well - the course helped me to do that.' 'I try to
work things out through proper channels instead of working on impulse.'

For other men there was only a fine line dividing the idea of
acting rationally and lapsing into violence: 'It's helped me to
stop and think before acting rashly.' 'It taught me to work out
what was for the best without becoming ill-tempered or depressed.'
'It made me think before I do anything and to bite my tongue before
I lose my temper.'

One man wrote to an officer, offering this advice for current
course members: 'Take your time and plan your moves if things get
desperate. STOP, THINK, LIST YOUR ALTERNATIVES and then ACT.'

And others saw even larger benefits: 'It has helped me to have
a purpose in life instead of living from day to day.'

The course files which many men took with them on release also
proved to be useful aids in problem-solving: 'Things have been far
from easy as we all knew they would be, but remembering the discussions we all had together and the situations that we enacted that
were of a similar nature to my recent experiences, you were with me
all the time. I often read through my file and by doing so I can
hear your own solutions to the same problems.' Another man used
his course file as a substitute for drink, retiring to his room and
reading it at times when he would otherwise have taken to the
bottle.

Table 8.4 shows the percentage reconviction rates for the three
groups at each prison, i.e. course members, unsuccessful applicants
and non-applicants. The figures in parentheses show the sizes of
each sample.

RECIDIVISM

Finally, the Criminal Records Office files were examined between
December 1977 and August 1978 to obtain information on reconvictions
for all the men in the study. The results were analysed in a number
of ways.

TABLE 8.4   Percentage reconviction rates to August 1978

Prison	Course members	Unsuccessful applicants	Non-applicants
Ashwell	23.0 (87)	31.4 (35)	26.3 (99)
Ranby	42.1 (114)	30.6 (36)	45.9 (98)

The simple reconviction rates show no significant differences between the groups. However, they only indicate the proportion of men
who were reconvicted up to August 1978 and they take no account of
the differences in release dates and reconviction dates. Men from
the first courses were released from April 1976 onwards and those in
the last courses studied were not released until December 1977.

One way of allowing for these time differences is to compare the
amount of 'crime free' time between each reconvicted man's release
date and his subsequent reconviction date to see whether one group
tends to stay relatively 'crime free' for a longer period than any
other group. Table 8.5 shows the mean time to reconviction for each
group of reconvicted men.

TABLE 8.5   Mean time to reconviction (months)

Prison	Course members	Unsuccessful applicants	Non-applicants
Ashwell	9.90 (20)	5.36 (11)	8.40 (25)
Ranby	7.40 (47)	6.64 (11)	8.09 (45)

The figures in parentheses show the numbers reconvicted.

The results show a similar picture to the previous table. Ashwell members appear to do slightly better than unsuccessful applicants and non-applicants, and Ranby members do slightly better than
non-applicants, but worse than unsuccessful applicants. The Ashwell
result does achieve statistical significance ($U = 59$, $p = < .025$),
but this is not true of the overall result so no simple benefit can
be claimed for release courses on either a straight reconviction
count or an average time to reconviction.

One further way of looking at the reconviction rates is to plot
the percentage reconvictions against time. Figure 8.1 shows this
plot and again no clear result emerges.

Proportionately fewer Ashwell course members were reconvicted
compared with other groups and this is most marked from six months
after release. Ranby course members were reconvicted at a similar
rate to non-applicants with a slight divergence after eighteen
months, but fewer unsuccessful applicants were reconvicted from
seven months onwards.

The pattern of reconvictions is similar to the one obtained by
Shaw (1974) in her study of the effects of extended contact between
offenders and welfare officers in Ashwell and Gartree. (1) However,

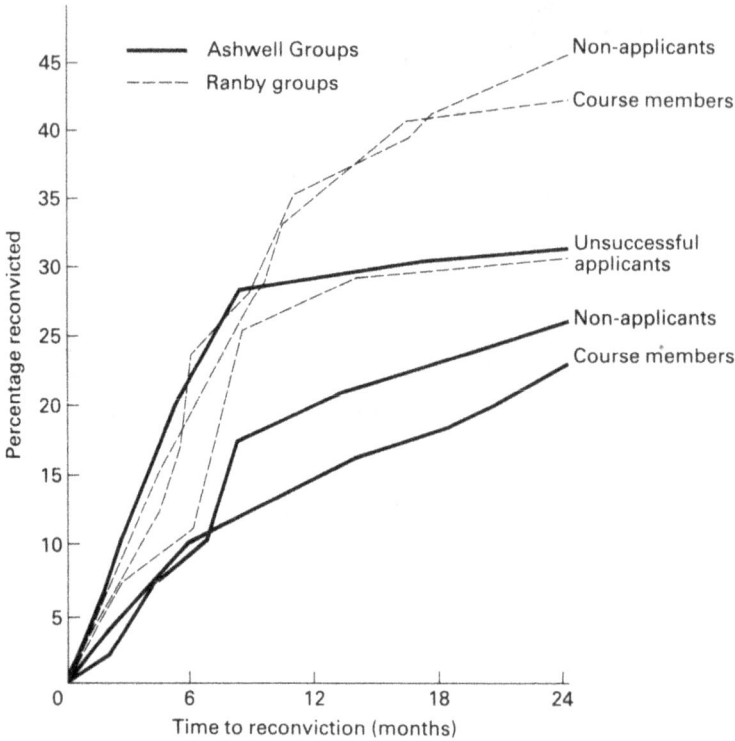

Figure 8.1   Percentage of group reconvicted over time

she obtained much higher proportions of reconviction within two
years after release and was able to demonstrate clear differences
between experimental and control groups (reconviction rates of 57
per cent and 76 per cent respectively).

It could be argued that the effects of social work interventions,
especially those involving uniformed prison officers, may be comparatively long-term in nature - you can't change the habits of a
lifetime overnight - so measures of a single reconviction are no
real indication of success or failure. This point will be answered
by looking at the proportion of men who were reconvicted to see how
many re-offended a second time. Table 8.6 shows these proportions
with sample sizes in parentheses.

TABLE 8.6   Proportion of reconvicted men who re-offended a second
time

Prison	Course members	Unsuccessful applicants	Non-applicants
Ashwell	30.0 (20)	72.7 (11)	28.0 (25)
Ranby	31.3 (48)	27.3 (11)	37.8 (45)

These results also show no clear differences between the groups
except that a much larger proportion of unsuccessful applicants at
Ashwell were reconvicted a second time, compared with other groups.
The sample sizes are inevitably small since we are only looking at
men who were reconvicted. So no clear conclusions can be drawn from
this comparison, one way or the other. Overall, the Ashwell course
members appear to have gained some benefits from attending a release
course, which are partly reflected in the reconviction rates, but no
similar benefits can be claimed for the Ranby groups.

Types of offences

A further question worth considering is whether there was any change
in the pattern of offences committed by men who attended a release
course and were subsequently reconvicted.

The analysis for this could only be done in a fairly crude way,
since there were a large number of different offences committed by
a relatively small number of men, especially in the Ashwell groups.
A comparison was made between the previous offence type (i.e. those
committed immediately before the study) and the current offence
type (those committed after release) for reconvicted men in three
broad groupings: offences involving violence, property offences,
and all other offences. The results of this comparison for course
members and non-applicants at Ranby are shown in Figure 8.2.

The histograms show a large drop in violence offences committed
by course members at Ranby with a corresponding increase in property
offences. There is no similar change in this pattern for non-applicants. These results are statistically significant (X_2 = 13.36,
p = < .01), and since there were no significant
differences between the type of previous offences committed by the
two groups at Ranby, it is likely that this is a real change.

The Ashwell results were examined but, as expected, there were no
differences in reconviction patterns between the groups, because the
proportions were small and offences involving violence are rare
amongst men who served their sentences at Ashwell.

A number of other factors were examined in an attempt to distinguish between the reconvicted groups, but there were no significant differences in biographical details, types of sentence, education and training histories, or employment histories.

The results presented so far in this chapter have been global
ones, treating the total membership of the prison courses as one
group to be compared with non-course members in terms of reconvictions. These can be illustrated more personally by looking at what
subsequently happened to the men who took part in the fourth Ranby
course described in chapter 6. Five of them were reconvicted in
the period from the end of the course in October 1977 and August
1978, a proportion almost identical to that for Ranby course members as a whole. The reconvictions of Ranby course 4 members are
set out in Table 8.7, together with predictions which the course
officers made about some of them at the end of the course.

TABLE 8.7   Reconvictions of Ranby course 4 members

Name	Present offence	Previous con-victions	Prediction	Reconviction
Alec J.	Arson, burglary		Possible return to prison unless selects company with care.	O
Carl W.	Theft	15	Another recidivist.	Theft - 6 mths suspended
Bill E.	Fraud	NK		NK
Roger M.	Robbery	6	The call of the bottle is still very real.	O
Ken D.	Wounding	8		Theft of elec-tricity - fined £10
John K.	Burglary	14		O
Alan T.	Burglary	17	If we got through to him at all it didn't show.	O
Terry Q.	Theft, actual bodily harm	14		O
Bob W.	Assault, poss. drugs	13	99% guaran-teed to return.	O
Kevin P.	Burglary, taking and driving away	13	The most likely to succeed.	Burglary - 3 mths; actual bodily harm - 6 mths imprisonment
Mick S.	Theft, deception	16		O
Neil M.	Burglary	10		Burglary - def. sent.; taking and driving away - fined £85
Buzz B.	Burglary	10		Burglary - fined £50

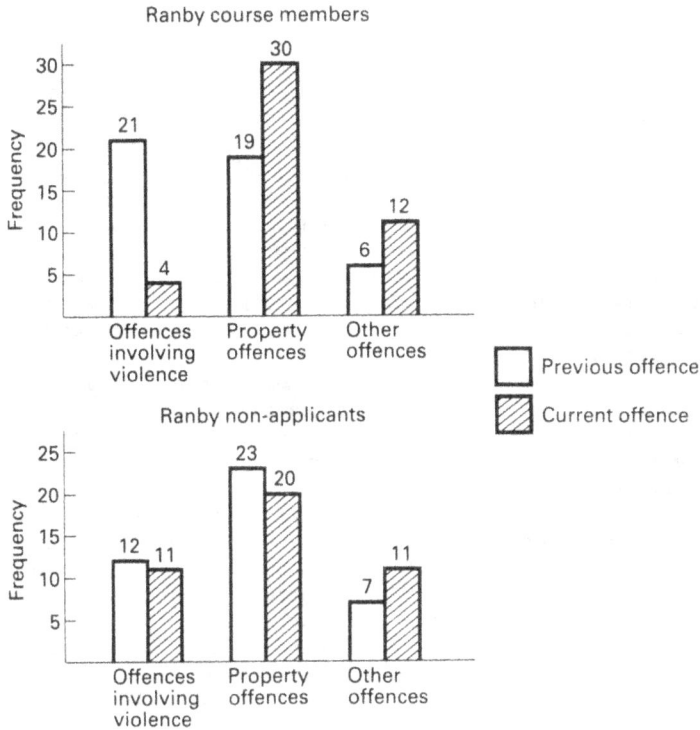

Note: Previous offences were those committed prior to the study. Current offences were those committed after release.

Figure 8.2 Comparison of previous offences with current offences for men at Ranby who were reconvicted

A final note on recidivism

As with most other studies of rehabilitative programmes, the efficacy of release courses cannot be simply demonstrated by a reduction in recidivism. Shaw (1974) (2) did obtain a remarkable reduction in reconviction rates at Ashwell with men who had received extended interviews with welfare officers, but this effect was not replicated in a later study. (3) The efforts of the majority of programmes are best summed up by a quote from Lipton et al.'s (1975) survey: 'With few and isolated exceptions the rehabilitative efforts that have been reported so far have had no appreciable effect on recidivism.' (4) Perhaps we have to turn to less 'hard data' to describe the effects of rehabilitation.

SHEFFIELD

Turning once again to Sheffield, we have already considered the responses of offenders to the course programme while they were still in attendance at the centre. Another source from which men's views on the centre can be gleaned is their recollections several months after their departure. One aspect of this response is whether or not men maintain some kind of contact with the centre on a voluntary basis - usually by paying an informal visit for a chat with members of staff. Savage (1977), in a follow-up study of the first twenty men to attend the day training centre during 1976, (5) reports that eight (40 per cent) of these men made some such contact with the centre after their required attendance was over; since six of the twenty men in her sample did not satisfactorily complete their sixty days (three were sent to prison for further offences, two were breached for non-attendance, and one had his condition of attendance removed), this is in fact a fairly encouraging proportion.

To obtain the views of course members in more depth, a follow-up meeting was organised in December 1977. This took place on a Saturday morning in South Yorkshire Probation's West Bar Day Centre, and was attended by fifteen former course members - just under a quarter of the sixty-four men invited -, by centre staff, and by most men attending the centre at that time. The meeting, which was analogous to those held for members of the release courses in Ranby and Ashwell prisons, consisted primarily of group discussions in which men were asked about the problems they had encountered, about the usefulness to them, viewed retrospectively, of the courses they had completed, about the problems they were facing at the time of the meeting, and about changes they would make in the centre programme in the light of their subsequent experience.

The men who came had attended the centre at widely dispersed intervals over the preceding two years. The commonest problems they had confronted since leaving were with money, and finding and keeping work; several also mentioned drink problems and frequent visits from the police. Five of the fifteen former course members had jobs at the time of the meeting; five had had jobs (in some cases up to four), but were currently unemployed; the remaining five had found no work at all since leaving the centre. In general their views of the centre were positive and echoed those voiced by men during and at the ends of courses; even though some had been stern critics of the programme while themselves in attendance. The patterns of their responses on rating scales included in a questionnaire were as shown.

How confident are you about keeping out of trouble?

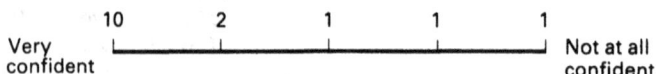

```
           10        2        1        1        1
Very       |_____|_____|_____|_____|  Not at all
confident                                         confident
```

Looking back, how much did you learn while you were at the DTC (1) about yourself?

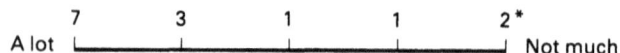

```
           7        3        1        1        2*
A lot      |_____|_____|_____|_____|  Not much
```

(2) about others?

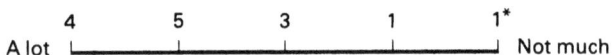

```
     4        5        3        1        1*
A lot └────────┴────────┴────────┴────────┘ Not much
```

* One man failed to complete the second two scales.

The majority of these men at least seem to have gained something of value from the centre - and something which has remained with them for some time after their departure. Obviously it can be said that men with a favourable view of the centre are more likely to attend a meeting of this kind: and therefore that those not present would be less approving in their opinions. However, attendance at a meeting like this - on a Saturday - indeed even stepping inside a probation office when it is not strictly necessary, are not the most natural inclinations of men like these. Placed in this context, their reaction on the whole adds further weight to the views expressed by men while still at the DTC.

Follow-up questionnaire for field probation officers

To find out more about the possible effects of the courses on those who had taken part in them, a short follow-up questionnaire was sent to the probation officers of those men who had attended the centre during 1976-7. Under ideal conditions, course members themselves would have been interviewed individually some time after leaving the centre; however the dispersal of the men and the time limits of the research project made this impracticable. Field officers could in any case provide some of the information that was being sought, and their views on the usefulness of day training to individuals amongst their case-loads are of interest in their own right.

A total of 118 questionnaires were distributed to probation officers who had referred men to the centre during the 1976-7 period. Clearly, staff changes, transfer of cases, and lack of time would ensure that only a proportion were returned; the questionnaire items were confined to one page in an attempt to maximise the response rate. Ninety-four questionnaires, of which eleven were in some way incomplete, were returned, a response rate of fractionally under 80 per cent.

The questionnaire asked first for some information; on whether or not men had been in trouble since leaving the centre, and on work; it then asked officers to identify any improvements they could see in the men; and invited their comments in general on the working of the day training centre.

Only one of the almost sixty different officers who replied said that he would not refer men for day training in future. This was a very positive result in view of the confusion, compounded occasionally by suspicion, surrounding the centre at a number of points in the past.

A primary concern of the field officers' questionnaire was with the kinds and extents of any benefits men might have derived from their sixty days. In response to a question on whether individuals

had benefited from attendance at the centre, the distribution of
answers was as follows:

Yes	63 (67.0%)
No	21 (22.4%)
Don't know/ no reply	10 (10.6%)
(Total = 94)	

Thus, a substantial majority of the officers said that men had
gained in some way, whilst a sizeable number could however detect
no advantage.

Probation officers were requested to expand if possible on the
nature of any changes they could identify. Some simply said the
individual had benefited and left it at that, but amongst the remainder, the comments paralleled and in some cases enlarged upon
evaluations made by course members themselves. Again a very common
type of statement referred to gains in motivation and self-confidence, often linked to other improvements of a more specific kind:

'Mr C. had become apathetic and through the DTC he found the
self-awareness and confidence to get out of his rut.'

'It gave him some confidence and a necessary push to think more
about his future.'

'He has greater levels of self-awareness, more confidence and
broader horizons.'

'It increased his confidence and ability to do things for himself, and be more reasonable about paying rent, electricity, etc.'

'He has increased confidence and ability to express himself.'

But as with the men's own reports, a great many practical and
interpersonal benefits were also pinpointed:

'He now has an ability to communicate which he did not have
before.'

'He felt secure at the DTC, and relaxed ... enjoyed himself and
the release of tension ... it boosted his self-confidence, improved
his reading and writing ... and he got the support he needed to get
out of the rut of unemployment and debts.'

'He benefited by realising that he had control over his life and
actions.'

'T. seems to have been brought to face up to himself in some
important ways. He has come to recognise his need for his wife and
to alter his behaviour in relation to her.'

'It kept him occupied, away from his "questionable" friends, and
controlled his drink problem.'

'He does not react to things not going his way as violently or
impetuously as before.'

'It made him give some thought to his difficulties over the last
ten years and to think of different ways of coping with people in
his trade ... he seems to have a more positive attitude towards
work.'

'He learned that there were various ways of examining problems
and attempting to solve them. Also, he seemed to gain more understanding of himself.'

'It boosted his morale; he enjoyed it. He discovered new
talents and interests and more confidence in relation to other
agencies; he believes probation is now worthwhile.'

'It enabled him to avoid prison for two years - the longest
period of freedom since childhood.'

Even of one man who would normally be considered.a 'failure' - in
that he was sent to prison not long after leaving the centre, a probation officer said: 'During his present sentence he has developed
many extra interests, and uses his time much more positively towards
release.'

Some of the men were regarded as having become remarkable successes by their field probation officers:

'He most certainly benefited, in fact one can but wonder at the
remarkable change in attitude, motivation, work record, and personal
insight.'

'A great success by almost any criteria. R. was a dosser, fast
becoming alcoholic, with gambling problems and little social confidence. He has now almost fully re-established himself.'

'He has been regularly employed since leaving DTC; he changed
jobs once for better pay. He became more approachable, responded
to interest taken in his future, is less anti-authority and more
verbally expressive. He seemed to gain more confidence and developed a sense of responsibility.'

Needless to say, there were criticisms too; some positive comments were tempered by reference to problems:

'DTC gave him a stabilising period which appeared to have a
positive effect. Unfortunately the end of his period at DTC proved
too much of an anti-climax.'

'Mixed benefits. In one sense he enjoyed the discipline of
having to attend and obeying the rules, but on leaving after sixty
days a great gap was left in his life which could not be filled with
anything half as stimulating.'

'The DTC did nothing to provide any motive to change; however it
did provide some social contact and temporary assistance.'

Finally, some officers said merely that men had gained little or
nothing; their comments speak for themselves:

'He seems to have looked upon DTC as a soft option.'

'It got him out of bed before midday while it lasted.'

The preponderance of comment, however, was on the positive side.
In order to build up a slightly more systematic impression of relative gains of different kinds, field officers were also asked to
rate individuals' improvements in a number of pre-selected areas
linked to the aims of the day training centre. These were: self-
confidence, ability to find work, ability to communicate, ability
to solve problems by himself, and relationship with the field probation officer. Improvements in each of these five areas were to
be rated on a simple scale: none - slight - moderate - considerable. Table 8.8 presents the results summed over all the questionnaires; no ratings whatever were available on eleven replies, while
on others particular areas were not rated. The totals available are
given in the right-hand column; percentages of this total are given
in brackets.

A consistent majority of the men for whom ratings are available
were seen as having shown some degree of improvement - in all five
areas under consideration. However, there are evident disparities
in the extent to which the centre was seen as achieving its goals
in the various 'target' areas. The areas in which, according to

TABLE 8.8   Probation officers' ratings of gains made by course members

	None	Slight	Moderate	Consider-able	Total
Self-confidence	18(22.8)	17(21.5)	26(32.9)	18(22.8)	79
Ability to find work	39(48.8)	17(21.2)	12(15.0)	12(15.0)	80
Ability to communicate	18(22.2)	26(32.1)	28(34.6)	9(11.1)	81
Ability to solve his own problems	24(30.4)	27(34.2)	25(31.6)	3 (3.8)	79
Relationship with probation officer	32(41.5)	17(22.1)	22(28.6)	6 (7.8)	77

field officers at least, course members made gains most frequently were those of self-confidence and the ability to communicate, followed by the ability to solve problems, ability to find work, and relationships with field probation officers. These results correspond broadly with the views expressed by course members themselves on ways in which the course had been of use to them, and are evidently associated with aspects of the course content and with working in groups.

Some of these results may be slightly misleading. In relation to the business of finding work, for example, the actual job-getting performance of the men outstripped their apparent ability to find work as perceived by field officers. The questionnaire also asked for details of course members' job histories since leaving the centre. These were then sorted into a number of categories according to the stability of individuals' employment patterns. The categories used were: first, those described as having been in stable employment for all or nearly all of the period since their departure; second, those in casual employment - having had one job or more with short periods of unemployment in between; third, those unemployed for most of their time since completing a course; fourth, those who had spent the largest proportion of this time in prison; fifth, those on whom no information was available. In reading these results it must be borne in mind that - as outlined in chapter 3 - every one of these men had shown great instability in his previous work record, and most had been unemployed for lengthy periods prior to arriving in the day training centre. Table 8.9 lists the numbers and percentages of men falling into each of the above groups.

TABLE 8.9 Job histories following day training

Category	n	%
In stable employment	23	24.5
Casual employment	16	17.0
Predominantly unemployed	33	35.1
Prison	17	18.1
No information	5	5.3
Total	94	100

   The above table simplifies the total picture in that three men
in the 'casual employment' and three in the 'unemployed' groups
suffered from some form of invalidity which made work difficult or
impossible to obtain; two others in the regularly employed group
had had accidents which debarred them from working (one whilst in
a job, his first in two years); another man in this category had
a long history of psychiatric illness and had returned to hospital
soon after leaving the centre; and some of the men in the 'prison'
group had been working prior to their sentences, or had obtained
jobs soon after their release.
   What this table implies, overall, is that there was a shift in
the work patterns of the group as a whole. A quarter of these men
had sustained regular work since leaving - in contrast to the not
unreasonable expectation that none might do so. Ten of the men in
the 'stable' group had been gone from the centre at least nine
months - in some cases up to two years - at the time of the return
of these questionnaires. Some of the jobs and workplaces of ex-
course members are listed in Table 8.10. While some of these describe the work of one man only, others (e.g. labouring) describe
the work of several.
   Though it cannot be said with absolute certainty, it seems likely
that the centre's impact on its course members' job-finding has been
steadily increasing over the years. Of the sixty-seven men leaving
the centre in the year June 1977-June 1978, for example, forty-six
had jobs to go to - a rate of 68.6 per cent or just over two-thirds.
This is impressive by any standards given the work histories of most
men sentenced to day training. A step has been taken towards
solving what, on their own account and also in the judgment of
others, constituted one of the central problems of their lives.

Results in general

What, in summary, seem to be the principal after-effects of day
training at Sheffield? Concerning the results presented in this
chapter, it is possible to identify a number of areas in which the
centre's current manner of working is of benefit both to the centre
and to its course members. According to both themselves and their
probation officers, they make a variety of personal gains: in self-

TABLE 8.10 Jobs obtained by course members

Labourer - in a rolling mill, engineering works, waterworks, public works department, building site, etc.

Handyman in council flats	Cook
New Careerist (temporary ancillary)	Gardener
Engineering inspector	Factory worker
Work on Job Creation projects	Work for the NCB
Self-employed - scrap trade	Coal merchant
Grinder	Warehouseman
Driver	Demolition worker
Work for a cutlery firm	Kitchen porter
Car park attendant	Work at Butlin's
Work in a wholesale butcher's	Work in a bakery
Casual work in a garage	Gravedigger
Crane driver	Barman

---

confidence, in information relating to many aspects of their lives, in skills of problem-solving and communication, and in relation to work. As far as can be ascertained from some men at least, these gains are still recognised as valuable many months after departure from the day training centre. Centre staff too are in agreement about the benefits which accrue to course members, which in their view include:

'a boost to their confidence; becoming generally motivated towards work; becoming more aware of outside agencies they can use to help them with their problems; and most become more articulate. The change in confidence is worthwhile in itself ... and is also a very definite tool.'

'an increase in self-confidence and self-awareness; straight factual information relating to daily life. Real knowledge about their rights which will be of use to them, temporarily or in the long term. A chance to genuinely re-assess their needs and expectations ... and at least the potential for change if they want it. Probably a fresh view of authority or the use of authority. Not a few are getting practical help - on employment capabilities, on a whole range of things; getting jobs, and sticking at them.'

Possibly as a complement to these effects, staff themselves enjoy a number of benefits from working in the way described here. One staff member said he derived

'far more satisfaction than as a field probation officer; moments of elation, moments of despair. I'm reasonably happy.

I didn't get the same extent of that in the field. You get
closer to the guys ... you can't do that when you only see them
for half an hour or so in a month.'

Another staff member described it as:

'the most satisfying way of working I have experienced. It tests
all my skills and abilities and my emotions. It does seem to
have some kind of purpose, achievable targets as its goals - not
castles in the air.'

In addition, therefore, to its usefulness for course members, the
centre's present way of working seems also to be congenial to staff.
   As noted at the outset of this chapter, no firm data are available on the possible effects of centre courses on subsequent re-
offending by course members. Forty-nine of those men on whom
questionnaires were returned had either been convicted of offences
during their period at the centre, were convicted some time after
they left, or were about to appear in court at the time the
questionnaires were returned. No conclusions can be drawn from this
information given the wide variation in intervals since these men
had departed the centre. In any case, as mentioned earlier, 'reducing recidivism' was not a fixed goal of this research and has
been achieved by very few studies in the entire field of penology.
What it may be possible to suggest - comparing the one-year follow-
up data of Payne and Lawton (1977) (6) with data in 'The Sentence
of the Court' (1969) (7), a crude comparison but the only one
available - is that the DTC is probably no worse than prison in
terms of numbers of reconvictions; it may, for all we know, be
better. Decisions about the value of day training should be made
on other grounds - in relation to social and financial cost and
other gains made by offenders.
   Overall, the results that emerged from the Sheffield centre's
'experiment' with new methods of working are similar to those obtained at the prison sites (see Barnitt et al., 1977; (8) Hardwick, 1977; (9) Priestley et al., 1978. (10)). The existence of
methods that are viable in both these settings suggests that they
may have applications elsewhere. This and a number of other questions are discussed in the final chapter which follows.

Chapter 9

Problems and prospects

This project was an ambitious and not too tidy attempt to do something different with offenders. It was different because it asked
prisoners and probationers to define their own problems and then
attempted to assemble a curriculum of activities for helping them
do something constructive about them. The contents of this curriculum were different because they drew on the insights and methods
which have flowed from the 'social skills' perspective in psychology
and education. And in the prison sites, they were combined with determined efforts to undermine the normal pattern of non-cooperation
between prison officers and their prisoners.

The project succeeded in some ways beyond what could reasonably
have been expected when it began; in others it failed disappoint-
ingly. On the credit side:

1 A large quantity of materials and methods was assembled and
   tested and found to be feasible with large numbers of offenders
   in prison and the community.
2 A problem-solving framework was evolved which makes possible the
   translation of these methods to other kinds of people and their
   problems.
3 Many of the participating offenders reported a wide range of
   personal gains, some of them confirmed by external observers -
   the subsequent employment records of Sheffield day training
   centre men, for example.
4 Some uniformed prison officers proved to be not merely capable
   of, but extremely good at running social skills based courses.
5 Some of the course members released from Ranby appeared to be
   less prone to violent re-offending.

On the debit side, we were unable to gather any evidence that the
work reported here produced any perceptible changes in the overall
reconviction rates of the offenders who took part in the project.

Outstanding items from this balance sheet will be considered
in this last chapter under the headings of materials, course
members, and staff, and some suggestions will be made about
future developments.

MATERIALS

The project began as a search for ways of working with offenders
which would meet a number of criteria:
1 that they should be addressed to problems which offenders themselves acknowledged and wished to tackle;
2 that they should be plausible and attractive to members of the
   target groups, and able to sustain their interest and attention
   in far from ideal circumstances;
3 that they should prove capable of being used, with relatively
   little preparation, not only by basic-grade prison officers but
   also by practising probation officers.
It soon became apparent that there was no shortage of suitable
materials scattered about in schools, colleges, training establishments, hospitals and prisons, and in the many special projects which
occupy that territory where the learning and helping environments
overlap, and in the specialist literatures that report and support
them. Many of these methods and materials were clearly relevant to
the range of problems that confront offenders, either as recently
released prisoners, or whilst attending non-custodial alternatives
to prison like day training centres. In their existing forms however they tended to be sets of fragmented items, rooted in different
disciplines and traditions of work, and not readily accessible to
those dealing with offenders. The single most usable source of
materials we came across was the Canadian 'Life Skills Coaching
Manual', produced by the Saskatchewan Newstart Programme. (1)   It
was not a ready-made answer to our search for material because it
was already 'ready-made' for a rather different purpose, that of
being administered by indigenous 'life-skill coaches' drawn from
the ranks of the target populations themselves. In consequence,
the life skills manual was an essentially prescriptive package intended to be taught in a tightly ordered and pre-set sequence. We,
on the other hand, were interested in developing a curriculum which,
whilst covering the same ground and using many of the same exercises, would permit constant and continuing adaptation to the needs
of separate groups and their individual members.
The key to doing this systematically emerged during the course of
the study as a reflexive 'problem-solving' framework; starting with
the assessment and self-assessment of personal problems, followed by
the formulation of specific learning goals, then a phase in which
all means possible are brought to bear on the achievement of these
goals, and a final stage in which progress, or the lack of it, towards them is critically evaluated. (2) This framework, it should
be stressed, was a product of the project and not its starting-
point, so that it remains to be properly tested as an articulated
approach to helping people solve their problems. Many of its con-
stituent parts have of course been used and appraised by their
original authors and others in a wide range of settings.
The most important general influence on release course content
was the theory and practice of social skills training, and some of
its derivatives in social and life skills programmes. It is a borrowing which raises interesting issues of principle and attracts
some recurring criticisms. One cluster of these hinges on the
behaviourist origins of social skills training methods. In some

quarters, the very mention of the word 'behaviourism' is like a red
rag to a bull - or perhaps a bell to a dog would be a better analo-
gy. It produces reflex accusations that anything to do with the
theory must be tainted with mechanistic notions of man and with
manipulative or coercive modes of 'treatment'. Ignoring for the
moment the humanistic transformations through which behaviourism
had passed in recent times, and the fact that some of its critics
subscribe to deeply held determinist doctrines of their own, both
psychological and sociological, a disclaimer ought to be entered at
this point. This research was not conceived as a scientific test
of theory, but as a feasibility exercise, and course materials were
chosen for their likely utility rather than theoretical purity. It
may be frustrating for those who prefer to judge research by defined
theoretical criteria, but the guiding spirit of this work not only
denied such an anchorage, it positively extolled the virtues of
theoretical agnosticism. It is true that we took from behaviourism
an emphasis on the minutiae of behaviour as a proper subject of
study and personal change, but it was re-presented in a way that
stressed the sovereignty of individuals in defining for themselves
and then tackling the problems they thought they faced in the outside world. It was applied, in fact, in a way that some behaviour-
ists might wish to disown or dismiss as 'unscientific'.

In part, this reflects the efforts that were made to distinguish
the courses as sharply as possible from their participants' previous
experience of schooling and the helping professions. They assumed a
style that de-emphasised the expert role of the worker, devolved
major responsibility for decisions about change to the people with
the problems, and deliberately turned its back on conventional
beliefs about 'growth through pain' in favour of an altogether more
light-hearted approach. Lest that sound frivolous it should be
understood that the purposes of the courses remained deeply serious
both to those who ran them and to those who took part in them. The
good humour and friendliness that eventually illuminated the best
of the sessions were not seen as ends in themselves but as outward
expressions of mutuality and also of hard work. The fact that it
proved possible to tackle serious issues in this fashion has profound implications for the conduct of many kinds of education and
social work. It is also a partial retort to some of the criticisms
made by social determinists, since the open style of the proceedings
which produced these results does not at all preclude the application of a problem-solving framework to social or political issues.

It does not however answer the more specific charges brought by
such critics against the use of social skills methods in the area
of job search. 'What is the point,' they ask, 'of preparing people
to look for jobs which are not there?' 'Is it not a cruel deception
to pretend that by improving letter-writing skills, or self-presentation in interviews, an individual is necessarily going to find a
job?' 'Would it not be better to direct the attention of the unemployed to the social and political causes of their plight, and urge
them to take concerted action to change the situation?' 'And even
if you do help this particular person to get a job, are you not
merely helping someone to jump the queue over the heads of other
unemployed people?'

All of these questions, and others in similar vein, are more

pointed now than in 1976, but they were valid even then. It is
true, of course, that no amount of social skills training will
create a single extra job - except for those who teach the subject -
and anyone working with the unemployed would be dishonest not to say
so, and to say so at frequent intervals. On the other hand, even
with very high levels of unemployment, many people eventually get
jobs of one kind or another, and the more skilful they are, the more
likely it is that they will secure something which yields them personal satisfaction. In addition, the skills which may be useful in
securing work are not so specific that they cannot be used to cope
with some of the problems of remaining unemployed, if that is to be
the person's lot for a period.

The queue-jumping allegation is more difficult to refute. Given
a competition for scarce resources, in this case increasingly rare
job vacancies, a really effective course of training in job search
skills does in fact confer an advantage on those to whom it is
given, provided other things are equal. The argument from equality
is that such training should either be given to everyone or to no
one; it is an argument for universal provision. But in the world
as it is, other things are not, however, equal, and in the case of
young people in general, black youth in particular, women returning
to the labour market, the disabled, ex-prisoners and convicted offenders, and a host of others suffering from an assortment of
mental, physical and legal handicaps, there is an equally strong
argument for positive discrimination towards them in such matters.

A version of this argument sometimes levelled against the project
in its earlier days was that social skills training might produce
more sophisticated, better organised and more effective criminals.
We are pleased to report that such fears were without foundation,
and can furnish statistical evidence which shows that prison course
graduates were just as likely to be reconvicted as their colleagues
who were not exposed to the benefits of social skills training.

COURSE MEMBERS

Two types of information were gathered in order to estimate the
effects of these methods on offenders: a set of qualitative data
recording their verdicts on the courses in the prisons and the day
training centre, and some quantitative data related to the reconvictions of the prisoners. The qualitative results were almost
wholly favourable. Allowing for some justifiable criticism, and some
personal dislikes, the mass of the evidence showed that offenders
saw this way of working as relevant and acceptable and enjoyable and
useful. There is also to be discerned in their responses to the
evaluative questions, a quite unlooked-for result. A conscious attempt had been made in the design and execution of the project to
create a style of working which was, if not 'anti', then at least
'non'-treatment in orientation, i.e. it did not seek to locate problems in the psychology of individuals, but in the wider social environment and their interaction with it. But among the quotations
presented in chapter 7 there are some which refer to things like
'understanding myself better', 'learning a lot about other people',
and 'getting on better with other people'. They refer in fact to

the achievement of 'insight' into themselves and other people, and to improvements in personal relationships. These are the classic goals of conventional 'therapeutic' methods such as psychoanalysis, casework, and some of their out-growths in the group-work movement. It appears to be the case, on the basis of our experience at Ranby, Ashwell and Sheffield that these goals can be achieved by briefly trained workers using simple, straightforward and unpretentious methods for tackling everyday problems.

Paradoxically, whilst arriving at these unexpected results, the courses failed to register success in one of the main aims of the original research commission, which spoke of keeping people 'out of trouble'. Although some of their members were perceptibly different following courses - better informed, more positively motivated, less lacking in confidence, and more skilful in certain areas of their lives, more likely to get jobs and to keep them, more able to size up situations and to make considered decisions - despite all that they were apparently just as likely to commit fresh offences as men who had not attended courses. One way of interpreting these results would be to say that the social skills procedures employed were in-effective. Reflection suggests a different standpoint from which greater leverage might be brought to bear on the unending riddle of re-offending. It appears likely, looking back, that those who com-missioned this research, and those who accepted and carried it out, subscribed to an 'implicit' and unadmitted theory of criminality, which was not spelled out in the research documents.

'Offending', according to this 'implicit theory', is the result of many interacting social and psychological factors: poverty, ignorance, subcultural values, unemployment, poor social skills, cultural disadvantage, poor self-esteem, lack of confidence, in-ability to make decisions etc., etc. The answer to the problem therefore is a broadly based effort to help individuals find work, manage their money better, make better relationships with others, use their leisure time more satisfyingly, etc. 'Then', the theory concludes, 'the offender will be less likely to re-offend.'

Perhaps the best test of such a theory would be a radical pro-gramme for the re-distribution of power and wealth to the alienated and impoverished individuals and communities it describes, but that would almost certainly lie outside the terms of reference of those agencies which currently fund criminological research.

Our experience leads us to believe that even if offenders are better equipped to deal with all these problems in their personal lives, even if they do get jobs, manage their money better, and make better personal relationships, they may still go out and commit of-fences as well. If that is indeed the case - and for the moment it must remain a speculation - then two possible courses of action are open to anyone wishing to work in this way with offenders. One is to double and redouble the efforts they make to rectify the de-ficiencies associated with the lives of delinquents until either there are discernible effects on subsequent reconvictions or it be-comes clear that the approach does not 'work' in that sense. The alternative is not to abandon all such work, but to add to it an element or elements that tackle directly the problem of offending behaviour. Rather than approach re-offending obliquely via all its allied difficulties, why not examine ways of avoiding becoming involved in actual offence behaviour? It is more than likely that some offenders get into trouble because they enjoy it, or because their friends expect them to, or for other 'good' reasons, and that for them, the costs of giving it all up outweigh even the likelihood of increasingly severe sentences from the courts. But if they do want to change, should there not be made available some systematic ways of helping them to do so?

The single statistic from Ranby which showed a reduction in violent re-offending amongst course graduates may point towards the possible success of a programme along these lines. Violent behaviour was looked at as part of the Ranby curriculum and although the time devoted to it was not extensive, and the materials not highly developed, they produced a statistically significant effect on behaviour which further work might consolidate and extend.

STAFF

Another major objective of the research in the prisons was to test the ability of basic grade prison officers to work successfully with men about to be released. The words of many prisoners, some of which appeared earlier in this book, are more eloquent testimony to their success in this direction than anything that could be said here. Not all the thirteen officers in the original training groups were able to do this kind of work; some were able to do it better than others; and not a few of those who were good at it found the strain so great that they fairly soon sought alternative postings in the prison system. Nor are we able to say anything about the representativeness or otherwise of the officers who worked with us. A subjective estimate would be that a sizeable minority of prison officers would be interested in and capable of working in this way with offenders, and that some of them could do it with great imagination and real commitment. The real question is not whether officers can do the work but whether prisons as presently constituted can permit them to exercise their talents. It was no part of our brief to examine the institutional impact of release courses on the prison establishments at Ranby and Ashwell, or to consider the organisational restraints which might militate against the successful implementation of courses either there or elsewhere in the prison system. But almost from the first day of the project it was obvious that the participating officers were to be engaged in a running battle with the middle managements of their prisons to secure the resources they needed to do their demanding and exhausting work properly. Many of the obstacles they faced arose out of the budgetary crisis that struck the prison service during 1976. On the other hand it is difficult to remember a recent time, or envisage even a medium-term future when the prison system was or will be other than in crisis. The reasons for that state of affairs lie outwith the remit of this research; all we can do in conclusion is to make some suggestions which would carry forward the constructive results that were achieved at Ranby and Ashwell and Sheffield.

POSSIBLE FUTURE DEVELOPMENTS

If release courses of the kind piloted in this study were to become
an established and expanding part of the prison service, it would
clearly require positive co-operation between the Prison Officers'
Association, which has so far shown little interest in the results
obtained by their members at Ranby and Ashwell, and the Prison Department at every level. There are no doubt perfectly defensible
administrative and economic reasons why release courses in the form
described in this book, or something like it, have not spread to
other prison establishments. None of these arguments have anything
to do with the declared aims of the prison service to do more than
contain men and women for the duration of their legally imposed
sentences. The results of this work present a variety of options
to prison administrators.

Long-term prisoners and lifers

Ranby and Ashwell are both low-security, short-to-medium-term-
sentence prisons, so that the most obvious development of release
courses is into longer-term establishments. This raises the immediate problem of parole. One or two men on courses at Ranby and
Ashwell were eligible for parole, and the uncertainty surrounding
their release dates caused considerable difficulties for courses
which operated on the block entry principle.

One answer to this problem might be to extend the period of
notice given to prospective parolees about their release dates or
to mount more frequent short courses for men who have been granted
parole.

Men with very long sentences, amongst whom lifers can be counted
as extreme cases, are in a very different situation which could be
tackled by adapting some of the release course materials to look at
how men can cope with long periods of incarceration. A series of
courses could be designed for use at different stages of a long
sentence, culminating in a modified, and possibly more elaborate
release course at the end.

Other establishments

Nor is there any apparent reason why some form of release course
based on the Ranby-Ashwell model should not be introduced into other
types of prison establishments, those for women for example, and
local prisons, youth custody and detention centres. For some very
short-sentence prisoners, the whole of their time inside could be
spent on a course, and the whole of the regime in selected detention
centres could be turned over to a social skills-based curriculum.

Types of offenders

Experience of constructing programmes for specific problems such as
drink and violence suggests that it might be worth developing more

substantial courses on special topics for particular types of offenders, such as violent or sexual offenders, alcoholics and near
alcoholics, take and drive away offenders, etc. Programmes like
these could be tested with some rigour as experimental procedures.

Training prisoners as tutors

One serious objection to extending release courses to other establishments is their potential cost in manpower terms. Spread across
the whole of the prison system even a modest provision of courses
could claim several million pounds annually. One way of reducing
these costs would be to train selected long-term prisoners to act
as tutors on release courses, either as aides to prison officers,
or to run their own courses. There is no doubt that just as the
ranks of the officer grades are full of talent and interest which
is waiting for a chance of self-expression, so are the even larger
ranks of the inmate population. In a large, long-term prison, three
or four officers and a dozen or so trained prisoners could make an
impact out of all proportion to their numbers. It would be difficult to overestimate the resistance which would be generated by such
a scheme, but it is worth serious consideration, not least because
of the effect it might have on the relatively few long-term prisoners involved in it in future.

Self-help groups

Recidivists Anonymous groups have existed in a small number of
prisons for many years, but the notion of prisoner self-help has
never taken root in the same way as, say, Alcoholics Anonymous.
There are many reasons for this failure, most of them beyond the
scope of this report, but amongst them, the absence of clear aims
and purposeful procedures must count high. Some of the methods and
materials used in release courses would lend themselves readily to
the formation of self-help groups, and one or two small-scale pilot
schemes along these lines might be fruitful.

An individual learning package

Release courses were built around group learning techniques, and a
considerable part of their success was due to the presence of others
with similar problems. There are, however, some individuals who
find group situations oppressive and who learn best on their own.
It would be useful to develop an individual learning package based
on the release course curriculum which could be used by serving
prisoners on a 'home study' or 'correspondence course' basis. This
exercise would require a lot of thought and could only proceed by a
process of trial and error, but the end product, if it worked,
would have applications in many other settings besides prisons.

Additional uses of day training centres and other applications

Programme development such as that done in Sheffield opens up the possibility that day training centres could adapt the methods and materials so produced to a number of other purposes. Given their position intermediate between custody and field supervision, the centres may be uniquely placed as potential testing grounds for other innovations.

For example, first, the usefulness of this way of working with younger offenders could be explored by using day training as an alternative to Attendance Centres on Saturday afternoons. A programme could be organised, run by centre or sessional staff, using methods derived from the mainstream of the centre's work but addressed to the needs of these groups. Even a short pilot study could make some initial evaluation of such a proposal. Second, as a supplement or alternative to prison release courses, day training centres could be used as sites for the running of end-of-sentence courses for suitable offender groups. Prisoners serving short to medium-length sentences, for example, might complete their final two or three months attending a day training centre, possibly with a condition of hostel residence attached. Third, day training centres could be more fully exploited as probation facilities, offering a variety of services such as evening 'problem-solving' classes for probation groups, brief one- or two-day life skills exercises, for example in job or accommodation search, rights, or violence, with selected groups such as unemployed, homeless, or alcoholic offenders, or to run short staff training seminars with interested area teams or other groups such as ancillaries, hostel staff, or New Careerists.

In a broader perspective, a number of other areas can be identified in which a 'package' like that used in the day training centre could have fruitful applications. For example, in community homes, some of the problems faced by children about to depart may be closely akin to those experienced by men in the Sheffield centre. The methods could also be used on a longer-term basis - on one afternoon, or one day, or one evening a week for example, as part of a home's integral activity. Again, day centres and probation hostels could make use of some of these methods, most likely on a sessional or one-off basis, with groups of offenders sharing a common problem; such an exercise has been successfully carried out by the West Bar Day Centre in Sheffield.

Alternatives to prison

Finally, a bridge can be made between the work at Sheffield and in Ranby and Ashwell by proposing the experimental use of some prisons as day training facilities. Local prisons in large centres of population are ideally placed to offer day training courses to their local courts as alternatives to full custodial sentences. And magistrates and Crown Court judges might welcome a sentence of day training which was actually carried out in a prison setting but which did not involve the social disruption and financial cost of conventional sentences of imprisonment. Prison officers too might welcome an opportunity to move away from a purely custodial role to one which looked outwards to the community. Day training centres in some prisons could also be run as joint enterprises between the probation and prison services.

One of the principal virtues of such a departure in the provision of alternative sentences to the courts would be to give to the prison service, for the first time in its long history, a direct interest in efforts to reduce the number of people held in captivity. The more successful the scheme, the less the pressure on other prison establishments, and the greater the likelihood that more and better rehabilitative work could be undertaken there as well.

Some seeds have been sown by this project, which with care and imagination could bring about a flowering of novel rehabilitative measures within the penal field, or like many of its more distinguished predecessors in the field, it could lead to nothing. Their implementation would be expensive in terms of money and manpower. But in the prison context, they define an opportunity, to put it no higher, for officers and men in a growing number of establishments to forge a working alliance which would have as its aim the pursuit of rehabilitation rather than that of the 'quiet nick'. And in the community, they suggest that growing numbers of offenders could come to terms with their problems in ways that were more congenial to themselves and less damaging to other people.

Appendix 1
Prison release questionnaire

Many of the situations which a man has to deal with after his release involve meeting and coping with other people - for example
in job interviews, finding accommodation, getting social security
payments, or fitting back into the family. We are interested in
finding out which of these situations are most important from the
prisoner's point of view.

The questions which follow are designed to ask you which situations *you* think are most important, and how confident you feel
about being able to deal with them. The information you supply will
be used to help design 'release courses' for men about to leave
prison. There is no need, therefore, for you to put your name on
these sheets.

1 First of all, how important do you think it is for you to be able
to deal with other people effectively in the period following
your release? Put a ring round the answer you agree with most,
where 1 = very important, 5 = not at all important, and 2, 3 and
4 are different shades of opinion in between.

Very important				Not at all important
1	2	3	4	5

2 In the following table, we would like you to list some of the
situations you will have to deal with after your release, in
rough order of importance. If you think some are equally important, put them beside the same number.
1
2
3
4
5
6
7
If you would like to add any more and can't find enough space
here, use the back of the sheet.

3 Do you plan what you are going to do after your release, or are
   you inclined to wait and see what happens?

4 Do you think that you could learn to handle people more effectively in some situations? Put a ring round your answer.

   Yes   No   I don't know

Appendix 2
Sheffield day training centre
Follow up questionnaire for field probation officers

We are carrying out a small follow-up study of some of the men who
have attended the DTC over the past two years, and would be very
grateful if you could complete the following short questionnaire
and return it to us in the SAE provided.

The man named below was on your caseload while attending the DTC;
if he has since been transferred could you complete the questionnaire as fully as possible and write down the name of the officer to
whom he was transferred at the foot of the page.

Name

1   Has this man appeared in court again since
    leaving the DTC? If so could you tell us the
    charge and the sentence if any.   Yes   No
                                                       (put a ring
                                                       where appro-
                                                       priate)

2   As far as you know has he been in employment since leaving the
    DTC? If you have any information about his work/unemployment
    could you write it down here.

3   In your view did he benefit from attendance at the DTC? If so
    how?

4   Would you say that since leaving the DTC he has shown any im-
    provement of the following kinds? (Put a circle where appro-
    priate.)
    In self-confidence   None   Slight   Moderate   Considerable
    In ability to find work   None   Slight   Moderate   Considerable
    In ability to communicate   None   Slight   Moderate   Considerable
    In ability to solve
    problems for himself   None   Slight   Moderate   Considerable
    In his relationship
    with you   None   Slight   Moderate   Considerable

5 Will you refer more men to the DTC in future?   Yes   No

6 If you have any comments on the DTC, or suggestions for improvement, please write them on the back. All of this information
   will be treated in the strictest confidence.

Thank you for your help.

Notes

CHAPTER 1   THE PROBLEM AND A PROJECT

1 N. Walker and H. Giller (eds), 'Penal Policy Making in
   England', Institute of Criminology, Cambridge, 1977.
2 'Report of the Commissioners of Prisons for the Year 1956',
   HMSO, 1957.
3 N. Fenton, 'Group Counseling', Institute for the Study of Crime
   and Delinquency, Sacramento, California, 1961.
4 'Report on the work of the Prison Department 1963', HMSO, 1964.
5 R. Caird, 'A Good and Useful Life', Hart-Davis, MacGibbon, 1974.
6 J.E. Thomas, 'The English Prison Officer Since 1850', Routledge
   & Kegan Paul, 1972.
7 P. Priestley, The prison welfare officer - a case of role
   strain, 'British Journal of Sociology', vol.XXIII, no.2, 1972.
8 Advisory Council on the Treatment of Offenders, 'The Organisation of Aftercare', HMSO, 1963.
9 Home Office Research Unit, 'Explorations in After-Care', HMSO,
   1971.
10 S.R. Brody, 'The Effectiveness of Sentencing', Home Office
    Research Study, HMSO, 1976.
11 Our prisons of squalor, degradation and despair, 'Observer',
    10 May 1970;   Judiciary blamed for 'gathering storm' in jails,
    'Daily Telegraph', 14 October 1970;   Prisons can no longer cope,
    'Times' leader, 14 October 1970.
12 Embodied in the Criminal Justice Bill, 1967.
13 Advisory Council on the Penal System, 'Reparation by the
    Offender', HMSO, 1970;   Advisory Council on the Penal System,
    'Non-custodial and semi-custodial penalties', HMSO, 1970.
14 G. Dendrickson and F. Thomas, 'The Truth about Dartmoor',
    Gollancz, 1954.
15 J.P. Martin and D. Webster, 'The Social Consequences of
    Conviction', Heinemann, 1971.
16 P. Morris, 'Prisoners and their Families', Allen & Unwin, 1965.
17 A.K. Taylor, 'From a Glasgow Slum to Fleet Street', Alvin
    Redman, n.d.
18 J.W. Fletcher, 'A Menace to Society', Paul Elek, 1972.
19 'Penal Practice in a Changing Society', Cmnd. 2303, HMSO, 1959.
20 A.S. Diamond, 'Primitive Law, Past and Present', Methuen, 1971.

21 N. Goldstein, Reparation by the offender to the victim as a method of rehabilitation for both, in I. Drapkin and E. Viano (eds), 'Victimology: A New Focus', vol.II, Lexington, 1974.
22 Sir E. duCane, 'An Account of the Manner in which Sentences of Penal Servitude are Carried Out in England', HMSO, 1882.
23 M. Foucault, 'Surveiller et Punir. Naissance de la Prison', Gallimard, 1975.
24 For details from a long history, see A. Bidwell, 'From Wall Street to Newgate', Bidwell Publishing, Hartford, Conn., 1895; W. Macartney, 'Walls Have Mouths', Gollancz, 1936; A. Hill, 'A Cage of Shadows', Hutchinson, 1973.
25 Zeno, 'Life', Macmillan, 1968.
26 R. Sykes, 'Who's Been Eating My Porridge?', Leslie Frewin, 1967.
27 B. Stratton, 'Who Guards The Guards?', Preservation of the Rights of Prisoners (PROP), 1973.
28 'Don't Mark His Face: Hull Prison Riot (1976)', Preservation of the Rights of Prisoners (PROP), n.d.
29 R. Barton, 'Institutional Neurosis', John Wright, 1966.
30 G. Rose, 'The Struggle for Penal Reform', Stevens, 1961.
31 A.E. Bottoms and F.H. McClintock, 'Criminals Coming of Age', Heinemann, 1973.
32 M. Davies, 'Prisoners of Society', Routledge & Kegan Paul, 1974.
33 J.E. Thomas, op.cit., has detailed the growing disillusionment of basic grade prison staff with the reformist pretensions of modern prisons and their increasingly successful opposition to further liberalisation of regimes.
34 The Role of the Modern Prison Officer, 'Prison Officers Journal', 1963.
35 The beginnings of a small-scale project for uniformed officers to undertake welfare work is described in the 'Report on the work of the Prison Department 1976', HMSO, 1977.
36 T. and P. Morris, 'Pentonville', Routledge & Kegan Paul, 1963.
37 W. Probyn, 'Angel Face', Allen & Unwin, 1977.
38 P. Priestley, 'Community of Scapegoats', Pergamon, 1980.
39 R.G. Andry, 'The Short-term Prisoner', Tavistock, 1963.
40 K. Vercoe, '614 Men Leaving Local Prisons', National Association for the Care and Resettlement of Offenders Regional Paper, Cheltenham, 1969.
41 Minutes of NACRO Regional Council for South Wales and Severn Valley, 1970.
42 P. Priestley, 'The problem of the short-term prisoner', mimeo, National Association for the Care and Resettlement of Offenders, 1970. See also P. Evans, Treatment outside gaols urged to cut prison population, 'The Times', 9 November 1970.
43 These assessment and selection policies were later changed in some fundamental respects.
44 D.H. Clark, 'Social Therapy in Psychiatry', Penguin Books, 1974.

CHAPTER 2 DESIGN AND DEVELOPMENT

1 J. Conrad, 'Crime and its correction', Tavistock, 1965; D. Briggs, 'In Place of Prison', Maurice Temple Smith, 1975.
2 S.R. Brody, 'The Effectiveness of Sentencing', Home Office Research Study no.35, HMSO, 1976.

3   S.R. Brody, op.cit.
4   D.J. West and D.P. Farrington, 'Who becomes delinquent?', Heinemann, 1973.
5   M.A. Yelloly, 'Social Work Theory and Psychoanalysis', Von Nostrand Reinhold, 1980.
6   P. Priestley, op.cit., 1972.
7   G. Goodman, 'Companionship Therapy', Jossey Bass, 1972.
8   See the references in Goodman, op.cit.
9   H.S. Sullivan, 'Conceptions of Modern Psychiatry', William Alanson White Psychiatric Foundation, 1947.
10 H.S. Sullivan, 'The Interpersonal Theory of Psychiatry', W.W. Norton, 1953.
11 I.R.H. Falloon, P. Lindley, R. McDonald and I.M. Marks, Social skills training of outpatient groups: a controlled study of rehearsal and homework, 'British Journal of Psychiatry', 131, pp.599-609, 1977.
12 M. Hersen, Modification of skill deficits in psychiatric patients, in A.S. Bellack and M. Hersen (eds), 'Research and Practice in Social Skills Training', Plenum, 1979.
13 A.P. Goldstein, R.P. Sprafkin and J.J. Gershaw, 'Skill Training for Community Living', Pergamon, 1976.
14 P. Trower, B. Bryant and M. Argyle, 'Social Skills and Mental Health', Methuen, 1978.
15 R. Paloutzian, J. Hasazi, J. Streifel and C.L. Edgard, Promotion of positive social interactions in severely retarded young children, 'American Journal of Mental Deficiency', 75, pp. 519-24, 1971.
16 P. Wehman and S. Schleien, Severely handicapped children: social skills development through leisure skills programming, in G. Cartledge and J.F. Milbur (eds), 'Teaching Social Skills to Children: Innovative Approaches', Pergamon, 1980.
17 C. Stephan, S. Stephano and L. Talkington, Use of modelling in survival skill training with educable mentally retarded, 'Training School Bulletin', 70, pp.73-8, 1973.
18 J.P. Curran, Skills training as an approach to the treatment of heterosexual-social anxiety: a review, 'Psychological Bulletin', 84, pp.140-57, 1977.
19 M.M. Linehan and K.J. Egan, Assertion training for women, in A.S. Bellack and M. Hersen (eds), 'Research and Practice in Social Skills Training', Plenum, 1979.
20 C. Twentyman and R. McFall, Behavioral training of social skills in shy males, 'Journal of Consulting and Clinical Psychology', 43, pp.384-95, 1975.
21 W.R. Lindsay, R.S. Symons and T. Sweet, A programme for teaching social skills to socially inept adolescents: description and evaluation, 'Journal of Adolescence', 2, pp.215-28, 1979.
22 S. Oden and S.R. Asher, Coaching children in social skills for friendship making, 'Child Development', 48, pp.495-506, 1977.
23 M.B. Whitehill, M. Hersen and A.S. Bellack, Conversation skills training for socially isolated children, 'Behaviour Research and Therapy', 18, pp.217-25, 1980.
24 L.W. Frederiksen, J.O. Jenkins, D.W. Foy and R.M. Eisler, Social-skills training to modify abusive verbal outbursts in adults, 'Journal of Applied Behaviour Analysis', 9, pp.117-25, 1976.

25 D.W. Foy, R.M. Eisler and S.G. Pinkston, Social-skills training to teach alcoholics to refuse drinks effectively, 'Journal of Studies on Alcohol', 9, pp.1340-5, 1975.

26 S.H. Spence and J.S. Marzillier, Social skills training with adolescent male offenders: 1. Short-term effects, 'Behaviour Research and Therapy', 17, pp.7-16, 1979.

27 M.H. Thelen, R.A. Fry, S.J. Dollinger and S.G. Paul, Use of videotaped models to improve the interpersonal adjustment of delinquents, 'Journal of Consulting and Clinical Psychology', 44, p.492, 1976.

28 I.G. Sarason and V.J. Ganzer, Modelling and group discussion in the rehabilitation of juvenile delinquents, 'Journal of Counselling Psychology', 20, pp.442-9, 1973.

29 I.G. Sarason, Verbal learning, modelling, and juvenile delinquency, 'American Psychologist', 23, pp.254-66, 1968.

30 D. Crawford, A social skills treatment programme with sex offenders, paper presented at the SHRU conference on sex deviance, London, 1976.

31 R.E. Kifer, M.A. Lewis, D.R. Green and E.L. Phillips, Training predelinquent youths and their parents to negotiate conflict situations, 'Journal of Applied Behaviour Analysis', 7, pp. 357-64, 1974.

32 M.J. Chandler, Egocentrism and anti-social behaviour: the assessment and training of social perspective-taking skills, 'Developmental Psychology', 9, pp.326-32, 1973.

33 P. Howe, Intermediate treatment: the development and operation of a 'social skills' group, mimeo, the Barton Project, Oxford, 1979.

34 B. Fawcett, E. Ingham, M. McKeever and S. Williams, A social skills group for young prisoners, 'Social Work Today', 47, pp.16-18, 1979.

35 Saskatchewan Newstart, 'Life Skills Coaching Manual', Training Research and Development Station, Department of Manpower and Immigration, Saskatchewan, 1973.

CHAPTER 3   TRAINING THE STAFF

1 By coincidence Vaughan College was host to an exhibition of sculptures by Jimmy Boyle, then resident in the Special Unit at Barlinnie Prison.

2 These were set out in a duplicated paper, 'Release Course Aims and Assumptions'.

3 Philip Bartlett, Rodney Cox and Erzsi Hurley.

4 Tom Douglas.

5 Sonia Coates and Peter Dawson.

6 Prepared by Roger Mottram and Kevin McKee.

7 A. Rodger, 'Seven Point Plan', National Foundation for Education Research, 1974.

8 Saskatchewan Newstart, op.cit.

9 H.J. Eysenck and G. Wilson, 'Know Your Own Personality', Penguin, 1976.

10 R.B. Cattell, 'Personality and Motivation Structure and Measurement', Harcourt, Brace & World, 1957.

11 H.J. Eysenck and S.B.G. Eysenck, 'Manual of the Eysenck Personality Inventory', University of London Press, 1964.

12 J.B. Rotter, Generalized expectancies for internal versus external control of reinforcement, 'Psychological Monographs', 80 (whole no.609), 1966.

13 A.W. Heim, K.P. Watts and V. Simmons, 'AH2 - a test of general reasoning, National Foundation for Education Research, 1972.

14 'Classification of Occupations and Directory of Occupational Titles' (CODOT) (3 vols), HMSO, 1972.

15 Careers and Occupational Information Centre, Signposts, Manpower Services Commission, Moorfoot, Sheffield.

CHAPTER 4   THE OFFENDERS AND THEIR PROBLEMS

1 The population sample consisted of every fourth case listed in the file of Initial Index Cards held in the Discipline Office, excluding men who were ineligible to apply, or who had applied for a place on a release course.

2 J. Baldwin, A.E. Bottoms and M. Walker, 'The Urban Criminal', Tavistock, 1976.

3 'Rates of Imprisonment in Magistrates' Courts 1976', Radical Alternatives to Prison, 70 Novers Park Road, Knowle, Bristol, 1978.

4 A.K. Bottomley, 'Decisions in the Penal Process', Martin Robertson, 1973.

5 Specifically these are: criminological data based on tables prepared by the administrative assistant in the centre; reports written by the centre staff; psychometric test scores.

6 In fact only sixteen groups started during the 'official' period of the research. Group 17 is included here because it was the first to begin in 1978, and some evaluative information that is available is included in chapters 7 and 8.

7 These numbers slightly underestimate the number of orders made. One man left on his first day; another was taken into custody for a new offence before he arrived; and two men who were to join groups were taken ill but have since attended the centre in 1978.

8 There were 121 referrals during 1977, but one man was referred to the DTC twice.

9 A statistically significant difference: t = 3.82, p = less than .01.

10 t = 0.67 (n.s.) Nor was a comparison made between the DTC group and six men not recommended for DTC, though the average number of convictions of the latter group was as high as 14; t = 1.41 (n.s.).

11 J. Holborn, Casework with short-term prisoners, part 2 of 'Some Male Offenders' Problems', Home Office Research Study no.28, HMSO, 1975.

12 D. Payne and J. Lawton, 'Day Training Centres', unpublished manuscript, Home Office Research Unit, 1977.

13 A. Anastasi, 'Psychological Testing', Collier Macmillan, 1976.

14 J. Holborn, op.cit.
15 These findings were obtained using the Heimler Scale of Social
    Functioning; see J. Holborn, op.cit., pp.62,69.

CHAPTER 5 METHODS AND MATERIALS

1 K.F. Jackson, 'The Art of Solving Problems', Heinemann, 1975.
2 A. Anastasi, op.cit., 1976.
3 In Saskatchewan Newstart, 'Life Skills Coaching Manual', op.
   cit., 1973.
4 J.B. Rotter, op.cit., 1966.
5 A. Osborn, 'Applied Imagination', Scribner, 1953.
6 T. Buzan, 'Use Your Head', BBC Publications, 1974.
7 A. Rodger, 'Seven Point Plan', National Foundation for Education
   Research, 1974.
8 M.L.J. Abercrombie, 'The Anatomy of Judgment', Penguin, 1969.
9 F.C. Bartlett, 'Remembering', Cambridge University Press, 1932.
10 K. Jones, 'Simulations: a handbook for teachers', Kogan Page,
    1980.
11 J.W. Pfeiffer and J.E. Jones, 'A Handbook of Structured Experi-
    ences for Human Relations Training', vol.2, Iowa University
    Associates Press, 1970.
12 Saskatchewan Newstart, op.cit., 1973.
13 J. McGuire and P. Priestley, 'Life after school: a social skills
    curriculum', Pergamon, 1981
14 A. Anastasi, 'Psychological Testing' (4th edn), Collier Mac-
    millan, 1976.
15 T. Buzan, op.cit., 1974.
16 A.F. Kinzel, Body-buffer zone in violent prisoners, 'American
    Journal of Psychiatry', 127, pp.99-104, 1970.
17 Saskatchewan Newstart, op.cit., 1973.
18 Ibid.
19 K.F. Jackson, op.cit., 1975.
20 E. de Bono, 'Teaching Thinking', Maurice Temple Smith, 1977.
21 Inner London Education Authority, Learning Materials Service,
    Publishing Centre, Highbury Station Road, London N1 1SB.
22 'Tenement', Shelter, National Campaign for the Homeless,
    157 Waterloo Road, London SE1 8UU.
23 'Connolly Occupational Interests Questionnaire', Careers and
    Occupational Information Centre, Manpower Services Commission,
    Moorfoot, Sheffield, South Yorkshire.
24 Saskatchewan Newstart, op.cit., 1973.
25 M. Seddon, Client as social worker, in D. Brandon and W. Jordan
    (eds), 'Creative Social Work', Basil Blackwell, 1979.
26 CODOT, op.cit., 1972.
27 Signposts, op.cit., 1972.
28 Saskatchewan Newstart, op.cit., 1973.
29 A.P. Goldstein et al., op.cit., 1976.
30 J.B. Rotter, op.cit., 1966.
31 A.H. Maslow, 'Motivation and work', Harper, 1954.

CHAPTER 7 THE RESULTS OF THE COURSES

1 A.E. Bottoms and F.H. McClintock, op.cit., 1973.
2 M.S. Folkard, D.E. Smith and D.D. Smith, 'IMPACT Intensive matched probation and after-care treatment vol.II', Home Office Research Study 36, HMSO, 1976.

CHAPTER 8 AFTERWARDS

1 M. Shaw, 'Social Work in Prison: An Experiment in the Use of Extended Contact with Offenders', Home Office Research Unit Study no.22, HMSO, 1974.
2 M. Shaw, op.cit., 1974.
3 A.J. Fowles, 'Prison Welfare: an account of an experiment at Liverpool', Home Office Research Study no.45, HMSO, 1978.
4 D. Lipton, R. Martinson and J. Wilkes, 'The Effectiveness of Correctional Treatment: A Survey of Treatment Evaluation Studies', Prager, 1975.
5 A. Savage, 'The Sheffield Day Training Centre - a study of 20 men', unpublished manuscript, South Yorkshire Probation Service, 1977.
6 D. Payne and J. Lawton, op.cit., 1977.
7 'The Sentence of the Court. A Handbook for Courts on Treatment of Offenders', HMSO, 1969.
8 R. Barnitt and others, Prisoners and prison officers - a new relationship? An experimental approach to pre-release preparation, Home Office Research Unit 'Research Bulletin', no.4, HMSO, 1977.
9 P. Hardwick, Discharged with confidence, 'Community Care', 2 November 1977.
10 P. Priestley and others, Release Courses: a new venture for prison officers, 'Prison Service Journal', April 1978.

CHAPTER 9 PROBLEMS AND PROSPECTS

1 Saskatchewan Newstart, op.cit., 1973.
2 P. Priestley, J. McGuire, D. Flegg, V. Hemsley and D. Welham, 'Social Skills and Personal Problem Solving', Tavistock, 1973.

Bibliography

ABERCROMBIE, M.L.J., 'The Anatomy of Judgment', Penguin, 1969.

ADVISORY COUNCIL ON THE TREATMENT OF OFFENDERS, 'The Organisation of Aftercare', HMSO, 1963.

ADVISORY COUNCIL ON THE PENAL SYSTEM, 'Non-custodial and semi-custodial penalties', HMSO, 1970.

ADVISORY COUNCIL ON THE PENAL SYSTEM, 'Reparation by the Offender', HMSO, 1970.

ANASTASI, A., 'Psychological Testing', Collier Macmillan, 1976.

ANDRY, R.G., 'The Short-term Prisoner', Tavistock, 1963.

BALDWIN, J., BOTTOMS, A.E. and WALKER, M.A., 'The Urban Criminal: a study in Sheffield', Tavistock, 1976.

BARNITT, R. et al., Prisoners and prison officers - a new relationship? An experimental approach to pre-release preparation, Home Office Research Unit, 'Research Bulletin', no.4, HMSO, 1977.

BARTLETT, F.C., 'Remembering', Cambridge University Press, 1932.

BARTON, R., 'Institutional Neurosis', John Wright, 1966.

BIDWELL, A., 'From Wall Street to Newgate', Bidwell, 1895.

BOTTOMLEY, A.K., 'Decisions in the Penal Process', Martin Robertson, 1973.

BOTTOMS, A.E. and McCLINTOCK, F.H., 'Criminals Coming of Age', Heinemann, 1973.

BRIGGS, D., 'In Place of Prison', Maurice Temple Smith, 1975.

BRODY, S.R., 'The Effectiveness of Sentencing', Home Office Research Study no.35, HMSO, 1976.

BUZAN, T., 'Use Your Head', BBC Publications, 1974.

CAIRD, R., 'A Good and Useful Life', Hart-Davis, MacGibbon, 1974.

CATTELL, R.B., 'Personality and Motivation Structure and Measurement', Harcourt, Brace & World, 1957.

CHANDLER, M.J., Egocentrism and anti-social behaviour: the assessment and training of social perspective-taking skills, 'Developmental Psychology', 9, pp.326-32, 1973.

CLARK, D.H., 'Social Therapy in Psychiatry', Penguin, 1974.

'Classification of Occupations and Directory of Occupational Titles' (CODOT), 3 vols, HMSO, 1972.

CAREERS AND OCCUPATIONAL INFORMATION CENTRE, 'Connolly Occupational Interests Questionnaire', Manpower Services Commission, Moorfoot, Sheffield, South Yorkshire.

CAREERS AND OCCUPATIONAL INFORMATION CENTRE, 'Signposts', Manpower
  Services Commission, Moorfoot, Sheffield.
CONRAD, J., 'Crime and its correction', Tavistock, 1965.
CRAWFORD, D., 'A social skills treatment programme with sex
  offenders', paper presented at the Special Hospitals Research Unit
  conference on sex deviance, London, 1976.
CURRAN, J.P., Skills training as an approach to the treatment of
  heterosexual-social anxiety: a review, 'Psychological Bulletin',
  84, pp.140-57, 1977.
Judiciary blamed for 'gathering storm' in jails, 'Daily Telegraph',
  14 October 1970.
DAVIES, M., 'Prisoners of Society', Routledge & Kegan Paul, 1974.
de BONO, E., 'Teaching Thinking', Maurice Temple Smith, 1977.
DENDRICKSON, G. and THOMAS, F., 'The Truth about Dartmoor',
  Gollancz, 1954.
DIAMOND, A.S., 'Primitive Law, Past and Present', Methuen, 1971.
duCANE, SIR E., 'An Account of the Manner in which Sentences of
  Penal Servitude are Carried Out in England', HMSO, 1882.
EVANS, P., Treatment outside gaols urged to cut prison population,
  'The Times', 9 November 1970.
EYSENCK, H.J. and EYSENCK, S.B.G., 'Manual of the Eysenck
  Personality Inventory', University of London Press.
EYSENCK, H.J. and WILSON, G., 'Know Your Own Personality', Penguin,
  1976.
FALLOON, I.R.H., LINDLEY, P., McDONALD, R. and MARKS, I.M., Social
  skills training of outpatient groups: a controlled study of
  rehearsal and homework, 'British Journal of Psychiatry', 131,
  pp.599-609, 1977.
FAWCETT, B., INGHAM, E., McKEEVER, M. and WILLIAMS, S., A social
  skills group for young prisoners, 'Social Work Today', 47,
  pp.16-18, 1979.
FENTON, N., 'Group Counseling', Institute for the Study of Crime
  and Delinquency, Sacramento, California, 1961.
FLETCHER, J.W., 'A Menace to Society', Paul Elek, 1972.
FOLKARD, M.S., SMITH, D.E. and SMITH, D.D., 'IMPACT Intensive
  matched probation and after-care treatment vol.II', Home Office
  Research Study no.36, HMSO, 1976.
FOUCAULT, M., 'Surveiller et Punir. Naissance de la Prison',
  Gallimard, 1975.
FOWLES, A.J., 'Prison Welfare: an account of an experiment at
  Liverpool', Home Office Research Study no.45, HMSO, 1978.
FOY, D.W., EISLER, R.M. and PINKSTON, S.G., Social-skills training
  to teach alcoholics to refuse drinks effectively, 'Journal of
  Studies on Alcohol', 9, pp.1340-5, 1975.
FREDERIKSEN, L.W., JENKINS, J.O., FOY, D.W. and EISLER, R.M.,
  Social-skills training to modify abusive verbal outbursts in
  adults, 'Journal of Applied Behaviour Analysis', 9, pp.117-25,
  1976.
GOLDSTEIN, A.P., SPRAFKIN, R.P. and GERSHAW, J.J., 'Skill Training
  for Community Living', Pergamon, 1976.
GOLDSTEIN, N., Reparation by the offender to the victim as a
  method of rehabilitation for both, in I. Drapkin and E. Viano
  (eds), 'Victimology: A New Focus', vol.II, Lexington, 1974.
GOODMAN, G., 'Companionship Therapy', Jossey Bass, 1972.

HARDWICK, P., Discharged with confidence, 'Community Care', 2 November 1977.

HEIM, A.W., WATTS, K.P. and SIMMONS, V., 'AH2 test of general reasoning', National Foundation for Education Research, 1972.

HERSEN, M., Modification of skill deficits in psychiatric patients, in A.S. Bellack and M. Hersen (eds), 'Research and Practice in Social Skills Training', Plenum, 1979.

HILL, A., 'A Cage of Shadows', Hutchinson, 1973.

HOME OFFICE RESEARCH UNIT, 'Explorations in After-Care', HMSO, 1971.

'Penal Practice in a Changing Society', Cmnd. 2303, HMSO, 1959.

'The Sentence of the Court. A Handbook for Courts on Treatment of Offenders', HMSO, 1969.

HOLBORN, J., Casework with short-term prisoners, part 2 of 'Some Male Offenders' Problems', Home office Research Study no.28, HMSO, 1975.

HOWE, P., 'Intermediate treatment: the development and operation of a "social skills" group', mimeo, the Barton Project, Oxford, 1979.

INNER LONDON EDUCATION AUTHORITY, 'Nine graded simulations', Learning Materials Service, Publishing Centre, Highbury Station Road, London N1 1SB.

JACKSON, K.F., 'The Art of Solving Problems', Heinemann, 1975.

JONES, K., 'Simulations: a handbook for teachers', Kogan Page, 1980.

KIFER, R.E., LEWIS, M.A., GREEN, D.R. and PHILLIPS, E.L., Training predelinquent youths and their parents to negotiate conflict situations, 'Journal of Applied Behaviour Analysis', 7, pp.357-64. 1974.

KINZEL, A.F., Body-buffer zone in violent prisoners, 'American Journal of Psychiatry', 127, pp.99-104, 1970.

LINDSAY, W.R., SYMONS, R.S. and SWEET, T., A programme for teaching social skills to socially inept adolescents: description and evaluation, 'Journal of Adolescence', 2, pp.215-28, 1979.

LINEHAN, M.M. and EGAN, K.J., Assertion training for women, in A.S. Bellack and M. Hersen (eds), 'Research and Practice in Social Skills Training', Plenum, 1979.

LIPTON, D., MARTINSON, R. and WILKES, J., 'The Effectiveness of Correctional Treatment: A Survey of Treatment Evaluation Studies', Prager, 1975.

MACARTNEY, W., 'Walls Have Mouths', Gollancz, 1936.

MARTIN, J.P. and WEBSTER, D., 'The Social Consequences of Conviction', Heinemann, 1971.

McGUIRE, J. and PRIESTLEY, P., 'Life After School: a social skills curriculum', Pergamon, 1981.

MORRIS, P., 'Prisoners and their Families', George Allen & Unwin, 1965.

Our prisons of squalor, degradation and despair, 'Observer', 10 May 1970.

MORRIS, T. and MORRIS, P., 'Pentonville', Routledge & Kegan Paul, 1963.

Minutes of National Association for the Care and Resettlement of Offenders (NACRO) Regional Council for South Wales and Severn Valley, 1970.

ODEN, S. and ASHER, S.R., Coaching children in social skills for friendship making, 'Child Development', 48, pp.495-506, 1977.

OSBORN, A., 'Applied Imagination', Scribner, 1953.

PALOUTZIAN, R., HASAZI, J., STREIFEL, J. and EDGARD, C.L., Promotion of positive social interactions in severely retarded young children, 'American Journal of Mental Deficiency', 75, pp.519-24, 1971.

PAYNE, D. and LAWTON, J., 'Day Training Centres', unpublished manuscript, Home Office Research Unit, 1977.

PFEIFFER, J.W. and JONES, J.E., 'A Handbook of Structured Experiences Experiences for Human Relations Training', vol.2, Iowa University Associates Press, 1970.

PRESERVATION OF THE RIGHTS OF PRISONERS, 'Don't Mark His Face: Hull Prison Riot (1976)', n.d.

PRIESTLEY, P., 'The problem of the short term prisoner', mimeo, National Association for the Care and Resettlement of Offenders, 1970.

PRIESTLEY, P., The prison welfare officer - a case of role strain, 'British Journal of Sociology', vol.XXIII, no.2, 1972.

PRIESTLEY, P., 'Community of Scapegoats', Pergamon, 1980.

PRIESTLEY, P. and McGUIRE, J., Preparing prisoners for release, discussion paper, 'State of the Prisons' conference, University of Kent, June 1977.

PRIESTLEY, P. et al., Release courses: a new venture for prison officers, 'Prison Service Journal', April 1978.

PRIESTLEY, P., McGUIRE, J., FLEGG, D., HEMSLEY, V. and WELHAM, D., 'Social Skills and Personal Problem Solving', Tavistock, 1978.

The Role of the Modern Prison Officer, 'Prison Officers Journal', 1963.

PROBYN, W., 'Angel Face', George Allen & Unwin, 1977.

RADICAL ALTERNATIVES TO PRISON, 'Rates of Imprisonment in Magistrates' Courts 1976', 70 Novers Park Road, Knowle, Bristol.

'Report of the Commissioners of Prisons for the Year 1956', HMSO, 1957.

'Report on the work of the Prison Department 1963', HMSO, 1964.

'Report on the work of the Prison Department 1976', HMSO, 1977.

RODGER, A., 'Seven Point Plan', National Foundation for Education Research, 1974.

ROSE, G., 'The Struggle for Penal Reform', Stevens, 1961.

ROTTER, J.B., Generalized expectancies for internal versus external control of reinforcement, 'Psychological Monographs', 80 (whole no.609).

SARASON, I.G., Verbal learning, modelling, and juvenile delinquency, 'American Psychologist', 23, pp.254-66, 1968.

SARASON, I.G. and GANZER, V.J., Modelling and group discussion in the rehabilitation of juvenile delinquents, 'Journal of Counselling Psychology', 20, pp.442-9, 1973.

SASKATCHEWAN NEWSTART, 'Life Skills Coaching Manual', Training Research and Development Station, Department of Manpower and Immigration, Saskatchewan, 1973.

SAVAGE, A., 'The Sheffield Day Training Centre - a study of 20 men', unpublished manuscript, South Yorkshire Probation Service, 1977.

SEDDON, M., Client as social worker, in D. Brandon and W. Jordan (eds), 'Creative Social Work', Basil Blackwell, 1979.

SHAW, M., 'Social Work in Prison: An Experiment in the Use of Extended Contact with Offenders', Home Office Research Unit Study no.22, HMSO, 1974.

SHELTER, NATIONAL CAMPAIGN FOR THE HOMELESS, 'Tenement', 157
  Waterloo Road, London SE1 8UU.
SPENCE, S.H. and MARZILLIER, J.S., Social skills training with
  adolescent male offenders: 1. Short-term effects, 'Behaviour
  Research and Therapy', 17, pp.7-16, 1979.
STEPHAN, C., STEPHANO, S. and TALKINGTON, L., Use of modelling in
  survival skill training with educable mentally retarded, 'Training
  School Bulletin', 70, pp.73-8, 1973.
STRATTON, B., 'Who Guards The Guards?', Preservation of the Rights
  of Prisoners (PROP), 1973.
SULLIVAN, H.S., 'Conceptions of Modern Psychiatry', William Alanson
  White Psychiatric Foundation, 1947.
SULLIVAN, H.S., 'The Interpersonal Theory of Psychiatry', Norton,
  1953.
SYKES, R., 'Who's Been Eating My Porridge?', Leslie Frewin, 1967.
TAYLOR, A.K., 'From a Glasgow Slum to Fleet Street', Alvin Redman,
  n.d.
THELEN, M.H., FRY, R.A., DOLLINGER, S.J. and PAUL, S.G., Use of
  videotaped models to improve the interpersonal adjustment of
  delinquents, 'Journal of Consulting and Clinical Psychology',
  44, p.492, 1976.
THOMAS, J.E., 'The English Prison Officer Since 1850', Routledge
  & Kegan Paul, 1972.
Prisons can no longer cope, 'The Times' leader, 14 October 1970.
TROWER, P., BRYANT, B. and ARGYLE, M., 'Social Skills and Mental
  Health', Methuen, 1978.
TWENTYMAN, C. and McFALL, R., Behavioral training in social skills
  in shy males, 'Journal of Consulting and Clinical Psychology',
  43, pp.384-95, 1975.
VERCOE, K., '614 Men Leaving Local Prisons', National Association
  for the Care and Resettlement of Offenders Regional Paper,
  Cheltenham, 1969.
WALKER, N. and GILLER, H. (eds), 'Penal Policy Making in England',
  Institute of Criminology, Cambridge, 1977.
WEHMAN, P. and SCHLEIEN, S., Severely handicapped children: social
  skills development through leisure skills programming, in G.
  Cartledge and J.F. Milburn (eds), 'Teaching Social Skills to
  Children: Innovative Approaches', Pergamon, 1980.
WEST, D.J. and FARRINGTON, D.P., 'Who becomes delinquent?',
  Heinemann, 1973.
WHITEHILL, M.B., HERSEN, M. and BELLACK, A.S., Conversation skills
  training for socially isolated children, 'Behaviour Research and
  Therapy', 18, pp.217-25, 1980.
YELLOLY, M.A., 'Social Work Theory and Psychoanalysis', Von
  Nostrand Reinhold, 1980.
Zeno, 'Life', Macmillan, 1968.

Index

Access to children, 150
Accommodation, 53; after release, 145
Advisory Council on the Penal System, 2
After-care, voluntary, 1
Aims and assumptions of project, 24
'Alan B.', case history, 151
Alcohol programme, 91
Alcoholics Anonymous, 146
Alternatives to prison, 174
Andry, Dr R.G., 7
Ashwell prison, 2, 7; courses at, 35; officers, 22; recruitment of prisoners, 35; self-reported problems, 52; training courses at, 7
Assessment, 28, 64; methods, 67-71
Atmosphere of courses, 114
Attendance at Sheffield day training centre, 126
Attendance centres, 174
Attitudes, 62

Baldwin, J., 43
Barbican Centre, Gloucester, 141
Belmont Hospital, 10
Blood feud, 3
Bottomley, K., 44
Bottoms, A., 43
Brainstorming, 68
Bristol Polytechnic, careers officer training course, 25

Broadmoor Hospital, 19
Budgetary control, 104
Budgetary crisis of 1976, 171
Bureaucracy, blind, 4

Canadian Life Skills Coaching Manual, 20, 29, 77, 106, 167
Catering, 98
Checklist of aims and objectives, 71
Chief officer, 103
CODOT, 30, 80
Confidence ratings, 117, 129; re. keeping out of trouble, 138
Confidentiality, 66
Community homes, 174
Community service, 2
'Community Training Centre', 8
Copyrighted tests, 29
Connolly Occupational Interests Questionnaire, 77, 78, 141, 146
Course atmosphere, 114
Course climate, establishment of, 65
Course design, 61, 63
Course files, 67, 152
Course length, 94
Course members, Ranby and Ashwell prisons: asked to leave, 112; characteristics of, 36-42: age, 37; comparisons between Ranby and Ashwell, 41; general ability, 41; jobs held before present sentence, 40; jobs, number held in pre-

vious two years, 40; marital status, 39; present offence, 37; present sentence, 38; previous convictions: number, 38; previous offences, 38; previous sentences, 39; Ranby course four, 95-6; unsuccessful applicants, 36; evaluations of courses: atmosphere, 114; choose to come on course again, 112; confidence ratings, 117; criticisms, 120-1; enjoyment, 114; expectations, 113; other reported gains, 120; self-assessment, 114

Course members, Sheffield day training centre: characteristics of, 44-51: accommodation type, 49; age, 45; intelligence, 50; marital status, 49; numbers, 45; present offence, 47; previous convictions, 46; previous offences, 47; work records, 50; evaluations of courses: attendance, 126; confidence ratings, 129; course completion rates, 127; criticisms, 130; reasons for not completing courses, 126; responses to courses, 128; unexplained absence, 127

Course officers: conditions of work, 104; evaluation of release courses, 123-6; expectations of prison work, 23; previous experience, 23

Course officers' training course, contents, 24-30: assessment, 28; group leading, 28; interviewing, 27; projects and placements, 31; social skills, 30; teaching, 29; vocational guidance, 30; expectations of training course, 23; evaluations of training course, 31-3; format, 25; style, 24; timetable, 26

Crawford, David, 19
Criminal Justice Act 1972, 2
Critical Incidents Analysis, 75, 82

Day training centres, 2, 6;

additional uses of, 174; experimental, 8; origins of, 7

'Desert', theory of, 3
Detail Principal Officer, 103
Deterrence, 3
DHSS, 55
Diary forms, 70
Direct teaching, 73
Dollinger, S.J., 18
Dorset magistrates, rates of imprisonment, 43
Dover Borstal experiment, 132
Drink, after release, 145-9
Drinking, 55
Driving, 56
Drugs, 57

Earliest date of release, 6
'Education' model for research, 14
Employment records, Sheffield day training centre, 166
Enjoyment of courses, 114
Evaluation, 64, 89, 94; officers' training course, 32-3; Ranby course four, 95-100; Sheffield day training centre, 126-30; value of, 131-4
Evidence of effectiveness, 111
Expectations of courses, 111

Family problems, 53
Fenton, Norman, 1
Films, 80, 97, 98
First day out of prison, 137-8
Fisherman's Mission, speaker, 98
Follow-up procedures: prison, 135-7; Sheffield day training centre, 157-8
Fry, R.A., 18

Gambling, 56
Ganzer, V.J., 19
Gardiner, Lord, 8
'Gate-fever', 2
Getting on with other people after release, 149-50
Glen Parva Borstal, 7, 35, 105
Goal-setting re. work, 79
Goldstein, A., 81
Grendon Underwood Prison, 1
Group discussion, 69, 74

Group leading, officers' train-
    ing, 28
Gym, 91

Home Office Research Unit, 6,
    12, 102
Hostels: pre-release, 1; volun-
    tary after-care, 1
Howard League conference, 8

ILEA Media Resources Centre, 76
IMPACT project, 132
Imprisonment: purposes of, 3;
    meaning of, 4
Individual learning package, 173
Industrial Training Research
    Unit, 147
Information, 61
Inmate subculture, 5
Intelligence tests, 40, 41, 50
Interaction programme, 81
Interview skills, 80
Interviewing, officers' train-
    ing, 27

'Jack-the-ripper', 141
Job histories following day
    training, 163-4
Job-search skills, 28; criti-
    cisms of training for, 168
Jobs held by Ranby course two
    members: before conviction,
    79; after release, 142
Jones, Ken, 76
Jones, Maxwell, 10

Keele University senior
    lecturer in social work, 25

'Learning' approach to problems
    of released prisoners, 21
Learning procedures, 73-7
Leicester Prison, 31, 32, 133
Leisure time, 56
Lex talionis, 3
Lifers, 172
Life-skills training, 20
Locus of control, 81
Long-term prisoners, 172

Magistrates' Association, 7
Management structures of
    prisons, 102
Manpower Review Team, 104

Marital problems, 55
Marzillier, John, 18
Maslow's hierarchy of human
    needs, 91
Materials and methods, 166,
    167-9
Midland Region Prison Depart-
    ment, 7
Modelling, 17, 18
Money, 53
Mooney Problem Checklist, 68
Motives for joining Ranby
    course four, 97

National Association for the
    Care and Resettlement of
    Offenders: Regional Paper,
    'The problem of the short
    term prisoner', 8; Regional
    Paper, '614 men leaving
    local prisons', 8; South
    Western Regional Council, 8
National Marriage Guidance
    Council College, Rugby, 22,
    25, 34
New Careerists at Sheffield day
    training centre, 109
New Careers posts, 77, 141
New Careers Project, Bristol,
    141
Non-applicants for prison
    courses: responses to inter-
    views, 42; samples, 36
'Norwich experiment', 1
Nottingham CID, 151
Nottingham Prison, 25, 31, 32,
    133

Oakham, Leicestershire, 7
Offence-behaviour, ways of
    avoiding, 170-1
'Offending', implicit theory
    of, 170
Over-crowding crisis in
    prisons, 2

P2 Division of Prison Depart-
    ment, 102, 104
Parole, 172
Paul, S.G., 18
Penal policy, English, 1
Pencil and paper assessment
    methods, 29, 69
People, 53

Personal goals, 65, 138-9
Personal problem-solving
    framework, 64; assessment,
    67-71; learning proce-
    dures, 73-7; setting
    objectives, 71-2
Personal space exercise, 71
Personality, 55; tests, 40
Pete K., case history, 146-9
Phases of involvement at
    Sheffield day training
    centre, 107-8
Police, 55, 73; contacts after
    release, 140, 150-1;
    harassment by, 82; percep-
    tions of, 74; session in
    Ranby course four, 98
Positive discrimination, 169
Preparing prisoners for re-
    lease, 1, 3, 6, 14
Prison: department, 102; local,
    6; long-term, 6; medium-
    term, 6; routine, 4
Prison officers: basic training,
    5; role of, 5, 135, 171, 175
Prison Officers' Association,
    5, 6, 172
Prison welfare officers, 8, 14
Prisoners as tutors, 173
Probation home/hostel, 6
Probation officers' evaluations,
    of day training centre
    courses, 159-63
Probation offices, 148-9
Problem-solving, 117-18;
    skills, 62; systems, 64, 75,
    82
Problems in running courses,
    100
Problems of implementation at
    Sheffield day training
    centre, 107-8
Programmes: alcohol, 91; inter-
    action, 81-2; violence, 99;
    work, 77-80
Progressive and Coloured
    Matrices tests, 50
Project, aims of, 12
Projects: information, 74;
    Ranby course four, 98

'Quiet nick', 175

Race relations speaker, 91

Ranby Prison, 2, 7; courses, 35;
    fourth course, 94-100;
    officers, 22; recruitment of
    members, 35; self-reported
    problems, 52; trade training
    courses, 35
Reasons for volunteering for
    courses, 111
Recidivism, 13; day trainees,
    165; prisoners, 152
Reconviction, rates of, 1, 12,
    13, 152-7
Recruitment to courses, 101
Referral and selection policies
    at Sheffield day training
    centre, 109
Relationships with women, 150
Removal of course members, 101
Research methodology, 12
Research team, previous experi-
    ence, 25
Responses of prisoners, 94
Retford, Notts, 7
Rights, 56

Sarason, I.G., 19
Saskatchewan Department of
    Immigration and Manpower,
    20; Life-skills Coaching
    Manual, 20, 29, 77, 106, 167
'Screws', good ones and bad
    ones, 6
'Screws and cons', 81, 121-3
Self-assessment, 63, 115
Self-confidence ratings:
    prisons, 116-17; Sheffield
    day training centre, 164
Self-control, 118
Self-help groups, 173
Self-presentation, 75
'Settling in', 57
Seven point plan, 28
Sex offenders, 19
Sheffield day training centre,
    2, 7, 8; activities, 9;
    aims, 8; course members:
    accommodation, 49; age, 45;
    first group, 108; intelli-
    gence, 50; marital status,
    49; New Careerists, 109;
    numbers attending, 44-5;
    present offence, 47; pre-
    vious offence, 48; self-
    reported problems, 58-9;

court decisions on referrals,
44; intake systems, 9; men
not sent to day training
centre, 44; numbers referred, 43; programme, 8; recruitment procedures, 43;
referrals to, 9; referral
and selection policies, 109;
rejection of applicants, 43;
validity of assumptions, 11
'Signposts', 30, 80
Simulations, 76; job search, 81
Skill centre, Leicester, 31, 80
Skill survey, 81
Skill training approach, 61-2
Smoking, 57
Social learning theory, 16
Social security after release,
143-4
Social skills training, 12, 30,
60, 63, 166; methods, 16-17,
75-6, 167; with offenders, 18
South Yorkshire magistrates,
rates of imprisonment, 43
South Yorkshire Probation and
After-care Service, 2
Speakers, 73, 91, 98
Spence, Sue, 18
Staff organisation at Sheffield
day training centre, 108
Strain on prison officers, 105
Street interviews, 75
Sullivan, Harry Stack, 16
Surveying marketable skills, 78
Suspended sentences, 2
Suspicion of prison officers, 97

Teacher, role of, 14
Teaching skills, officers'
training course, 29
'Tenement', 76

Thelen, M.H., 18
Therapeutic community, 1, 10
Timetables: Ranby and Ashwell,
83-6; Ranby course four, 97;
Sheffield day training
centre, 88-9
'Training' model for research,
15
'Treatment and training', 1
'Trouble', 55
Trust, 56
Turnkey, 5
'TV Covingham', 76

Uniformed prison officers, 3

Vaughan College, Leicester, 22
Vercoe, Kate, 7
Video, 28, 71, 75, 76, 91, 98;
at follow-up meetings, 151;
and social security claims,
144
Violence, 56; programme, 98-9;
after release, 151, 166
Violent re-offending, 171
Vocational guidance, 30
Voluntary nature of release
course attendance, 112

Walker, M.A., 43
Walton Prison, Liverpool, self-
reported problems of
prisoners, 52
West Bar Day Centre, Sheffield,
174
'Whispers', 76
Wootton, Lady, 2
Work, 53, 64, 87, 118; programme, 77-81; after
release, 139-43

For Product Safety Concerns and Information please contact our EU
representative GPSR@taylorandfrancis.com
Taylor & Francis Verlag GmbH, Kaufingerstraße 24, 80331 München, Germany

www.ingramcontent.com/pod-product-compliance
Lightning Source LLC
Chambersburg PA
CBHW050442280326
41932CB00013BA/2211

9 781032 571164